KABBALAH AND JEWISH MODERNITY

THE LITTMAN LIBRARY OF JEWISH CIVILIZATION

Life Patron
COLETTE LITTMAN

Dedicated to the memory of
LOUIS THOMAS SIDNEY LITTMAN
*who founded the Littman Library for the love of God
and as an act of charity in memory of his father*
JOSEPH AARON LITTMAN
and to the memory of
ROBERT JOSEPH LITTMAN
who continued what his father Louis had begun
יהא זכרם ברוך

'*Get wisdom, get understanding:
Forsake her not and she shall preserve thee*'

PROV. 4: 5

*The Littman Library of Jewish Civilization is a registered UK charity
Registered charity no.* 1000784

KABBALAH AND JEWISH MODERNITY

◆

RONI WEINSTEIN

London
**The Littman Library of Jewish Civilization
in association with Liverpool University Press**

The Littman Library of Jewish Civilization
Registered office: 14th floor, 33 Cavendish Square, London WIG OPW

in association with Liverpool University Press
4 Cambridge Street, Liverpool L69 7ZU, UK
www.liverpooluniversitypress.co.uk/littman

Managing Editor: Connie Webber

Distributed in North America by Longleaf Services
116 S Boundary St, Chapel Hill, NC 27514, USA

First published in English 2016
First published in paperback 2024

A longer version of this book was published in Hebrew as
Shavru et hakelim: hakabalah vehamoderniyut hayehudit
© The Haim Rubin Tel Aviv University Press 2011

Abridged English edition © Roni Weinstein 2016

Catalogue records for this book are available from the
British Library and the Library of Congress

ISBN 978–1–837640–54–6

Publishing co-ordinator: Janet Moth
Copy-editing: Mark Newby
Indexing: Meg Davies, FSI
Designed and typeset by Pete Russell, Faringdon, Oxon.

Printed and bound by CPI Group (UK) Ltd, Croydon, CR0 4YY

Acknowledgements

THE publication of this book would not have been possible without the assistance and kindness of several people to whom I wish to express my gratitude. Professor Aviad Kleinberg of the Tel Aviv University Press consistently encouraged the publication of the original Hebrew version, which was awarded the Goldstein-Goren International Prize for the Most Important Book in Jewish Thought, 2011–13. I would also like to thank him for his permission to publish the English version. For the publication of the English version by the Littman Library of Jewish Civilization, I wish to thank Ludo Craddock, chief executive officer, and Connie Webber, managing editor, for the encouragement they offered me from the very first moment of our encounter. Lastly, my gratitude to Dr Mark Newby, for his meticulous and lucid editing.

Contents

Note on Transliteration

THE transliteration of Hebrew in this book reflects consideration of the type of book it is, its content, purpose, and readership. The system adopted therefore reflects a broad approach to transcription, rather than the narrower approaches found in the *Encyclopaedia Judaica* or other systems developed for text-based or linguistic studies. The aim has been to reflect the pronunciation prescribed for modern Hebrew, rather than the spelling or Hebrew word structure, and to do so using conventions that are generally familiar to the English-speaking reader.

In accordance with this approach, no attempt is made to indicate the distinctions between *alef* and *ayin*, *tet* and *taf*, *kaf* and *kuf*, *sin* and *samekh*, since these are not relevant to pronunciation; likewise, the *dagesh* is not indicated except where it affects pronunciation. Following the principle of using conventions familiar to the majority of readers, however, transcriptions that are well established have been retained even when they are not fully consistent with the transliteration system adopted. On similar grounds, the *tsadi* is rendered by 'tz' in such familiar words as barmitzvah. Likewise, the distinction between *ḥet* and *khaf* has been retained, using *ḥ* for the former and *kh* for the latter; the associated forms are generally familiar to readers, even if the distinction is not actually borne out in pronunciation, and for the same reason the final *heh* is indicated too. As in Hebrew, no capital letters are used, except that an initial capital has been retained in transliterating titles of published works (for example, *Shulḥan arukh*).

Since no distinction is made between *alef* and *ayin*, they are indicated by an apostrophe only in intervocalic positions where a failure to do so could lead an English-speaking reader to pronounce the vowel-cluster as a diphthong—as, for example, in *ha'ir*—or otherwise mispronounce the word.

The *sheva na* is indicated by an *e*—*perikat ol*, *reshut*—except, again, when established convention dictates otherwise.

The *yod* is represented by *i* when it occurs as a vowel (*bereshit*), by *y* when it occurs as a consonant (*yesodot*), and by *yi* when it occurs as both (*yisra'el*).

Names have generally been left in their familiar forms, even when this is inconsistent with the overall system.

A Social Historian Looks at Early Modern Kabbalah

Historians dislike the idea of sudden changes, preferring to view history as a continuous process. However, the end of the Middle Ages and the beginning of the modern period in Europe saw many and varied developments, which confront historians with the question of whether it was primarily a period of continuity or of radical transformation. This book focuses on one aspect of the period: the role of tradition and innovation in early modern kabbalah and how it shaped modern Jewish life, religion, and culture. What was it about Jewish mysticism as it evolved in the small Galilean town of Safed that enabled it to free itself from centuries of esotericism and exclusivity and become a dominant force in Jewish culture and religion? What was so alluring about the complicated teachings of figures such as Isaac Luria (Ari, 'the lion'), Hayim Vital, Moses Cordovero, Joseph Karo, Elijah de Vidas, and Eleazar Azikri? Why did increasingly large parts of the Jewish public acquiesce in changes to important elements of their tradition? The mystical sayings and writings of the Safed kabbalists were addressed to the public in an attempt to change its habits and religious conceptions and were therefore crafted with the aim of responding to the needs of this public no less than they were intended to express the sublime experiences of the exceptional few who produced them.

Highlighting continuity is the preferred approach to the study of Jewish mysticism, as shown by recent research on early modern kabbalah.[1] This research could, without exaggeration, be described as a real historiographical renaissance. Books, monographs, articles, and conferences have revealed many fascinating aspects of the lives of the kabbalists, the relationships of

---

[1] See Elior and Liebes (eds.), *Lurianic Kabbalah* (Heb.).

masters and disciples, their innovations in theology and religious practices, and their attitudes to magic, liturgy, and music. Yet common to most of them are three features: the attempt to uncover the precedents of the mystical thinking and writings of the great names of kabbalah; a focus on the text— that is, identifying mystical thinking and practice mainly with literary products rather than with oral traditions; and the presentation of the theological issues—the secrets of the divine realms—as the main point of interest, from which all other aspects of kabbalistic discourse are derived. Modern research into Jewish mysticism thus joins hands with the long tradition of the 'history of ideas'. Jewish mystical writings are supposed to have developed primarily in reaction to the work of previous generations, a 'republic of Jewish scholars' conducting a kind of internal, intergenerational dialogue. Such an understanding is reasonable for a tradition that assigns major importance and sanctity to the interpretation of its sacred texts, and Jewish mystical works are often a dense web of references to and elaboration of earlier mystical works and the Jewish canon. Again and again the major figures of Jewish religion and culture return to the same textual fountains and offer their own reading. The dense commentaries on *Sefer hazohar* (the Zohar, literally the 'Book of Splendour', described by Yehuda Liebes as the 'mystical Bible'[2]) seem to support this point, as if early modern kabbalah was nothing more than a new reading of this book. Contemporary kabbalists—especially Luria, whose theology is indeed an intergenerational dialogue within the family of Jewish scholars—humbly presented themselves as nothing more than loyal readers of the Zohar. The canonical text apparently overwhelms its historical context, and change is seen very much as a threat rather than as a positive development. What is particularly problematic in this approach is the very issue of change, an issue that is all the more important as other indicators of change in the Jewish world point independently to the same period. My perspective as a social historian does not diminish the theological motives of the kabbalists but relates them and their writings to their social, economic, and political

---

[2] See Liebes, 'Zohar and Eros' (Heb.). The Zohar has inspired some fascinating research in recent years: see Dan (ed.), *The Age of the Zohar*; Wolfson, *Luminal Darkness*; Meroz (ed.), *New Developments in Zohar Studies* (Eng. and Heb.); id., 'The Middle Eastern Origins of Kabbalah'; Helner-Eshed, *A River Flows from Eden*; Abrams, *Kabbalistic Manuscripts and Textual Theory*; Benarroch, '"The Mystery of Unity"'.

contexts. Mystics, like any other creators, are not detached from their surroundings and respond to contemporary cultural conditions and events.

This book stresses the innovative aspects of early modern kabbalah and attempts to overcome the constraints placed by canonical texts upon how mystical phenomena can be understood in the Jewish context. Something crucial and quite unprecedented happened in the sixteenth and seventeenth centuries: from a highly secretive and esoteric tradition, kabbalah developed into a missionary movement, spreading its doctrines throughout the Jewish world. The goal was ambitious: no less than the remodelling of the religious and ethical attitudes of the entire Jewish population, a wholesale reformation of Judaism. This dramatic transformation cannot be understood aside from the wider historical changes occurring in Europe, such as the rift between Catholicism and Protestantism, the rise of the modern state, colonial expansion, and the new philosophical and scientific positions that undermined traditional social and cultural conventions. These changes are barely mentioned in most works on early modern kabbalah.

This book examines kabbalah's passage from the esoteric to the public domain. Few aspects of Jewish life and religious practice were not touched, commented upon, and eventually changed as a result of the spread of kabbalah. Kabbalah was based on innovative and daring theological ideas regarding the inner recesses of God and their implications for human behaviour. As it reached into the public sphere, it led to the rise of *kedoshim* (holy ones) as authorities in halakhah (religious law) and community regulation; inspired the establishment of confraternities (*ḥavurot mitsvah*); influenced family life and the education of the young; promoted religious conscience and awareness of sin and guilt; fostered interest in the human body, especially its erotic aspects; introduced public confession and the practice of making reparations (*tikunim*: repairing the divine and human realms); and increased the role of emotion in religion through music and *piyutim* (liturgical chants).

These innovations originated mainly in the town of Safed in Galilee. Its leading figures, both kabbalists and halakhists, were not acting in a vacuum: they addressed their messages to people for whom they needed to make sense in terms of their everyday lives. Given such a dialogical situation, the impressive kabbalistic corpus produced over the course of the sixteenth and seventeenth centuries needs to be reinterpreted not only as a further elaboration of

earlier mystical experiences and a secretive literary tradition but also as a
response to the needs of Jewish communities in their concrete historical
context.

Such a reading does not underestimate the deep mystical dimensions in
the writings of Luria, Cordovero, Vital, or any of the other leading figures of
Safed, nor does it explain religious experiences solely in terms of their social
or economic circumstances. It suggests that a broader evaluation of Jewish
mystical texts is needed, along similar lines to the recent research of the *storia
religiosa* school in Italy.[3] Religion is concerned with the interaction between
humans and the divine, yet in order to function in a broad setting it needs
other dimensions as well. The urge of the Safed kabbalists to reform Judaism
obliged them to respond to social and cultural circumstances and institutions,
such as family life, community regulations, legal traditions, and religious
practices. Furthermore, according to Yehuda Liebes, fundamental elements
of Lurianic theology reflect the personal psychology of Isaac Luria and the
problems that concerned him and his disciples.[4] When they spoke about
the processes within the divine realms—processes of growth, crisis, and even-
tual recovery—they were speaking about themselves. They were highly sensitive to the voices of life around them—in the small town of Safed but also in
Jewish communities all over the Mediterranean basin and beyond—and to
the historical changes taking place. Early modern kabbalah was part of a religious ferment occurring across Europe and the Ottoman empire. It needs a
global reading.

The effect of early modern kabbalah on Jewish culture was nothing short
of revolutionary. Like other revolutions—be they political in character, such
as the French, American, or Russian revolutions, or social and cultural in
character, such as the industrial, feminist, or even internet revolutions—what
I call the kabbalistic revolution was initiated by people who considered themselves pioneers. It deeply affected people's lives at the time and also laid the
foundations for more profound changes in the future. Surprisingly the daring
attitude of early modern kabbalists has not been passed on to modern scholars of kabbalah, who refuse to acknowledge the sixteenth and seventeenth

[3] Prosperi, *Tribunali della coscienza*; see also Seidel Menchi, *Erasmo in Italia*; for a compendium of writings in this historiographical tradition, see De Rosa and Gregory (eds.), *Storia
dell'Italia religiosa*, vol. ii: *L'età moderna*.   [4] Liebes, "'Two Young Roes of a Doe'" (Heb.).

centuries as a period of dramatic cultural and religious changes. Instead they mostly concentrate on textual aspects and the literary dialogue between mystics of different schools and succeeding generations. The Zohar is frequently the focal and paradigmatic point of reference, and the impression given is of the discussion and extension of a well-known literary canon. The exegesis of the past marginalizes innovation. According to Amos Funkenstein:

[Most researchers] assume continuity and innovation to be disjunctive, mutually exclusive, predicates. The 'new' often consists not in the invention of new categories or new figures of thought, but rather in surprising employment of existing ones. Of the variety of ways in which a new theory can be said to have been prepared by an older one, two ideal modes are particularly pertinent to our discussion: the dialectical anticipation of a new theory by an older, even adverse, one; and the transplantation of existing categories to a new domain—employing them under a new perspective.[5]

This attitude is unable to divest itself of the classical Jewish ethos of the chain of transmission as the foundation of Jewish religion. I believe the time has come to re-examine this attitude and consider how citation of old canonical books merely provides a common substratum and how 'citation culture' could actually provide future generations with the freedom to innovate.[6] By focusing on the textual aspects, modern Jewish studies effectively accepts and justifies the orthodox Jewish ethos, which emphasizes the common core of Jewish culture throughout the centuries, despite the ceaseless internal disagreements on almost every issue.

There is a tension between tradition and continuity, on the one hand, and innovation and revolution, on the other, throughout all of early modern kabbalah, because, in this context, innovation does not imply the dismissal of the past. This was by no means the intention of the kabbalists, as it would have made it impossible for them to spread their new message: they had to present their doctrines as the continuation of what went before. A similar dynamic characterized the beginnings of modern science in Europe. The new scientific discoveries—the biological cell, astronomical observations, the vacuum, surgery—are often presented as a break with old scientific patterns and their replacement by new paradigms, yet recent research suggests a more

---

[5] Funkenstein, *Theology and the Scientific Imagination from the Middle Ages to the Seventeenth Century*, 14. [6] Compagnon, *La Seconde Main*.

complicated process, in which the old and the new were intertwined, and scientific advances were not necessarily linear:

Thus, new early modern approaches to natural inquiry should not be seen in the first instance as an attack on the doctrines and methods contained in the works of Aristotle and his medieval Arabic and Latin commentators. . . . Such attacks, although the stuff of popular historiographic legend—crystallized around heroic figures such as Galileo and Francis Bacon (1561–1626)—were less common than one might gather from the many textbooks on the history of early modern science that embrace, with varying degrees of enthusiasm, the premise of a 'Scientific Revolution'. . . . The process of change was gradual and sporadic, shaped well into the first half of the seventeenth century by serious, widespread and accepted efforts to accommodate ancient texts to newer methods and discoveries. . . . It was only toward the middle of the seventeenth century that the weight of scholarly opinion—and even then there were many objectors—shifted from gradual, accommodationist strategies to calls for more fundamental change, as more and more voices argued that the old edifice of natural knowledge needed to be torn down and a new one constructed, however unclear the shape of that new edifice might be.[7]

If the kabbalistic turn of the early modern period was a marked change due to new applications of old traditions, several questions are raised. How valid was Luria's claim to be continuing the path of the Zohar? Granted that religious practice attracted the main interest of the kabbalists, did they continue the classical tradition or divert it into entirely new streams? If the latter, what was their attitude to classical halakhah, Torah study, and traditional yeshivas? To what extent was the composition of the *Shulḥan arukh*, Joseph Karo's comprehensive and constitutive code of law, related to kabbalistic missionary endeavours? Why was there such an intense preoccupation with the human body, and why was it used as the point of departure for the discussion of so many other issues? Was Safed kabbalah predominantly a Mediterranean phenomenon, or was it influenced by events in other areas of the Jewish diaspora? And last, but certainly not least, was there common ground between the kabbalists and their non-Jewish neighbours? This last query highlights the fact that modern research into Jewish mysticism has disregarded the possibility of contact with and inspiration from religious and mystic traditions in Islam and Catholicism, with which contemporary Jewish mystics would

---

[7] Park and Daston, 'Introduction', 8–9; on the re-elaboration of past traditions, see Grafton, *Bring Out Your Dead*; Grafton, Shelford, and Siraisi, *New Worlds, Ancient Texts*.

have been very familiar. The following chapters will attempt to answer these questions.

Chapter 1 argues that the similarities between scientific progress and Lurianic kabbalah are not coincidental. Both needed to adapt old texts and mental attitudes to a flood of new information. The chapter begins with an explication of the aspects of the divine realms which stood at the core of early modern kabbalah. I do not intend to delve into the minutiae and technicalities but outline the fundamental features, especially the innovations, and attempt to answer the fundamental question of how such intricate and detailed theological positions, requiring years of arduous and dedicated study, could excite the imagination of so many common people.

Chapter 2 discusses the rise of the *kadosh*, the Jewish holy man, as a source of religious creativity and an authority on the pious life, sin, guilt, and repentance.

Chapter 3 considers the encounter between kabbalah and halakhah as the two pillars of early modern Jewish religion. The legal tradition was certainly more dominant in Jewish life, yet some of the leading mystics were also distinguished halakhists. They used their position to propose entirely new meanings for religious practices and halakhah and to introduce remarkable innovations in ritual.

Chapter 4 looks at the institutional aspects of Safed kabbalah, especially religious confraternities. Confraternities existed in both Jewish and Christian societies in the sixteenth and seventeenth centuries. In the Jewish context, their members contributed to the study of kabbalistic writings, spreading their ideas among new members and translating them into concrete acts. Much kabbalistic literature was composed in response to requests from confraternities. Confraternities later served as the model for other organizations, such as educational institutions for the young.

Alongside its communal aspect, kabbalah was also concerned with social control. Chapter 5 discusses the place of the body in the socialization process. The human body and its concrete physiological functions were paralleled in the divine realms by Adam Kadmon, the primeval man. Regulation of sexual behaviour was the most important part of the refinement of basic instincts and emotions, which was held to have such a central role in the 'civilizing process' taking place in contemporary Europe.

Chapter 6 examines the kabbalists' preoccupation with sin. Never before had sin and evil been so much discussed in Jewish writings. Sin called for constant vigilance and knowledge of the external circumstances and internal processes that gave rise to immoral acts and thoughts. This increased sensitivity was apparent in the mystical diaries and autobiographical writings of the kabbalists. These writings also discuss the place of the emotions in religious life, especially the negative role of anger, and the centrality of conscience to religious activity. The major response to the challenge of evil was the practice of confession and reparation similar to those of Catholicism.

Chapter 7 highlights the contribution of the Iberian diaspora to the expansion of kabbalah. The new Sephardi communities included former Conversos, whose lives as Catholics or secret Judaizers had made them into an intermediate group between the two religions. As such, they acted as a conduit between Counter-Reformation Catholicism and Judaism, bringing with them many of the ideas discussed in the earlier chapters and making Safed kabbalah an agent of modernization.

Information about the social history of kabbalah must be sought in a variety of genres, not just in the great theological works of kabbalistic speculation. These include *musar* literature, ethical writings addressed to the Jewish public; 'ego documents', such as the diaries and journals in which the major kabbalists examined their innermost thoughts and emotions; community regulations and rabbinic responsa; and Catholic sermons and theological works, which reveal the religious background of the Conversos who so influenced the course of early modern Judaism. Catholic religiosity has never been as prevalent in Jewish culture as it was during this period, and Safed kabbalah served as its main point of entry.

The shift from the theological to the sociological reading of mystical texts highlights a number of methodological considerations: the importance of the non-Jewish environment in understanding texts that seem intimately Jewish; the role of Ottoman culture and religious traditions in the modernization of Judaism; Jewish modernity as primarily a process of ripening within the Jewish context supported by a long cultural heritage rather than something enforced from the outside during the Enlightenment; the acknowledgement that Jewish modernity began in the late sixteenth century in the Mediterranean world rather than in eighteenth-century Berlin; and, finally, the importance of a broad range of sources for early modern kabbalah and its impact on Jewish life—theological tracts, ethical literature, hagiography, mystical diaries, halakhic rulings and responsa, community and confraternal regulations, material objects, mystical techniques, the testimonies of non-Jewish travellers, and Catholic religious literature of all kinds.

This English edition is shorter than the Hebrew original primarily because the arguments made in rabbinic and mystical texts have generally been summarized rather than presented in full, and I have focused on presenting the main conclusions rather than entering into historiographical debates. I have also assumed that much of the explanation of the Catholic context relevant to an understanding of early modern Jewish kabbalah could be abridged for English-speaking readers.

A New God
Theological Innovation

THE JEWISH GOD has a long history.[1] Various faces of God appear throughout the biblical stories and prophetic messages, in the intricate ritual cycle of the Temple, and all through the rabbinic canon. Later the Jews' encounters with the other monotheistic religions—Christianity and Islam— and especially with medieval philosophy, science, and pietistic movements, had a significant influence on their understanding of God. Jewish mystical texts—whose production started in the rabbinic period and flourished during the Middle Ages when kabbalistic systems were increasingly put into writing, mainly in Spain and neighbouring countries—provided a new vision of the godhead. No longer was God merely active in human history, wishing to be obeyed through well-defined religious praxis; God in and for himself carried his own history which began before the creation of the world and the appearance of human beings. All the traditional theosophical elements were taken for granted in early modern kabbalistic writings; however, the bold and innovative theology of Isaac Luria would fuse them into something radically new.

The divine realms which stand at the heart of Lurianic kabbalah are characterized by a ravishing richness and effulgence. Never before had there been such a fascination with, or so much energy dedicated to expounding, every minute detail of worlds beyond the mundane. Theology was the creative force behind early modern kabbalah, initiating innovations in such areas as the interpretation of the Torah, ecstatic mystical experiences, and religious practice. Any discussion of its impact on the Jewish public cannot avoid the theological starting point.

However, it is not the theology itself which matters for the analysis offered in this study but the link between the theological and sociological

[1] See Idel, *Ben*.

aspects of Lurianic kabbalah. How did such a complicated perspective on God—with its complex terminology and presentation, its high intellectual requirements for even a basic understanding, and its rigorous religious standards—manage to fire the imagination of increasingly large sections of the Jewish public? Why were these esoteric and scarcely accessible texts sanctified more than any other mystical books? It is surprising how limited discussion of this question has been. The only broad answer was offered by Gershom Scholem, who claimed that the secret lies in the correlation between the traumatic experiences of the Spanish Jewish refugees and the theology of crisis within the Lurianic God. This claim was refuted by Moshe Idel, who pointed out that Lurianic kabbalah only started to appeal to the public during the early seventeenth century. Idel's assertion was later supported by Zeev Gries's work on the spread of kabbalistic ethical works and Yosef Avivi's study of the dissemination of Lurianic texts in manuscript and print.[2] I wish to make a triple claim in this chapter: Lurianic theology was highly innovative and much more radical than any previous Jewish mystical system; its innovative character was intimately linked to new concepts of knowledge developing in early modern Europe; and, much like these new ways of organizing knowledge, it provoked an active and involved attitude to the world and a wish to reform human life and age-old social and religious traditions and institutions. These changes affected more and more people in Europe, influencing such diverse things as the arrangement of libraries, nautical navigation, mining, surgery and anatomy, and political science. Lurianic theology suggested a similar dialectics in regard to divine knowledge: the deep secrets of God remained within limited and esoteric circles, but they became an agent of change.

Biographical facts about Luria are rather scant and are mostly found in the hagiographical stories about him and the writings of Hayim Vital.[3] He was born around the year 1540 in Jerusalem, although little is known about his family background. He grew up in Egypt, where he became a disciple of the famous halakhic scholar Bezalel Ashkenazi, and devoted most of his time to studying the Talmud. At some point he became acquainted with the Zohar

---

[2] Scholem, *Lurianic Kabbalah*; Idel, "'One from a Town and Two from a Family'" (Heb.); Gries, *Conduct Literature* (Heb.); Avivi, *Lurianic Kabbalah* (Heb.).

[3] See Pely, 'Lurianic Kabbalah' (Heb.), 92–108.

and turned most of his attention to deciphering its mystical secrets. In 1570 he moved to the Land of Israel and settled at Safed, where he lived until his death in 1572. Although he developed his mystical theories before leaving Egypt, he was practically unknown on his arrival in Safed; nevertheless, he managed to study under Moses Cordovero, then the leading kabbalist there. Very few of his own writings have survived—as opposed to those attributed to him by later generations—and 'Lurianic theology' is mainly preserved in the writings of his closest disciple and his heir, Hayim Vital. Luria was not a scholar who communicated through the written word but an oral teacher who addressed his thoughts to a group of devoted disciples, and Vital minutely documented his master's teachings while he was alive and maintained a strict monopoly over his heritage after his death. Vital's magnum opus, *Ets ḥayim* (The Tree of Life), is the most elaborate and comprehensive version of Luria's theology. Other versions did survive, but they gained little prestige and their diffusion was rather limited.[4] Non-Lurianic kabbalistic writings were also produced in late sixteenth-century Safed, mainly by Moses Cordovero and his disciples.[5]

A Radical and Innovative Theology

The Creation is a great enigma. How is it possible to have a material world alongside the endless plenitude of God? Does the created world not set limits to the divine, being somewhere that is not God? No clear-cut answer to this question was provided by Luria or his followers, but they depicted Creation as an ongoing process, not a one-off event. According to the most fundamental axiom of Lurianic kabbalah, the creation of the world was analogous to human birth and development. We shall see the consequences of this in what follows.

In the Lurianic scheme, God withdrew from himself to himself, creating a spherical internal space within which all decisive events would later take place. Into this space, a pipe, rather like the umbilical cord, penetrated, from

---

[4] On the special role of Vital's *Ets ḥayim*, see Avivi, *Lurianic Kabbalah* (Heb.), i. 36, 47, 53, 56, 110–15; ii. 636, 640–1, 673. Vital also composed a shorter version of the Lurianic emanation system, *Kitsur seder ha'atsilut*.

[5] Luria's disciples occupied themselves with the question of whether the Lurianic or the Cordovan version had priority and even asked dead kabbalists for their opinions (see Avivi, *Lurianic Kabbalah* (Heb.), i. 260–1, 287, 467; iii. 1072, 1461).

which the divine opulence or emanation (*shefa, ha'atsalah*) poured. The cord emanates light from each and every point. The light is structured as a human figure known as Adam Kadmon (primeval man), who serves as the archetype of every activity and revelation beyond himself. Light radiates from all of his bodily parts, arranged into conglomerations called 'Faces' (*partsufim*). There are five Faces. The first, Atik Yomin (the Old One, also known as Arikh Anpin, the Long-Faced), is almost completely hidden, but the rest are related like a human family: Abba and Imma (Father and Mother), their son, Ze'er Anpin (Small Countenance), and Nukba Deze'er Anpin, his consort. Later in this cosmic chain of being appear the ten *sefirot*, the angelic worlds, the material creation—including human beings—and the demonic domain. The attention of the Lurianic kabbalists was attracted more to the domain of the Faces than to that of the *sefirot*, which lies beneath it and had such an important place in the zoharic tradition from the thirteenth century.[6]

Many details of this scheme, such as God's withdrawal (*tsimtsum*) from himself to himself in order to enable the creation process to begin, can be found in earlier kabbalistic literature.[7] However, the degree of innovation becomes apparent when the Lurianic schema is compared with that of the Zohar. The Zohar and the Lurianic corpus are the two most important points in the history of Jewish mysticism, and there is an undeniable continuity between them. Throughout history they have mutually reinforced each other's legitimacy and prestige. The Zohar represents the particular tradition of Iberian Jewry, which increasingly dominated early modern Jewish culture, and the spread of kabbalah and its modernizing effects were, to a large extent, the work of the Sephardi diaspora. The kabbalists of Safed, especially the followers of Luria, presented themselves as nothing more than adherents and interpreters of the zoharic tradition, and the Zohar provided the starting point for their discussions of the divine Faces and Adam Kadmon. This has led modern scholars to concentrate on the continuity of early modern

[6] Systematic presentations of Luria's positions are found in the writings of his direct disciples and later kabbalists, along with their own elaborations. Among them were Menahem Azaryah da Fano, Naftali Bacharach (*Emek hamelekh*), Emmanuel Hai Ricchi (*Mishnat ḥasidim*), and Shalom Sharabi.

[7] Idel, 'On the Concept of *Tsimtsum*' (Heb.); Huss, *The Kabbalah of R. Simeon ibn Lavi* (Heb.), ch. 10; Garb, 'Magic and Mysticism' (Heb.); Sack, 'R. Moses Cordovero's Doctrine of *Tsimtsum*' (Heb.). The concept of withdrawal might have precedents in classical rabbinic thinking (see Hoshen, '*Tsimtsum* and R. Akiva's School' (Heb.)).

kabbalah with the zoharic literature. However, this approach tends to mask the radical newness of Lurianic kabbalah, for two reasons: the first is that the Jewish scholarly tradition is a 'culture of citation', relying heavily on earlier texts even when it is suggesting completely new readings of those texts; the second is that, until the zoharic corpus was printed, it was not even conceived as a literary unity. Before then it consisted of various manuscripts, circulating among small groups of mystics. In a comprehensive study of the diffusion of the Zohar from thirteenth-century Spain onwards, Boaz Huss marked the sixteenth century as a watershed. Not only was the Zohar printed for the first time (in Italy, twice), but it also became the focus of intensive exegesis, which played an important role in shaping kabbalistic positions and influenced Jewish ethical traditions and halakhic decisions.[8] According to Daniel Abrams, the canon of the Zohar—that is, what of the vast zoharic literature was included or excluded—was only decided once the work was printed.[9] Its canonization in the second sense—that is, its acceptance as sacred alongside the classical Jewish texts of the Bible and the Talmud—was the result of the Safed kabbalists considering it the fundamental text of the Jewish mystical tradition: the 'kabbalistic Bible'. Several major kabbalists wrote comprehensive commentaries on it, such as Cordovero's *Or yakar*, Abraham Azulai's *Or ḥamah*, Shimshon Lavi's *Ketem paz*, and Moses Zacuto's *Igerot haremez*. These overshadowed the original texts, in much the same way that the Catholic Church's interpretations monopolized the Bible and prevented common readers from gaining direct access to it.

Luria saw himself as the direct successor to and reincarnation of the imputed creator of the Zohar, Simeon bar Yohai, and his circle of disciples as a reincarnation of the group that escorted bar Yohai on his mystical journeys.[10] Of the very few genuine written works that Luria has left, the longest and most elaborate is a commentary on part of the Zohar, called *Safra ditseniuta* (The Secret Book).[11] The Lurianic reading of the Zohar was so

[8] Huss, *Like the Radiance of the Sky* (Heb.), 4–5; an English edition is published by the Littman Library.   [9] Abrams, *Kabbalistic Manuscripts and Textual Theory*, ch. 4.

[10] *Sefer toledot ha'ari* (Heb.), 179–81. On the mystical rank of early modern kabbalists compared with previous generations and Luria and his disciples' sense of superiority, see Chapter 2 below.

[11] On Luria's authentic writings, see Benayahu, 'The Commentaries of R. Bezalel Ashkenazi and R. Joseph Ashkenazi and Their Original Version' (Heb.); id., 'The Commentaries on *Mishneh torah* on the Original Maimonidean Copy and the Commentaries Ascribed to R. Bezalel

influential that it became almost impossible to read it except through Luria's eyes,[12] and his dominance led to the rejection of other readings of the Zohar, especially Cordovero's. Luria's revelations, visions, and encounters with holy figures from the Jewish past made his position superior even to that of bar Yohai.[13] Once his position was established, Luria combated the common opinion of his time—supported by Cordovero—that the Zohar was accessible to any reader willing to spend the time and effort required to understand it. The concept of 'open knowledge' was replaced by 'closed knowledge', and reading the Zohar was permitted only to those who had reached the same spiritual level as its creator. Luria also distinguished between more secretive parts of the Zohar, to be restricted to esoteric circles, and open sections, occupied with deportment and etiquette.

Vital took Luria's stand a step further and claimed that his master's theology had a serious advantage over the Zohar:

Do not think that the ten *sefirot* called in the Zohar 'the ten *sefirot* of emanations' are primeval and higher than any other emanations, since several [divine] realms preceded them, and due to their secrecy they were not even mentioned in the Zohar . . . . Still, to the best of our capacity, we shall start by explaining [higher aspects than the *sefirot*] . . . starting with Adam Kadmon, being so elusive he was not even referred to in the Zohar.[14]

According to Vital the central text of Jewish mysticism contained only partial knowledge and provided limited access to God and needed to be completed through Lurianic theology. The supremacy of Luria in relation to bar Yohai is reflected in the superiority of his theology over the zoharic writings.

The Zohar was 'revealed' and written down in thirteenth-century Castile. Throughout the fourteenth and fifteenth centuries it was largely ignored and was rarely mentioned in either rabbinic or mystical circles. Only at the end of the fifteenth century did it begin to be cited by Sephardi sages as part of their battle for hegemony in the places they arrived in after their expulsion from

Ashkenazi and to R. Isaac Luria' (Heb.) (my thanks to Hagai Pely for drawing my attention to these articles).

   [12] See Liebes, 'New Directions in the Study of Kabbalah' (Heb.).
   [13] Huss, *Like the Radiance of the Sky* (Heb.), 183, 191, 208–10, 214–15, 218–83; see also Hallamish, 'Luria's Status as a Halakhic Authority' (Heb.).
   [14] Vital, *Ets ḥayim*, i. 34–5; see also i. 42; ii. 60.

the Iberian peninsula. The Zohar served them well in the battle against philosophical ideas, which they saw as weakening belief and adherence to the Jewish tradition, and allowed them to replace local halakhah and customs with Sephardi ones.[15] The Sephardi diaspora brought the traditions of the west to the eastern end of the Mediterranean and to the Italian communities on the way. It was precisely after the Iberian expulsions that Spanish kabbalah prospered and left its deep imprint on other Jewish traditions.[16]

The main body of the Zohar offers a mystical reading of the weekly portions of the Torah, but this seemingly traditional framework can barely mask its revolutionary character:

Rabbi Simeon began: 'I have put my words in your mouth. How vital it is for a human being to engage in Torah day and night! The Holy One listens to the voice of those who occupy themselves with Torah, and every word *innovated* in Torah by one engaged in Torah fashions one heaven. We have learned: The moment a *new word* of Torah originates from the mouth of a human being, that word ascends and presents herself before the blessed Holy One, who lifts that word, kisses her, and adorns her with seventy crowns. . . . But an *innovated word of wisdom* ascends and settles on the head of the Righteous One. From there, it flies and soars through 70,000 worlds, ascending to the Ancient of Days. . . . When that secret word of wisdom, *innovated* here, ascends, it joins those words of the Ancient of Days. . . . So each and every word of wisdom is transformed into a heaven, existing enduringly in the presence of the Ancient of Days. He calls them *new heaven, newly created heavens*, hidden mysteries of supernal wisdom. As for all other *innovated words of Torah*, they stand before the blessed Holy One, then ascend and are transformed into earths of the living. Then they descend, crowning themselves upon one earth, which is renewed and transformed into a *new earth* through that *renewed word of Torah*. Concerning this is written: 'As the *new heavens* and the *new earth* that I am making endure before me'. The verse does not read 'I have made' but rather 'I am making', for he makes them continually out of those *innovations* and mysteries of Torah.[17]

The inventive and the new stand at the heart of the mystical activity.

The Zohar revolves around a group of mystics following their master on the road, encountering the wonders of nature and unexpected events outside the traditional loci of Jewish learning—the *beit midrash* and the yeshiva—

---

[15] Huss, *Like the Radiance of the Sky* (Heb.), 167.
[16] Idel, 'Jewish Thought in Medieval Spain'.   [17] *The Zohar*, i. 4*b*–5*a*.

which act as a spur for the revelation of heavenly secrets. This leads to new interpretations of the Torah and, concurrently, to the creation of new mystical worlds. The mystics and God co-operate in generating new divine realms, and, in this mystical creativity, man is creating God as much as God created man. Moments of exhilaration reflect the mystics' liberty, 'delectation' (*sha'ashua*), and positive attitudes to material reality, their bodies, and even sexuality. The Zohar is one of the greatest literary and aesthetic achievements of medieval Jewish culture. It is not a systematic work, nor was it intended to be; its profoundness lies, to a great extent, in interpreting isolated biblical verses or narratives, which might later be loaded with more and more complementary or even contradictory interpretations.[18]

Almost every passage from Vital's *Ets ḥayim* reveals the distance between the zoharic and Lurianic writings. Most conspicuous are the linguistic differences:

I need to compare and explain the current claim with what is stated elsewhere. For the tools have two aspects, external and internal, which are body and soul. And the body has incubation, suckling, and intelligence, which lead to NHY [the *sefirot* Netsah, Hod, and Yesod], and later SE [six edges, six further spheres], and then the head, TF [the three first spheres]. And the head is called external intelligence . . . and the spheres of Netsah, Hod, and Yesod of incubation, which are vessels, contain the intelligence of minor incubation, which is the internal aspect of vessels. While the six edges of suckling contain the intelligence of suckling, which are the internal aspect of vessels.[19]

This is far from the graceful, enigmatic poetry of the Zohar. The language of *Ets ḥayim* lacks any rhetorical or aesthetic dimension; its tone is cumbersome, full of technicalities and rabbinic shorthand. Zoharic lyricism is replaced with the severe style of a textbook providing precise information. The Zohar was translated from its original Aramaic into Hebrew, Latin, and many modern languages; *Ets ḥayim* was never even translated into Latin by contemporary Christian kabbalists. As I shall demonstrate, the avoidance of any aesthetic dimension was not accidental but was related to fundamental points of Lurianic doctrine. *Ets ḥayim* offers an exact and comprehensive depiction of divine secrets, creating the clear impression that they can all be revealed. Vital did

[18] See Liebes, 'Zohar and Eros' (Heb.).   [19] Vital, *Ets ḥayim*, ii. 278.

include stern warnings against stepping outside the permitted domains of knowledge, stressing the need to take precautions and to observe the revelations 'hastily and as if looking through peepholes', especially in those passages containing bold anthropomorphic, and indeed sexual, metaphors in relation to God. Still, these admonitions should not be taken too literally, as they clearly mark the passages where the crucial pieces of information are. Fundamentally, so Vital hints, there are no secrets: theology and the divine realms are open, open to those who have access to the secret writings and the teachings of Luria and his followers. He even goes as far as to provide a new twist to the famous rabbinic story in which God orders Moses to keep silent and ask for no further explanations (BT *Men.* 29*b*). According to Vital this is another occasion for revelation, so that in fact there exists no barrier to the exposure of divine secrets.[20]

The divine realms are open in a double sense: there are no obstacles to anyone who has gained access to the kabbalistic community, and, once initiated, the seeker can explore them ad infinitum. But in a traditional society any new knowledge has to be grounded in the familiar, in earlier, accepted knowledge, and much of Lurianic theology was grounded in the Jewish tradition. However, the information was arranged according to three new and related paradigms: encyclopedism, mnemonics, and mechanics. This placed the new Jewish theology squarely within the knowledge revolution then occurring in Europe.

'Too much to know': The Organization of Information in Early Modern Europe

Europe witnessed considerable changes during the sixteenth and seventeenth centuries in politics (the rise of modern nation states, colonial expansion), religion (the schism between the Catholic and Protestant churches), economics (crises following unprecedented price rises, new sources of gold and other precious metals), geography (the discovery of the New World), and scholarship (the 'new science'). New scientific methods and the accumulation of information in many fields—biology, botany, physics, mathematics, mineralogy, mechanics, warfare—not only restructured the real world but also

---

[20] Ibid. i. 400.

formed the basis for major changes in how information was organized. This was an urgent task because of the sheer amount of new information.[21] Unlike previous achievements in science and philosophy, the knowledge revolution in early modern Europe affected increasingly large numbers of people, not all of them even aware of the changes.

Encyclopedism

European encyclopedism dates back to the medieval period.[22] The modern terminology became customary during the fifteenth and sixteenth centuries, in, for example, the writings of François Rabelais; but, according to Jacques Le Goff, the change was not merely semantic but an indication of the passage from medieval to modern patterns of thought. The twelfth and thirteenth centuries marked the high point of the production of *summae* and *encyclopaediae*, which presented comprehensive summaries of contemporary knowledge in a well-structured and organized manner and noted where information was lacking. Most of the people involved in these projects lived in monasteries, and the huge volumes they produced were the result of teamwork, unlike the work produced in the universities. One consequence of this was that knowledge acquired religious overtones. The medieval encyclopedists could not detach themselves from the moral-allegorical perspective—in which comprehension of the cosmos leads to a closer relationship with God—and see knowledge as an end in itself.

These huge volumes left an important legacy for later generations, including an awareness of how important methodological considerations were in organizing quantities of information too large to allow any specialization, and the dissemination of them beyond limited circles of theologians and academics. Despite these achievements the encyclopedists stimulated sharp criticism on the part of two leading intellectuals, the Franciscan friars Roger Bacon and Raymond Lull,[23] both of whom had a great influence on sixteenth-

---

[21] Gilbert, *Renaissance Concepts of Method*; see also Blair, *Too Much to Know*.

[22] See König and Woolf (eds), *Encyclopaedism from Antiquity to the Renaissance*; Fumagalli Beoni Brocchieri and Parodi, 'Due enciclopedie dell'occidente medievale'; Alessio, 'Conservazione e modelli di sapere nel medioevo'; Picone, 'Il significato di un convegno sull'enciclopedismo medievale'; Le Goff, 'Pourquoi le XIIIe siècle a-t-il été plus particulièrment un siècle d'enciclopedisme?'; see also Voorbij, 'Purpose and Audience'.

[23] See Blackburn, *Oxford Dictionary of Philosophy*, *s.v.* 'Bacon', 'Lull'; Fumagalli Beoni Brocchieri, 'Le enciclopedie'.

and seventeenth-century thought. Bacon criticized the simple acceptance of earlier texts as true and authoritative without any consideration of how their information was obtained. Lull left a vast number of writings, many of which are concerned with the expansion of knowledge. According to him, any discussion must begin from utterly reliable premises, following which it is possible to validate the truthfulness of any proposition with mathematical precision. One of his most important contributions was combinatorial theory, which was both logical and metaphysical and based on the common principles of all fields of knowledge. Simple components were combined with each other in order to analyse known facts and to produce new ones. This method was part of a project aimed at creating a new, artificial language, capable of coping perfectly with any and all types of information.

Many kinds of encyclopedia were compiled in Europe during the early modern period, and the term itself was not completely unambiguous. Johann Heinrich Alsted, who himself produced an important one, enumerated fifteen different types.[24] Their modern character is clear from the fact that they were usually intended for a popular audience and not confined to erudite circles. A typical example is *Universum naturae theatrum* (Universal Theatre of Nature) by Jean Bodin—better known for his contribution to modern jurisprudence and political thought[25]—in which he stated explicitly that he was presenting the knowledge of all 'natural sciences' to the general public.

The classical tradition of natural science was challenged by the massive flow of new information following discoveries, observations, and reports from the New World, and it became imperative to organize this unexpected and disorderly flood of facts. Leading figures—such as Peter Ramus, Francis Bacon, René Descartes, and Gottfried Leibniz—occupied themselves with questions of methodology. What were the preconditions for gaining knowledge? By what means could it be validated? How could human knowledge be expanded? Questions of this sort led to great interest in Lull's theories. He was not merely concerned with details but aspired to produce a guide to all science and religious doctrine. He not only sought to organize all the knowledge then available but to broaden its horizons to encompass the entire cosmos, following methodological principles that were considered to be

---

[24] See Blair, 'A Europeanist's Perspective', 204–5.
[25] See Blair, *The Theater of Nature*.

analogous to human cognition.[26] Lull's methodology was well known among Spanish Jewish intellectuals early in the fourteenth century.[27] The importance of this will become clear in Chapter 7, where I examine the role of the Sephardi diaspora in the promulgation of the Lurianic corpus throughout the Mediterranean world and beyond.

The storing and retrieval of knowledge were increasingly described using visual metaphors. Bodin referred to his work as a 'theatre', and other compilers of encyclopedias and works on methodology produced tables, 'trees of knowledge', maps, landscapes, and other images to present their readers with large quantities of information at a glance. These images also revealed lacunae in knowledge, which provided an incentive for further research. One of the most striking examples comes from the field of botany and reveals the fantastic increase in knowledge in this period. A tract published in 1530 contained 258 items; one published in 1715 contained more than 20,000.[28] The organization of so many samples was made possible by Carl Linnaeus's invention of botanic taxonomy, which he presented as a map, enabling every plant to be given a precise name which expressed its relationship to similar plants and their place in the classificatory system. A plant's name now carried information about the history of its discovery and its place in nature. The development of this nomenclature was a direct consequence of colonial endeavours, which led to encounters with vast numbers of plants previously unknown in Europe. I will discuss the similar role of libraries and *Kunstkammern* below.

The development of visual metaphors was paralleled by an increased criticism of language. Human languages were said to misrepresent reality and to prevent close acquaintance with it. Furthermore, the diversity of languages in the world created divisions and misunderstanding between people and hindered the spread of Christianity. Only a universal language could enhance cooperation among scholars and serve the goal of religious and spiritual unity. This led to attempts by the leading intellectuals of the sixteenth and seventeenth centuries to invent rigorous and accurate new languages—even going as far as to use mathematical signs for verbal expressions—which could label every object correctly and relate it to others of the same kind in an expanding network of absolutely certain facts.[29]

[26] Rossi, *Logic and the Art of Memory*, 30–8.   [27] See Hames, 'It Takes Three to Tango'.
[28] Rossi, 'La memoria, le immagini, l'enciclopedia', 230–2.
[29] Rossi, *Logic and the Art of Memory*, esp. ch. 7.

Interest in encyclopedism was not confined to intellectuals but started to spread into the general population as well, as is evident from the work of Johann Alsted. He was a follower of Lull and Ramus, publisher of the writings of Giordano Bruno, and the mentor of John Amos Comenius, the leading educational reformer of his day. Alsted's encyclopedic works were intended to enable the easy comprehension of all the sciences and provide verification criteria for every field of study. He related his method to kabbalistic traditions as part of a common search for the 'universal tree of knowledge'. Alsted's interest in the project was not theoretical but practical. He sought a comprehensive reform of education and the passing on of knowledge to future generations. This influenced a variety of other fields, such as jurisprudence, where legal codices were found to be easier to use when organized along general (and visual) principles,[30] the Bollandists' attempt to classify all the saints according to their feast days,[31] and the organization of collections of relics, including the immense one belonging to the Spanish king Felipe II.[32] The encyclopedic paradigm fell from favour in the late seventeenth century and was harshly criticized by Enlightenment intellectuals.

Mnemonics

The increased amount of information flooding into early modern Europe placed pressure on human memory and the traditional methods of memorization inherited from the Middle Ages and the Renaissance. Francis Yates has demonstrated how medieval culture preserved and developed the methods the Greeks and Romans used to enhance memory (*mnēmotechnē*, *ars memoriae*).[33] The most common technique was to create an imaginary architectural edifice with various rooms and spaces within which the information was 'deposited'. The process of recollection involved mentally strolling through the edifice and 'locating' the required information. Mary Carruthers

---

[30] See Fioravanti (ed.), *Lo stato moderno in Europa*; see also Hespanha, 'Cultura giuridica, libri dei giuristi e tecniche tipografiche'.

[31] Société des Bollandistes, *Acta Sanctorum*, <http://acta.chadwyck.co.uk/>.

[32] On the collection and its relationship to the library at the Escorial palace and the idea that it memorialized Catholic history and testified to the might of the Spanish kingdom, see Lazure, 'Possessing the Sacred'. The article contains interesting references on 'collectionism' in early modern Europe.

[33] Yates, *The Art of Memory*. On the contribution of this work to the study of memory, see Rossi, *Logic and the Art of Memory*, pp. xxii–xxiii.

and Lina Bolzoni criticized Yates's model as being too static, as if memory were a warehouse from which information could simply be collected.[34] They argued that this suits the modern conception of memory, which sees past events as finished and distinguishes memory from imagination, but it does not suit the medieval period, when memory was an active and creative process with an important role as a source of new religious and cultural insights.

Carruthers reconstructed mnemonic techniques as developed and prac-tised in medieval monasteries. Knowing and remembering things were not ends in themselves but means to spiritual salvation. Thus the model for the recollection process was not a stroll through a building but a browse through the chapters and verses of the holy books. Significant verses were kept deep within the mind where they interacted with one another:

The memory techniques, as shown by Mary Carruthers, are tightly connected to the way in which texts were read, ruminated on, assimilated, and transformed into an internal treasure that could be further reused in order to produce new texts or make moral decisions. Seen from this perspective, the text is not closed and never actually finished: it passes through the generations and functions as an authority, as much as it is fragmented, digested, made alive in other forms and other models of behaviour. Above all, it is a mental process, which leaves traces on the body. It is a long tradition in which the memory techniques of classical rhetoric interact with monastic meditative techniques. These techniques show how to shape one's mind and to create a map of 'places': here memories of things read and experienced are positioned and from here one draws material and associations for new thoughts, new words, and new deeds. The force of the mind enables one to construct mental temples, tabernacles, palaces, gardens, and routes to follow during the process of mental elevation and to transform the memory into an archive capable of reproduc-ing and generating. It is a memory nourished by the Bible, or better by some pas-sages of the Bible, imprinted in the mind, so as to create a network of places. It is a memory which aims at the celestial Jerusalem and the eternal world of the afterlife. It is a memory which mobilizes the emotions, and closely connects the reading, maintaining, and inventing of Holy Scriptures.[35]

Human memory, according to Hugh of St Victor, one of the innovators of medieval mnemonics, requires order and organization.[36] Its enemy is not ob-livion but chaos and the deplorable fault of *curiositas* (being over-inquisitive).

[34] Carruthers, *The Craft of Thought*; Bolzoni, *La stanza della memoria*.
[35] Bolzoni, *La rete delle immagini*, pp. xviii–xix (my translation).
[36] Carruthers, *The Craft of Thought*, 81–2.

What is needed is a well-structured mental framework, with information organized according to themes and sub-themes, so that one look can encompass them all: a method perfectly suited to reading the holy books in order to meditate on them later. The internal taxonomy is a pre-condition for both recollection and creative thought. This imaginative and creative process was called *machina animae* (the machine of the soul).

Lina Bolzoni has examined the continuation of these monastic practices into the Italian Renaissance. The intimate link between written texts and visual images in the Augustinian tradition was stressed in monastic meditation texts which instructed the reader to represent textual messages by human figures (for example, seven women for the seven cardinal virtues): these were to be mentally connected to important personal emotions, which could then lead to the creation of other images. Alternatively, the information might be organized along different branches of the 'tree of life', each with its own character which could interact with all the others. Visualization techniques were also used in public sermons in Italian cities, such as the preaching of Bernardino of Siena. He turned the entire city into a huge mnemonic device: local landmarks became visual symbols for his listeners, reminding them of the content of his sermons. Imagination, memory, bodily senses, canonical texts, spirituality, and the city were all woven into one fabric.[37]

The classical technique of using places to aid memory was augmented by adding human figures, either real or imaginary, who had some significance for the practitioner. Bolzoni discusses a tract written for a nun in the fifteenth century by a Franciscan monk in Pisa. During meditation she was instructed to visualize a space in which the tracts she had studied appeared as familiar people. They would then interact and create new insights and texts. She could also use the technique to reconstruct the Stations of the Cross or recall the canonical hours.[38]

The preoccupation with mnemonics continued into the sixteenth century, especially in Italy. But in contrast to previous periods it was not limited

---

[37] Ibid. 103.
[38] Bolzoni, *La rete delle immagini*, 71–2. The Stations of the Cross is a sequence of fourteen events from the day of Jesus's death, including his trial, crucifixion, and burial. Images of them are often placed on church walls, and the faithful move along the sequence saying a prayer at each one. The canonical hours are the divisions of the monastic day separated by prayers, including matins, lauds, and vespers.

to monastic circles or brief moments of enthusiasm during religious festivals. The issue now was the harnessing of human memory to cope with knowledge in fields as diverse as rhetoric, philosophy and theology, theatre and other pastimes, and physiognomy. The aim—to memorize all available knowledge —was not a modest one, nor was it theoretical; it was considered entirely practical and feasible, since the compilers of memory books intended them for students' use and needed to sell them to make a living.

Undoubtedly the father of modern mnemonics was Giulio Camillo.[39] Very little is known about this fascinating person—alchemist, kabbalist, friend of artists and writers, a man of literature and philosophy. Those who knew him not only praised his phenomenal memory but described him as a 'divine man'. He is best known for his life's work, the Teatro del Mondo (Theatre of the World) and the theoretical writings which preceded it. The theatre was a physical construction, erected and exhibited at least twice— in Italy and Paris—which presented visually all the information about the physical world and cosmic order. It was described by contemporaries as a 'theoretical book' comprising all the books available in the sixteenth century. It was a huge and complex machine, wherein movable plates produced end-less new combinations of the relatively simple elements of the universe. However, it did not just present the external world: it required a deep intel-lectual and emotional involvement, and watching the spectacle was supposed to influence the mental processes of the spectator. Camillo considered Jewish kabbalah an important element of his mnemonic system and machines, and the classical Ciceronian memory techniques were replaced by seven eternal principles of reality borrowed from seven of the zoharic *sefirot*.

Another innovative figure was Orazio Toscanella.[40] Toscanella claimed that his motivation for writing a book on memory was not honour or fame but the fatigue caused by the amount of reading necessary to be considered learned in any field. This inspired him to find a quicker method of memoriz-ing the contents of a book. Using his experience as a university professor, he produced diagrams, trees of knowledge, and tables, which would allow his students to reduce any work to its basic elements and recompose it in a more

[39] See Bolzoni, *La rete delle immagini*, and *La stanza della memoria*; see also Bologna, 'Esercizi di memoria dal "Theatro della sapientia" di Giulio Camillo agli "Esercizi spirituali" di Ignazio Loyola'.   [40] Bolzoni, *La stanza della memoria*, 53–75.

easily memorized form. Another of Toscanella's books was a dictionary, which he worked on throughout his life, expanding it in an attempt to encompass all existing knowledge. Machines were an important source of inspiration for those involved in developing mnemonic techniques. An illustration in a contemporary work *Diverse et artificiose macchine* (Diverse and Artificial Machines) explicitly depicts a man sitting operating a machine with cogs which produces new books by combining others.[41] Toscanella, in fact, proposed rhetorical machines or mechanisms that could not only enhance memory, but also digest every literary and rhetorical text and produce new ones. In his *Armonia di tutti i principali retorici* (Harmony of all Major Rhetoricians) the rhetorical tradition is presented graphically to suggest that every element is the centre of a circle of knowledge, of which every point is also the centre of a circle of knowledge, and so on and so on.

Early modern mnemonic techniques began to be used in new areas such as botany, music, games, library cataloguing, and museum curating. They were perceived as ever more important, since the theatrical structures and memory machines were taken to reflect the actual processes of the human mind:

Machines, then, are the prolongation and projection of the mental mechanism, but the relation might be turned upside down [and the human mind viewed as an extension of the machine]. . . . For Giovanni Fontana, numbers furnish an efficient instrument for the art of memory, and they are located in a territory in which the fascination of machines is mingled with the search for refined perspective techniques and extraordinary illusionistic effects. In a culture influenced by Neoplatonism and kabbalah, the construction, use, and deciphering of numbers implies a contact with the most profound and secretive elements of reality.[42]

The seventeenth century saw an abrupt end to the intensive preoccupation with memory as a basis for polymathy and a way to organize general knowledge:

The widespread dissemination of the printed book (and thus of repertories, dictionaries, bibliographies and encyclopedias), and the progressive development of new logical methods (from Ramus to Bacon, from Descartes to the logicians of Port Royal) had dealt a mortal blow to the popularity and credibility of the mnemotechnical works which, during the fifteenth and sixteenth centuries and in

[41] See ibid. 61–4.   [42] Ibid. 104–5 (my translation).

the first decades of the seventeenth, had literally invaded Europe. It is only by taking into account the widespread popularity of mnemotechnics, not only in literary and philosophical circles, but also schools, universities and pedagogical programmes, that we can begin to understand the vehemence of the many criticisms and satires which were levelled against it in the Renaissance.[43]

Mechanics

Machines, in our highly technological era, are often seen as alienating and a threat to individuality, despite their immense usefulness. It was very different in the Middle Ages and, certainly, during the early modern period. One of the most important medieval machines was the treadwheel crane, which could lift very heavy weights with minimal effort, and it became an important metaphor for lifting the mind to spiritual heights. Lifting bodies was one of the themes discussed in medieval mechanics, as part of the general discussion of how bodies moved and interacted.[44] Important advances were made by the *calculatores*, who tried to provide a quantitative calculation (hence their name) of the movements of bodies using mathematical tables. However, their calculations and insights were not to be applied to actual bodies; they dealt with the interactions of abstract bodies in abstract space.

A great leap forward in mechanics was achieved in Italy during the sixteenth century as a result of the unusual co-operation between mathematicians, such as Niccolò Tartaglia and Giovanni Benedetti, and craftsmen and architects. In 1577 Count Guidobaldo del Monte published *Liber mechanicorum* (The Book of Mechanics), which established mechanics as an independent, legitimate, and respectable domain of knowledge and not solely the concern of craftsmen, proficient only in practical matters and lacking any theoretical background.[45] Del Monte's book was commissioned by the prince of Urbino to serve very practical ends: the construction of war machines and fortifications. The book is representative of how knowledge spread from small circles of erudite people, usually affiliated with universities, to more and more of the general population, who had no access to the theoretical

---

[43] Rossi, *Logic and the Art of Memory*, 2; see also pp. xvi–xviii, 6, 29–30, 58, 61–3, 97.

[44] Clagett, *The Science of Mechanics in the Middle Ages*. On further developments in mechanics in Italy, see Wallace, 'Mechanics from Bradwardine to Galileo'.

[45] Henninger-Voss, 'Working Machines and Noble Mechanics'; Micheli, *Le origini del concetto di macchina*, esp. 32–5, 144–61.

level but nevertheless wished to benefit from the information. Fear that the spread of knowledge would be uncontrollable was expressed by Del Monte in his book and his private letters, and he was right: machines began to appear in other contexts as well, such as publishing houses, mines, and mills.[46] However, machines did not serve only military, economic, and trade purposes: they became part of a profound cultural shift that broke down the distinction between respectable theoretical knowledge and despised practical work that went back to the medieval period if not earlier. This distinction was strongly criticized during the early modern period as pedantic, lacking in any scientific basis, and typical of class bias.[47] Indeed many of the important achievements of this period were the joint labour of theoreticians of abstract knowledge and those in possession of practical experience acquired in workshops and on construction sites.

Machines played an important role in putting theoretical achievements to practical use, but their contribution went further, as research into mechanics provided the knowledge to not only ameliorate nature but to overcome it.[48] Some of the more radical theoreticians, such as the French mathematician Henri de Monantheuil, presented God as a divine mechanic, creator of an elaborate *machina mundi* (world machine). The clock served as the archetype of the mechanical exactitude of natural law and appears in the works of Johannes Kepler, for example. Some of the most famous utopian visions of the period were inspired by machinery and scientific innovation, such as Tycho Brahe's *Urania*, Tommaso Campanella's *Città del sole*, and Francis Bacon's *Nova Atlantis*.

An important visual expression of this process were *Kunstkammern*, 'cabinets of curiosities', well-ordered collection rooms. According to Horst Bredekamp, they represented the entire universe in a physical encyclopedia.[49] They contained three sections—one for minerals, plants, and animals (the natural world), one for artistic objects (history and culture), and one for artificial items, mainly new machines (human ingenuity)—demonstrating

---

[46] Rossi, *Philosophy, Technology and the Arts in the Early Modern Period*, 37–42; Henninger-Voss, 'Working Machines and Noble Mechanics', 239.

[47] See Rossi, *Philosophy, Technology and the Arts in the Early Modern Period*.

[48] Bredekamp, *The Lure of Antiquity and the Cult of the Machine*, esp. 37–9, 58–62. Bredekamp mentions Descartes's claim that he did not perceive any differences between machines constructed by craftsmen and natural objects (ibid. 39). [49] Ibid. 40, 49–53, 72–4.

humanity's rise from and mastery of nature and embodying the belief that humanity could imitate God and participate in the process of creation. *Kunst-kammern* reflected the classic conflict between nature and art and, in this context, between stagnation and progress. They were both a laboratory and an incentive for further discoveries, and their wealthy owners often funded expensive scientific projects.

The period was one of intense religious debate as a result of the rise of Protestantism, and scientific innovation was imbued with theological implications.[50] The link between the new science and theology contributed much to secular and modern attitudes.[51] These attitudes can be characterized as secular because they were influenced by lay people—Galileo, Descartes, Leibniz, and Newton—as opposed to professional theologians or church dignitaries, but they were also secular in a deeper sense, since their implicit premises about God were radically different from those of the Middle Ages. The search for a concise and exact universal language was already present in the medieval scholastic tradition, but the laws of nature as discussed and presented in the language of early modern science were applicable equally and universally on earth and in heaven. In order to have scientific validity they could not be limited only to the earthly domain, as medieval thinkers claimed. Teleological reasoning, the idea that everything that happens serves some higher goal, was rejected in favour of mechanistic reasoning: things happen because they follow natural laws.

Descartes united some the fundamental elements of this new discourse:

The new method purported to be universal, a canon of principles and procedures overarching all disciplines. Descartes claimed that it was a tool for the discovery of new truths, not only for the exposition of old ones . . . [a method] whose practitioners know what they talk about because they start with simple intuitions and combine them according to infallible rules. The method proceeded by resolution and composition. It succeeded in uniting algebra and geometry, in the mathematization of mechanical laws and the mechanization of natural phenomena. It had built philosophy, physiology, and psychology on new foundations. Most 'mechanical

---

[50] An obvious example is the science conducted in Jesuit institutions (see Gorman, 'The Scientific Counter-Revolution'; see also Feingold (ed.), *Jesuit Science and the Republic of Letters*.

[51] Funkenstein, *Theology and the Scientific Imagination*, esp. 3–7, 12–14, 28–30, 176–9, 291–9, 317–27; see also Feldhai, *Galileo and the Church*.

philosophers' of the seventeenth century embraced many of these hopes and claims.[52]

The old boundaries between God and humankind needed redefinition in response to the new claims of knowledge. The way God knows the world and its natural laws is not essentially different from how humanity learns about the world through deduction and discursive thinking. Furthermore, attributing temporal and spatial predicates to God is unavoidable if he is to intervene in the world. While testing his theories practically, Galileo stated that natural laws can be verified only by quantification and measurement. Later he claimed this as a basic criterion for understanding the *machina mundi*.[53] The *machina mundi* was a huge mechanism of interacting objects and dynamics that followed strict rules and formed a self-contained closed system. No external force, such as the will of God, was needed. Understanding this immense mechanism required the meticulous acquisition of many details and the examination of patterns in various domains (chemistry, mineralogy, physics, biology). True knowledge implies both general criteria and specific details. Interest in mechanics was not confined to the philosophical and scientific elite. It was also manifested in popular passions for clocks, machines for performing astronomical calculations, and automata. It was even claimed the human body was nothing more than a vastly complicated machine.

The Lurianic God

Encyclopedism

Jewish encyclopedias were being compiled during the Middle Ages, mainly using Aristotelian taxonomy.[54] In the fifteenth and sixteenth centuries the Jewish communities of Italy witnessed a noticeable rise in encyclopedic writing, with works by Yohanan Alemano, Abraham Portaleone, Abraham Yagel-Gallico, Solomon Joseph del Medigo, Jacob Tsahalon, and Tobias Hakohen (the last two were both doctors of medicine) and, later, Isaac Cardoso and Leone Modena.[55] The contribution of Vital's *Ets ḥayim* to Jewish culture

---

[52] Funkenstein, *Theology and the Scientific Imagination*, 296.

[53] Dear, 'The Meaning of Experience'; see also Daston and Park (eds.), *Early Modern Science*.

[54] Harvey (ed.), *The Medieval Hebrew Encyclopedias of Science and Philosophy*; Berger and Fontaine, 'Something on Every Subject'.

[55] Melamed, 'The Hebrew Italian Renaissance and Early Modern Encyclopedias'.

must be considered as part of the rise of the encyclopedia genre in the early modern Jewish context (the most famous examples being Joseph Karo's *Beit yosef* and *Shulḥan arukh*[56]).

The Lurianic corpus can be considered encyclopedic simply on the grounds of its size. It was expanded throughout the seventeenth century and was quite exceptional in contemporary Jewish culture, although Moses Cordovero also left a massive quantity of writings, and prolific writing is an interesting feature of other early modern authors, such as Judah Loew (Maharal) of Prague. Luria's followers claimed to possess the keys to under-standing all levels of reality: even what was not stated explicitly could be restored by those who knew the recurring patterns in extant knowledge and possessed the noetic tools. However, the corpus is also encyclopedic in its content. There is no significant issue in Jewish religion not dealt with—sin and punishment, the next world, religious practice, prayer, body and soul, salvation, halakhah, and preaching—but there are also novel themes—lan-guage and its value, religious practice as a means of spiritual elevation, family life, the body and corporeality, sexuality as central to human life, death, rais-ing and educating children, and magic and popular beliefs. These themes are not discussed separately but woven together throughout the corpus, cross-referenced into an enormous web of knowledge, which, in its holism and methodology, recalls early modern encyclopedism.

Both the Lurianic and Cordoveran schools attributed great weight to knowledge of the divine realms as the basis for religious life and ritual prac-tice. When Luria's esoteric sayings and Cordovero's *Or ne'erav* became known beyond the circles of their disciples, their systems were given more structure and order. In later kabbalistic literature, the theologization of the religious heritage is much clearer.[57] The Lurianic cosmos as it finally appears is one comprehensive fabric, from the divine realms through the material world to the demonic domain. In Lurianic terms it runs from Ein Sof (infin-ity) to Adam Kadmon, whose body is an emanation of light containing the divine Faces, to the ten *sefirot* and three created worlds (*beri'ah*, *yetsirah*, and *asiyah*) to the angelic kingdom, the system of wheels (*galgalim*) that move the

[56] On the printing of the *Shulḥan arukh* and its impact on the early modern Jewish world, see Raz-Krakotzkin, 'Law and Censure' (Heb.).
[57] See Idel, 'On the Theologization of Kabbalah in Modern Scholarship'; see also G. Cor-dovero, 'Introduction' (Heb.), to M. Cordovero, *Or ne'erav*, 3a.

stars, and the material world (*olam hahomer*)—the scene of human existence —with its four elements, and finally to the demonic region (*sitra ahra*).

Adam Kadmon is not only the first to appear, but his image is repeated at every level of reality.[58] Even though any discussion of Ein Sof is prohibited in Lurianic theology (as in earlier kabbalistic traditions), a cautious analogy is suggested: that Ein Sof relates to Adam Kadmon as Adam Kadmon relates to the emanated domain, since the divine essence is reflected at every level of existence:

[The relationship of] Adam Kadmon [to the emanated domain] is analogous to the relationship between Keter [Crown, the first *sefirah*] and the rest of the ten *sefirot*, and this analogy is valid in every world. For Adam Kadmon is the crown of four mystical levels of emanation. Consequently Adam Kadmon provides the root of all five worlds . . . be it of souls, bodies, garments, or palaces.[59]

Furthermore, the members of the human body are organized in the same manner as Adam Kadmon's.[60]

The emanation processes within and beyond Adam Kadmon are described in meticulous detail: each and every division and subdivision of his light is named, measured, and documented.[61] The most dramatic of these processes preceded the Creation: the Breaking of the Vessels (*shevirat hakelim*) and the Dispersal of the Divine Sparks (*hitpazrut hanitsotsot*). The divine light had to be restricted in order to allow space for Creation to take place. It was poured into vessels, but they could not contain the infinite light and broke, and it spilled everywhere. Most of it returned instantly to its divine source, yet some sparks remained trapped in the world. The third process, the Reparation of the Worlds (*tikun ha'olamot*), is the return of these divine sparks to God. This is achieved through repairing the world and humanity, since the divine sparks are present in both of them.

The endless division of the light of Adam Kadmon is necessary since the divinity is infinite and comprises all aspects of reality: a claim made earlier in the history of Jewish mysticism, especially in *Sefer yetsirah*, which records the

---

[58] Vital, *Ets hayim*, i. 37, 48, 51; ii. 33, 301, 315.

[59] Ibid. i. 48; see also i. 33; ii. 301. [60] Ibid. i. 31, 49, 149; ii. 359.

[61] Ibid. i. 32, 41, 43, 46–7, 53, 56, 62, 75–6, 80, 82, 89, 90, 97–8, 105, 109–11, 120, 144, 150, 158, 161, 172–3, 179, 203, 208, 212, 215, 223–4, 229–31, 234–5, 240, 253, 256, 262, 267, 272, 276, 280, 283, 287–8, 291–3, 295, 301, 311, 315–16, 327, 329–32, 336; ii. 3, 22, 31, 42, 44, 49–51, 55–6, 90, 117, 119, 231–2, 244, 262–3, 265, 269, 272, 280–1, 298–9, 321, 328.

infinite measurements of God, although even in this enigmatic composition no internal divine mechanism is described. In the Lurianic corpus this is elucidated at extraordinary length: the location of every component within the divine structure is noted. The obsession with fine detail borders on intoxicating, and the sheer amount of data threatens to become overwhelming; however, it remains controlled by Adam Kadmon's image repeating itself at each level of creation. The parallels between levels are very exact and are presented with the soberness of a talmudic legal discussion.

Thus was elaborated the order of the angels' souls produced from the coupling of Abba and Imma, and by analogy from the coupling of Ze'er Anpin and Rachel . . . and by analogy from the coupling of Israel and Leah, and by analogy from the coupling of Jacob and Rachel, and by analogy from the coupling of Jacob and Leah, and all this in the emanated divine world and by analogy in the three divine worlds beneath them. So you should understand the existence of various kinds of souls and of angels, for there are infinite grades, all distinct one from the other.[62]

As the same deductive rules are applied from one legal discussion to the next, the structures of Adam Kadmon, the Faces, the ten *sefirot*, and so on are the same: 'And now we shall expose a fundamental rule, concerning all four divine worlds. . . . We shall start with the Face Ze'er Anpin, from which [the reader] can deduce [the rules] for the other Faces.'[63] As in a talmudic discussion, the Lurianic mystic encounters logical and textual inconsistencies, which must be resolved. These resolutions may not be valid for the entire Lurianic construction, yet they do solve local difficulties. As in a yeshiva, the discussion leans on canonical texts which provide the starting point for discussion and elaboration.[64] The analogy ends with the material world and minute details of how human life reflects the secret life of God (for example, the five aspects of the human mind reflect the five divine Faces). The tone is not one of ecstatic revelation but of methodological teaching, using the discursive mode and deductive logic of a textbook. At other times it borrows technical terms from the Talmud such as legal exegesis (*perushim*) and judicial controversy

---

[62] Vital, *Ets ḥayim*, ii. 233, 280.   [63] Ibid. ii 307.

[64] Ibid.; see also i. 33, 35, 37, 43, 44–5, 46, 53, 61, 66, 68, 76, 77, 80, 81, 84–5, 87–90, 93, 107, 108, 132, 139, 149, 153, 166, 171, 207, 212, 215, 220, 224, 232, 250, 252, 277, 288, 295, 300, 326, 329, 330, 333, 336; ii. 3, 7, 10, 21, 24, 43, 51, 57, 61, 75, 110, 220, 229, 231, 232, 233, 247, 254, 255, 256, 261, 266, 269, 270, 274, 285, 286–7, 292, 297, 300, 302, 322, 329, 348, 379, 384, 401, 402.

(*maḥloket*),[65] and the atmosphere is that of a typical Sephardi yeshiva any-where in the Ottoman empire, where heated discussions were terminated by the final, decisive word of the head of the yeshiva.[66] At other times Vital borrows terms from the philosophical tradition, such as 'prolegomenon' (*hakdamah*), 'deduction' (*hekesh*), or 'unavoidable result' (*hekhreaḥ*).[67]

However, Lurianic theology is not a static system. The infinite diversity of divine revelation makes any attempt at a final description impossible. Every claim, every proposition put forward in *Ets ḥayim* is countered by oth-ers restricting its validity or limiting its application. Every generalization turns out to be only partial. The eternal movement and ceaseless motion of emanations of God are never the same. The principal metaphor used to con-vey this is the endless rotations of the stars and the unique constellations thus created:

In each and every minute the worlds change, and no one hour is like any other. Whoever looks at the stars and zodiac signs rotate will understand the endless divine worlds and how they change, and according to these changes thus transform the readings of the Zohar. And these are all divine revelations.[68]

While allocating a fundamental role to the Zohar, it is also claimed that only the Lurianic mystics held the key to expounding it and reading its secrets, which only extended as far as the *sefirot* and avoided exposing the structure of Adam Kadmon and the divine Faces. Endless variety posed the same prob-lem that confronted early modern compilers of encyclopedias: the tension between the need for an all-encompassing structure as the basis for any sig-nificant and comprehensive compendium of knowledge, and the necessity of including the masses of small details, local particularism, and variety. Variety suited the Lurianic tradition, as every aspect of Jewish religion and scholar-ship could be linked to some aspect in the divine economy.

Mnemonics

One of the most fundamental Lurianic claims is that no 'event' in the divine world ever gets 'lost': it always leaves some mark or sign. These signs remain

---

[65] Ibid. i. 101–4, 107, 119, 120, 131, 151, 152–3, 189, 192, 204, 206, 209, 241, 251, 258–60, 267, 282, 295, 297–8, 304, 310, 317, 329, 331.

[66] Avivi, *Lurianic Kabbalah* (Heb.), ii. 601, 609; iii. 1052, 1177, 1183. On the Sephardi educa-tional tradition in general, see Grossman, 'Characteristics of the Yeshivas in Islamic Spain' (Heb.).   [67] Vital, *Ets ḥayim*, i. 46, 80, 81, 87–9, 93.   [68] Ibid. i. 42–3.

in the cosmic memory, since the divine activity needs to leave its inner recesses and radiate itself onto its surroundings. This radiation leaves memory-
signs (*reshimu*) on everything it encounters.[69] *Reshimu* is related to both
roshem ('impression') and *lirshom* ('to write'). The divine Faces and the *sefirot*
interact and reflect their lights upon each other, and these events result in
memory-signs that provide a record of divine activity. A fundamental metaphor of this encounter, recorded in the cosmic memory, is the sexual act
between the masculine and feminine aspects of God. As human coupling
leads to the creation of new life, the divine encounter gives birth to another
aspect of God which is the memory-sign of such an encounter.[70]

Lurianic thought took earlier kabbalistic traditions of providing everything in the universe—thoughts, abstractions, the mutual reflections of divine Faces—with a name and ontological position of its own to new heights.
The process of treating abstractions as if they were real, existing things is
called 'reification', and Luria's reificatory tendency was so strong that his
mystical language needed to be rigorous and rich enough to provide a semantic map of God. It thus not only offers a system for representing the divine
realms but also serves as a bottomless memory reservoir, capable of containing all the mystical data. All the classifications and sub-classifications of divine
activity and its continual flux needed to be explicitly expressible. This was
similar to the contemporary European search for a universal language
capable of expressing all knowledge and is also why the Lurianic corpus is so
technical and unaesthetic.

Originally Luria's teachings were transmitted orally to his disciples in no
particular order.[71] Later generations, under the influence of Vital, restructured the material in order to impart it to their disciples. At first the tradition
was conveyed mainly through the exegesis of holy scriptures and the explanation of the commandments. The divine memory-signs were presented as
waymarks on a mental map of the sacred texts, and every aspect of Jewish life
and tradition was plotted onto this map. A map is a useful concept for understanding Lurianic kabbalah, since all the inner processes of the divinity and
the divine Faces are described in spatial terms. Despite the Jewish abhorrence
of anthropomorphic descriptions of God, an abhorrence occasionally ex-

---

[69] Vital, *Ets ḥayim*, ii. 44.   [70] See ibid. ii. 232.
[71] Avivi, *Lurianic Kabbalah* (Heb.), i. 34; ii. 637, 720; iii. 1113–15, 1174.

pressed in Vital's own writings, the mystical approach is saturated with visual and spatial similes. In the Lurianic system, every divine element has its own particular place,[72] which overlaps with that of the elements adjacent to it, implying that every aspect of the divine shared its nature with each of the others.[73] In a very common sixteenth-century trope, the divine body is seen as analogous to the human body, and every member is seen to contain all the others and internal equilibrium as necessary for its correct functioning.[74]

Vital employed a rich vocabulary to describe the interaction between the various members of the divine body and the mutual imprint of memory-signs. 'Emanation of lights' (*ha'atsalat orot*) is a central simile. It is always a two-stage process: light flows out from a divine Face or *sefirah* and then returns, bringing some memory-sign back with it. This creates a sophisticated structure in which each component draws meaning from each of the others and shares some of their contents.[75] The technical term for this interaction is *behinah*, a Lurianic neologism meaning 'reflection'. Another common simile is the 'root of the spheres' (*shorshei hasefirot*), which refers to the fact that every aspect of God remains in intimate contact with its source. 'Donning of clothes' or 'wrapping' (*hitlabshut*) refers to an intimate encounter between *sefirot*.

The memory-signs mark an endlessly dynamic system of lights flowing out and returning, creating new lights and new aspects of God in a complicated network of interdependent elements. 'Their ends lies in their beginning' was a key expression in Vital's writings. The great chain of divine being, from Ein Sof to humanity, upwards and downwards, was constantly changing and being changed, its elements constantly reflecting and being reflected by memory-signs of themselves and of others, forming a dynamic, self-contained system of storing memory-signs with its own rules and activities.

Some elements of the Lurianic memory machine had clear parallels in the contemporary European preoccupation with memory: holy scriptures as the basis for the restoration of divine memories; the combination of memorized facts as a source of new religious insights; acquaintance with divine realms as a starting point for meditation; visual imagery and especially memory and mystical language as tools for mapping knowledge of God; emotions

---

[72] 'Place' in the double sense of location and role.   [73] Vital, *Ets hayim*, i. 2, 50.
[74] Ibid. ii. 325.   [75] Ibid. i. 75, 179; ii. 82; see also Wolfson, 'Assaulting the Border'.

as a means of maintaining memories; memory as a road to individual and collective salvation; the use of memory techniques to expedite the mastery of rabbinic texts. The European and Lurianic traditions came together in their use of the biblical 'tree of life' as a basis for memory techniques and for encountering God, and their use of the image of a circle, all the points on the circumference of which were themselves centres of circles—the 'infinity of infinities' of Toscenalla and Bruno. In both Jewish and Catholic contexts memory was not restricted to organizing knowledge but provided a tool to influence the outside world.

Mechanics

Vital had a deep interest in the application of the new science to daily life, and in one work he describes a system of measuring the height of objects based on geometrical theorems.[76] In *Ets ḥayim*, the descriptions of God are full of mechanical imagery: the most significant act, the emanation of light between divine Faces and *sefirot*, is compared to the passage of water from one vessel to another.[77] In another context the balance of lights is said to follow the natural law that regulates the height of water in two connected vessels, 'as one can clearly perceive in nature'.[78]

The central element of this model is physical space. Following the Aristotelian principle—still current in sixteenth-century Europe—that all objects occupy space, in *Ets ḥayim*, every aspect of God is assigned a place.[79] The ceaseless changes and interactions within the divine realms are described exactly,[80] and Vital recorded their lengths and breadths.[81] The overlaps between divine realms are analysed according to quantity and quality.[82] The direction of every divine aspect is described: if a divine Face is showing its front to one, logic demands that it must be showing its back to another.[83] Every process takes time, and no intermediary phase can be skipped.[84] As the divine Faces interact with each other, every one of their aspects is divided into mathematical sections—halves and quarters, thirds and sixths, and their combinations, ad infinitum—in a process entirely unprecedented in Jewish mysticism. Statements about God are always accompanied by some concrete

---

[76] Vital, *Sefer hape'ulot*, 25.   [77] Vital, *Ets ḥayim*, i. 47.
[78] Ibid. ii. 345–6; see also i. 203–4, 250; ii. 160; id., *Sha'ar hakavanot*, i. 9*a*, 71*a*, 163*b*, 280.
[79] Vital, *Ets ḥayim*, i. 112, 293; ii. 124, 323.   [80] Ibid. ii. 210.   [81] Ibid. i. 292.
[82] Ibid. i. 57.   [83] See esp. ibid. i. 93, 109.   [84] Ibid. i. 96, 313, 320.

numerical evaluation or measurement, which might lead at times to paradox: the *sefirah* Netsah (Eternity) has to pass through the same mechanistic grinder that evaluates every aspect in numerical terms: 'It is well known that Eternity is divided into three parts.'[85] Passages from the rabbinic canon are also subjected to this analysis: in a discussion of the saying that women are light-minded (BT *Shab.* 33*b*), the term 'light' is valued as quantitative statement, implying that women received half of the emanated light that men did.[86] The mind–body distinction, so important to mysticism in general, is described in quantitative parameters: the presence of various parts of the mind in the body can be measured as part of the parallel growth of God and man, as the mind physically fills more and more of the members of the body.[87] As machines in early modern Europe were explained by precise mathematical principles, so, in *Ets ḥayim*, is God. This mechanistic analysis of God led to some of the most graceless writing in *Ets ḥayim*, devoid of any aesthetic merit, as any literary diversion might interfere with the transmission of the precise mechanical details.

Mechanics added another dimension to the Lurianic understanding of God. Not only did aspects of the divine overlap and leave memory-signs in each other, the activity of each of them was limited by the others as described by one of the more profound readers of Luria's teachings, the prominent eighteenth-century Italian kabbalist Moses Hayim Luzzatto, who described the function of the *sefirot* as a 'horologe [chronometer], whose wheels encounter one another' in such a way as to ensure they move in unison.[88] The aspects of the divine were connected to each other like cogs: if one moved, the others had to move accordingly. The divine Faces were not only great conglomerations of lights but were also components of a huge machine.

Summary

During its initial phase, Lurianic literature was a jealously guarded secret circulated among close friends and trusted disciples. It was highly technical and apparently lacked any rhetorical finesse or poetic inspiration, and yet it

[85] Ibid. ii. 110. [86] Ibid. i. 253. [87] See ibid. i. 250.
[88] Cited in Avivi, *Lurianic Kabbalah* (Heb.), ii. 764. The clock metaphor was important in early modern European culture (see Mayr, *Authority, Liberty, and Automatic Machinery in Early Modern Europe* (my thanks to Ido Ya'avets for drawing my attention to this work)).

appealed to increasingly large sections of the Jewish population from the late sixteenth century onwards. Lurianic theology contained many traditional elements and often relied on the hermeneutics of earlier generations, but it was not so much a continuation of the mystical heritage as a rupture. It originated in the need to find a new organizing framework for the Jewish tradition, in the same way as early modern Europe needed to find a new organizing framework for the vast amounts of knowledge then being accumulated—although there is no evidence for the direct influence of any European intellectual figure on Luria or Vital. The revelation of new divine realms, the divine Faces, beyond the zoharic *sefirot* obliged Luria to stretch the Hebrew language to its limits, giving new meanings to old terms and producing a whole series of neologisms.

Vital's *Ets ḥayim* is very different from earlier mystical tracts, as shown by a comparison with the Zohar, the inspiration for the Lurianic tradition. The difference is not confined to the stylistic or linguistic level: daring anthropomorphic statements about God appear in the zoharic sections *Idra raba* and *Idra zuta*, but nowhere do we find such detailed references to any aspect of God and the divine realms or divisions and subdivisions into halves and quarters, thirds and sixths.

There are three aspects of late sixteenth-century European culture which can serve as paradigms for the Lurianic discourse: encyclopedism, mnemonics, and mechanics. Luria's God has distinctly mechanistic traits: his inner dynamics are governed by strict mechanical laws—like cogs in a chronometer—and ceaselessly produce new knowledge by combinations of his basic elements. None of this knowledge is ever lost but is preserved by memorysigns in the endless reservoir of God. Place held a central role in memory techniques from late antiquity to the early modern period, especially in the systematic representation of knowledge in tables, charts, trees of knowledge, maps, and memory theatres. This contributed to the visual and spatial representations in Lurianic kabbalah. Visualizing techniques provided a way to approach God, as Giulio Busi noted in his discussion of 'visual kabbalah' and the spread of manuscripts containing charts of God.[89] The divine machine and memory reservoir contained all the knowledge available, from the most hidden recesses of God down to the physical cosmos. Lurianic theology

---

[89] Busi, *Qabbalah visiva*.

encompassed all aspects of human life, even those not previously considered religious, as each and every one of them provided reflections of divine life and its dynamics.

Encyclopedism, mnemonics, and mechanics have been presented here as distinct elements for the purpose of analysis, but it is clear from modern research into the baroque period that they shared the same cultural platform and premises:

There is a univocal relation between signs and things, and every sign corresponds to a particular thing or action ('a distinct mark was assigned to every thing and notion'): the project of a universal language, then, presupposes an encyclopedia; it presupposes, that is to say, a complete and orderly enumeration and rigorous classification of all those things and concepts which were to correspond to a sign in the perfect language. Since the efficacy of the universal language depends on how much of the field of experience it aims to encompass and describe, it requires a preliminary classification of everything which exists in the universe and all objects of discourse—it requires, in fact, a total encyclopedia, the construction of 'perfect tables'. In order to facilitate this total classification and reduction of things and concepts into 'tables', a classificatory method needs to be elaborated, based on the division of things into general categories, genera and differences. . . .

Wilkins's insistence on the mnemonic value of the universal language was not incidental: a language of this kind seemed to fulfill the hopes and realized the aspirations of all those theorists of artificial memory who wished (to use the words of Giulio Camillo) 'to arrange in an orderly manner . . . enough memory-places to hold in the mind all human concepts and all things which are in the world'. All the major theorists of the universal language insist on its mnemonic advantages.[90]

These concepts are important for the way in which they transformed complex bodies of knowledge, requiring years to achieve proficiency in them and restricted to professionals, into popular and accessible versions through the printing press, co-operation between professionals and craftsmen, libraries, and public lectures and demonstrations.[91] The leading lights in these areas often announced their intention not to leave the world as they found it. New knowledge served as a lever to change the human environment and improve nature. It also had a religious value, as it provided a comprehensive

[90] Rossi, *Logic and the Art of Memory*, 159–61, 168; see also id., 'La memoria, le immagini, l'enciclopedia'; Bolzoni, *La stanza della memoria*, 253–4.
[91] Rossi, *Logic and the Art of Memory*, 133–8.

perspective on the cosmos and allowed humans to perceive it as God did. Contemporaries often connected these conceptions with Jewish kabbalah: Federico Borromeo, bishop of Milan and a prominent figure of Counter-Reformation Italy, explicitly declared the link between Camillo's basic terminology and the Jewish sefirotic system.[92]

Unlike previous generations of kabbalists, who insisted on restricting their secrets to intimate circles, the followers of the Lurianic tradition spread their teachings as widely as possible. The esoteric aspects of divinity were still kept strictly secret, but they could now influence the lives and religious behaviour of people at large. Fundamental concepts such as 'withdrawal', 'death of the kings' (*mitat hamelakhim*), 'straight line' (*kav yosher*), and 'circles' (*igulim*) created a bridge between the human world and the divine realms, where the divine womb gave birth to Adam Kadmon. As well as its new reading of the entire Jewish literary heritage, another appealing feature of Lurianic theology was this opportunity for intimacy with God (*devekut*). By portraying God using aspects of human birth, life, and death, the story of God became the existential story of humanity. It was clearest in regard to the human body:

You should know that man was born in the shape of God, and from my flesh I shall envision God. . . . Indeed we shall now refer to the completed foetus, what kind of mind he has, and later when he is born, and later when he grows . . . and always the divine Face Ze'er Anpin has different phases when he is small and when he grows up.[93]

The growth of Ze'er Anpin from infant to adult and his role in the interaction between the human and the divine will be examined in Chapter 4.

There are many ways of investigating divine dynamics—reciting the names of God, studying the emanations of light, the exegesis of holy scriptures—yet in the Lurianic tradition they constantly led to the human model. From this perspective, the weight of discussion was shifted from knowledge of divine secrets as an end in itself (the noetic aspect) to their implications for

---

[92] Bolzoni, *La stanza della memoria*, 80. For a fascinating precedent for the impact of Jewish kabbalah on Giovanni Fontana's memory machines in the fifteenth century, see ibid. 103–5.

[93] Vital, *Ets ḥayim*, i. 308–10; see also i. 1, 11, 26–8, 33, 36, 43–5, 48–53, 97, 103–6, 121, 130, 329–33; ii. 61, 64, 233, 297, 300–2, 315–16, 320–3, 351, 359–60, 404–5; on the growth of the human figure, see M. Pachter, 'Smallness and Greatness in Lurianic Kabbalah' (Heb.).

and effect on human life (the performative aspect).[94] Indeed, in the earlier books and manuscripts—those that show the least sign of having been re-worked by Vital and his followers—the Lurianic teachings were not occupied solely with theological issues but included hermeneutics of holy scriptures, instructions about religious practices, new kabbalistic customs, meditative techniques, and atonement for sin. The first printed book of Lurianic kab-balah, Abraham Tsahalon's *Marpe lanefesh* (Healing for the Soul), contained much practical instruction and very little theoretical discussion. Hence, the point of all the meticulous descriptions of the divine machinery was to allow humans to approach God and make him present in their daily lives. This will be discussed further in Chapters 2, 5, and 6, but for the moment suffice it to point out that one of the commonest religious practices in Jewish life, the daily prayer, was changed dramatically, as the liturgical sayings were not only a formal obligation but were supposed to reflect and influence the divine dynamics.[95]

[94] On the need to link and raise the material world, not only the spiritual world, to its divine origins, see e.g. Vital, *Sha'ar hakavanot*, i. 120a.

[95] Kallus, 'The Theurgy of Prayer in the Lurianic Kabbalah', ch. 4.

TWO

'Like giants sitting on the shoulders of dwarfs'
The Rise of the *Kadosh*

T HE FIRST CHAPTER outlined the innovative aspects of Lurianic theology. The following ones will explore the continuity between Lurianic kabbalah and earlier kabbalistic traditions as well as its new developments. The success of Lurianic kabbalah did not result from excluding or marginalizing older religious traditions but from charging them with new and vibrant content. The traditions supplied the substratum for changes that were presented as continuations, thus avoiding any opposition that might have been aroused by too much novelty.

The early modern period saw the rise of the Jewish saint (*kadosh*) throughout the Mediterranean. Many *kedoshim* acquired significant power in their communities and often posed serious challenges to more traditional authority figures, such as the rabbi, the *posek halakhah* (halakhic decisor), and the talmudic scholar. This power was not derived from endorsement by a religious institution, or from erudition, wealth, or legal standing, but from personal charisma: they were seen as possessing an intimate relationship with God which was manifest in their exemplary lives, profound religious devotion, and, often, the performance of miracles. Their rise was related to other contemporary religious developments, such as the ferment in Catholic Europe following the Council of Trent (1545–63) and the intense activity of the Sufis in the Ottoman empire. This is not to say that the *kedoshim* were influenced by either of the majority societies: they were a Jewish response to similar religious dynamics. They were also largely responsible for the spread of Safed kabbalah.

However, holy people in any religion are also characterized by their relationship to their communities: how they respond to the very earthly needs of their co-religionists and how they behave in social and political life. Holy people and holiness have their own histories, because they do not perform the same role in every society and every historical context. The story of the holy person is also the story of the religious community in which they operate. The rise of the *kadosh* in the early modern period marks a significant change in Jewish culture.

The *Kadosh* in the Rabbinic Tradition

Exceptional religious figures are present in the Jewish tradition from the earliest times: the Bible tells the stories of patriarchs, judges, kings, and prophets. Rabbinic sources mention individuals of late antiquity, the formative period of classical Judaism, whose authority did not derive from the learning acquired at schools of Jewish law nor from expounding the Torah but from their intimate relationship with God and their miraculous powers, mainly relating to rain: some of them are even compared to biblical figures.[1] They are often described as existing on the margins of society, performing hard physical labour, and being exceedingly poor. However, very little else about them is recorded, because rabbinic circles viewed them as lax in halakhah, especially in relation to purity regulations, and had little room for personal mediation between God and his followers: study was the primary channel to God and knowledge of his will.[2] Furthermore, the ability to perform miracles was not one the sages possessed or valued, however much it might appeal to the common people.[3] That they were recorded in mainstream rabbinic literature at all provided them with some legitimacy, but legitimacy was conferred only when the miraculous acts followed or were adapted to halakhic normativity. At the margins of the rabbinic world, a charismatic stream continued to flow, sought out by the common people in times of distress, yet regarded by the sages with deep suspicion.

The need for holy figures who maintained a personal relationship with

[1] Safrai and Safrai, 'Rabbinic Holy Men', esp. 76–8; Green, 'The Zaddiq as Axis Mundi in Later Judaism'.

[2] Fenton, 'La Hiérarchie des saints dans la mystique juive et dans la mystique islamique', esp. 52–3; Fine, *Physician of the Soul, Healer of the Cosmos*, 123.

[3] On the complicated interaction between sages, *kedoshim*, and prophets, see Sarfatti, 'Pious Men, Men of Deeds and the Early Prophets' (Heb.).

the divine and could change the course of nature if need be continued in Judaism throughout the Middle Ages. So too did the tension between the rabbinic establishment and the marginal *kadosh*. *Kedoshim* continued to excite religious sentiment through their devotion and piety, their ecstatic mystical experiences, their novel readings of the holy books, and the circles of disciples that gathered around them. The *kedoshim* responded to developments in the other religious traditions, absorbing such practices as the veneration of individual holy people during their lifetime and pilgrimages to their tomb after their death, as was customary in both Islam and Christianity. However, Jewish veneration of holy people remained a marginal practice compared with talmudic study and the collective notion of the uniqueness of the 'Chosen People'. Such a cultural ethos made divine revelations to exceptional persons less relevant: they remained part of the shared local traditions that transcended religious boundaries and included magical beliefs and archaic folkloric customs.[4] Not surprisingly, such practices evoked strong criticism from the rabbinic authorities in both Christian and Muslim lands, who characterized them as *darkhei ha'emori*, 'idolatrous traditions'. Veneration of *kedoshim* was never provided with any wider halakhic or theological underpinning during the Middle Ages.

From the late eleventh century onwards, holy people became more important in all three monotheistic religions. Their veneration was particularly pronounced in Sufism, a movement which left its mark on Egyptian Jewry,[5] especially as mediated by Abraham Maimuni (1186–1237), the son of Maimonides. Maimuni inspired others to follow Sufic practices of prayer and meditation as a means of attaining intimacy with God, either in isolation or as part of a group of Jewish Sufis.[6] He and his descendants initiated reforms in synagogue ritual, introduced meditation in secluded places including the repetition of God's name (as in the Sufic *dhikr* ritual), night vigils, and the construction of separate synagogues for very pious Jews. These changes were justified by claims that they were a return to long-forgotten prophetic traditions. Jewish awareness of Catholic patterns of veneration of saints is clear in

[4] See Heschel, 'The Holy Spirit in the Middle Ages' (Heb.).

[5] On Sufism in early Islam, see Karamustara, *Sufism* (my thanks to Guy Burak for drawing my attention to this work); on the impact of Sufism on Jewish culture, see Fenton, 'Influences soufies sur le développement de la Qabbale à Safed'; id., 'Devotional Rites in a Sufi Mode'.

[6] See Fenton, 'Abraham Maimonides'.

the important testimony of Obadiah of Bertinoro (*c.*1445–*c.*1515). Passing through Palermo on his way to Jerusalem, he summed up his impression of the local Jews: 'Whatever the Catholics would do to their saints, they did to me.'[7] His testimony is all the more important since it is not otherwise documented and preserves a genuine popular tradition.

Holy people were considered not only religious leaders and spiritual guides but also a fundamental part of the universe itself: a certain number of righteous people of a certain spiritual standing was believed to be necessary to sustain the world. Such beliefs led to extended pilgrimages by large numbers of people to graves and other places connected with righteous biblical characters: the Cave of the Patriarchs at Hebron, the Damwa Synagogue in Cairo, which was associated with Moses, or the tomb of the prophet Ezekiel near Baghdad.[8] These holy places were often visited by Muslims and, to a lesser extent, Christians, as well as Jews, and had developed fixed ritual practices, such as the lighting of olive-oil lamps, by the end of the thirteenth century. The rabbinic response to these pilgrimages was far from unanimous. Some Spanish rabbis asserted that the interred body of the *tsadik* maintained its power and could mediate between the earthly and divine realms.[9] Even Maimonides, who opposed the veneration of dead *kedoshim*, did not prohibit it completely.[10] The Ashkenazi rabbis, in the context of an ongoing polemic with Catholicism about saints as divine mediators, relics, and the talmudic idea of corpse contamination, were more critical. Yet the first institutionalized Jewish pilgrimage shrine was in Regensburg in Germany: the tomb of Rabbi Judah the Pious, leader of the German Pietist movement. The collective work of this movement, *Sefer ḥasidim* (Book of the Pious), is one of the first to explicitly discuss the role of *kedoshim* and *tsadikim* in the Jewish tradition.

Medieval Jewish literature hardly mentions *kedoshim*. The first signs of change appeared not in the kabbalistic milieu, but in the increased preoccupa-

---

[7] See E. Horowitz, 'Towards a Social History of Jewish Popular Religion', 140.

[8] *Sefer toledot ha'ari*, 326–7; Vital, *Sefer haḥezyonot*, 2: 46 (ed. Faierstein, 95). On pilgrimage to Meron, near Safed, following the Sephardi tradition based on the Zohar, see Huss, 'Holy Place, Holy Time, Holy Book' (Heb.), 256; see also Lichtenstein, *Consecrating the Profane* (Heb.), 296–8, 300–10, 324–35; Meri, *The Cult of Saints among Muslims and Jews in Medieval Syria*, 60–6, 123–4, 200, 209–13, 232–4, 242–50, 281–5; Reiner, 'Pilgrims and Pilgrimage to the Land of Israel' (Heb.).

[9] Lichtenstein, *Consecrating the Profane* (Heb.), 330–2.   [10] Ibid. 315–23.

tion with *kedushah* (sanctity), such as in the section of Abraham ben David of Posquières' *Ba'alei hanefesh* known as the *Sha'arei kedushah* (The Gates of Sanctity) and Nahmanides' commentaries on the Torah, neither of which reached an audience beyond esoteric circles. *Kedoshim* became a serious topic in Jewish literature only from the second half of the sixteenth century onwards,[11] mainly in writings supportive of Safed kabbalah and critical of much traditional religious and ritual practice, such as Elijah de Vidas's *Reshit hokhmah* (The Genesis of Wisdom)—a major kabbalistic ethical and penitential work—and Aaron Berakhyah of Modena's *Ma'avar yabok* (The Passage of Jabbok) and *Seder ashmurot haboker* (Morning Vigils). The last book is of great importance as it contained special prayers and meditative practices for a kabbalistic confraternity. By the seventeenth century *kedushah* was practically a code word for new standards of behaviour, not only among those who devoted their lives to the esoteric but among the Jewish public at large.

Kabbalistic ethical literature sought to bring kabbalistic ideas to large parts of the Jewish public, yet there were also other channels. The interest in making contact with *kedoshim* among the common people changed the patterns of pilgrimage to the Land of Israel. Tombs of *tana'im* such as Hillel and Shammai were abandoned in favour of those of kabbalistic figures, such as Simeon bar Yohai. The increasing popularity of such visits can be gauged by the rabbinic opposition to them—especially to men and women mixing together and indulging in frivolous behaviour—and the printing of a comprehensive list of tombs of *tsadikim*, their locations, and the correct prayers to say at each one, which became very popular. In the second half of the sixteenth century it was translated into the idiom of Spanish Jews as *Libro intitolado yihus hatsadikim, stan intirados los tsadikim in erets yisra'el* (Genealogy of the Righteous Ones Buried in the Land of Israel),[12] addressing directly the Iberian diaspora throughout the Mediterranean.

A clear change in popular attitudes to *kedoshim* was marked by the appearance of hagiographical stories in the sixteenth century, among them *Mayse bukh* (Book of Stories), a Yiddish compilation of tales of both Jewish and Christian origin passed down orally over several centuries and first printed in

---

[11] Idel, *'Ganz Andere'*, pp. v–xliv. Idel's discussion of early modern saints leans on kabbalist authors such as Cordovero, Isaiah Horowitz, Haim Yosef David Azulai, and Moses Hayim Luzzatto (see ibid., pp. xxiv–xxv, xxxii, xli).

[12] Printed in Constantinople by 'Reina Widow of Don Yosef Nasi' in 1595.

1527.[13] It contains a section of apocryphal stories about the pious lives of famous Ashkenazi sages, written long after their deaths. These tales managed to escape their local context and became known throughout all the Ashkenazi lands, eventually reaching Italy—where they were reproduced in the historiographical *Shalshelet hakabalah* (The Chain of Transmission) by Gedalyah ibn Yahya—and Safed.

'Praises of Luria': The Beginning of Jewish Hagiography

The heroes of Jewish history—the patriarchs, Moses, the prophets, the sages of the Land of Israel and Babylonia—attracted admiration and respect, as reflected in the canonical literature, yet none of them became the subject of hagiographical literature, let alone personal veneration. Their prestige was linked to their contribution to developing, restoring, or continuing the tradition that became classical rabbinic Judaism. This holds true for the medieval period as well: key figures in the long history of Jewish law in Babylonia, the Ashkenazi lands, and the Iberian peninsula served as leaders of their communities, yet very little is known about them beyond their learning and renown. What is known about them—such as the stories of Judah the Pious's miracles or the legend about Maimonides turning from philosophy to mysticism—crystallized long after their deaths.

All this changed with the leader of the new kabbalistic school in Safed. Meir Benayahu makes the important point that during his lifetime Isaac Luria was known only among the Iberian communities of the Ottoman empire, such as Safed, Cairo, and Istanbul.[14] The development of his legend can be seen from changes in the stories told about him, beginning with his obituary by a local rabbi, Samuel Ozeida, who extolled him mainly for his knowledge of Torah rather than of divine mysteries, and mentioned no miraculous or supernatural abilities.[15] Only a little while later other descriptions started to

---

[13] See e.g. Zfatman, '*Mayse bukh*' (Heb.); Elstein and Krasney, 'The *Mayse bukh*' (Heb.). Several of these traditions have been preserved only in manuscript, such as the stories of Simeon the Liturgist, modelled on Simeon bar Yohai (see Raspe, 'Payyetanim as Heroes of Medieval Folk Narrative'; ead., 'Jewish Saints in Medieval Ashkenaz'; for extensive background, see ead., *Jüdische Hagiographie im mittelalterlichen Aschkenas*).

[14] Benayahu, notes (Heb.) to *Sefer toledot ha'ari*, 108.

[15] Ozeida, *Derashat hesped al mot ha'ari*. Pachter claims that it is reasonable to suppose that Ozeida preferred not to mention any of Luria's personal traits, which were known in esoteric

spread into Europe and the eastern Mediterranean basin, mainly through minor members of his school, such as Meir Poppers, Benjamin Halevi, Jacob Tsemah, and Israel Saruk.[16] One of the most significant contributors to the Luria legend was Solomon Shlomiel of Dresnitz, who sent enthusiastic letters from Safed to eastern Europe about Luria's extraordinary divine character. Shlomiel was probably the first to realize the effectiveness of hagiographical stories in spreading the new kabbalistic message. He asked his readers to copy his letters and pass them on, and, according to Benayahu, they served as the basis for *Shivḥei ha'ari* (Praises of Luria), the first elaborate exposition of Luria's theology and messianic vision, which became very popular but aroused strong criticism from other kabbalists.[17] Another source of information about Luria is *Sefer toledot ha'ari* (Stories of Luria), which gained even greater popularity, especially in Italy, which was a centre for disseminating kabbalistic traditions in Europe.[18] Both works were compiled when the stories of Luria were still fresh, benefiting at times from eyewitness testimonies, and both were dedicated entirely to aggrandizing Luria. This was the birth of the new genre of Jewish hagiography. Earlier hagiographical legends were also linked to Luria. According to the earlier Castilian version, the protagonist in the mock-execution of a sinner described in Chapter 5 below was Moses de Leon.[19]

According to the stories, Luria was a *kadosh* because he was immersed in the divine realms and everything he said and did revealed the presence of God. He is described as predestined to *kedushah* from before birth, the roots of his soul being in Adam Kadmon, who exists at a higher divine level than the Faces and the *sefirot*. He led an ascetic life, avoiding worldly pleasures. His magical and miraculous powers became more prominent in later hagiographical stories, but the supernatural was never isolated: it was always linked to his ability to see into people's hearts and to inspire them to repentance.

circles. In any case his words reflected the common opinion in Safed about Luria's personality (M. Pachter, introduction (Heb.) to Ozeida, *Derashat hesped al mot ha'ari*, 39–40).

[16]   See Avivi, *Lurianic Kabbalah* (Heb.), vols. i and ii.

[17]   *Sefer toledot ha'ari*, 13–37, 41–67, 71–110; see also *Safed Spirituality*, 61–5; Fine, *Physician of the Soul, Healer of the Cosmos*, 2, 84–7. The letters were collected and published by the halakhic scholar Naftali Bacharach in *Emek hamelekh*. On Bacharach and his writings, see Liebes, 'Towards a Study of the Author of *Emek hamelekh*' (Heb.).

[18]   *Sefer toledot ha'ari*, 13.   [19]   Solomon Shlomiel of Dresnitz, *Sefer ha'ari vegurav*, 106–8.

He excelled in all kinds of techniques, such as physiognomy and palmistry, the languages of palm-trees and poultry, of flames and angels. He inferred from a man's forehead what sins he had committed and his kind of soul and his mission of reparation [in his current reincarnation]. He could tell if the soul was once or twice reincarnated and its relations to previous sages. . . . He knew what sins a man had committed from his young childhood up to the present. He also knew the thoughts of people, drawing their souls from their bodies in order to talk to them.[20]

The *kadosh*, from his very first appearance on the Jewish stage, had a strong social aspect, and the story of Luria's revelation—his passage from esoteric secrecy to public figure—connects him to a quasi-legal institution called the *va'ad berurei averot* brought to the Land of Israel by the Spanish exiles. Luria was a member of a court which served in parallel with the formal halakhic courts in major communities to investigate the private life of community members and enforce social control through scorn and ostracism. During one of the sessions of this court, Luria's prophetic powers prevented a miscarriage of justice against an innocent woman.[21] He was also the centre of another social institution, his group of devoted disciples. Such gatherings around a master were not exceptional in Safed: Moses Cordovero, Joseph ibn Tabul, Eleazar Azikri, and Moses ben Makhir all had their followers.[22] The members of the group were intended as models of the pure human life, and this led to a preoccupation with sin and repentance. Lawrence Fine described Luria as the 'physician of the soul':

Among the most significant roles Isaac Luria played in the lives of his disciples was that of physician of the soul. Before they could practice rituals intended to enable them to bind their souls to the divine realm and to repair that realm in accordance with the teachings of Lurianic mythology, his disciples had first to mend their own souls, to cleanse and purify them of all imperfections. No one whose own soul had failed to achieve a certain level of perfection could hope to engage successfully in the intricate and elaborate contemplative rituals Luria devised.[23]

[20] Ibid. 156–7.
[21] Ibid. 159–60; on social control in Mediterranean Sephardi communities, see Ben-Naeh, *Jews in the Realm of the Sultans*, 205–10, 291–310, 412–25; Lamdan, 'Deviation from the Norms of Moral Behaviour' (Heb.).
[22] On the group around Ibn Tabul, see Fine, *Physician of the Soul, Healer of the Cosmos*, 117. Simeon Bacchi attributed the superhuman capacities that others attributed to Luria to his own master, Ibn Tabul (see Z. Rubin, 'The Zoharic Commentaries of Joseph ibn Tabul' (Heb.), 363–87). On Cordovero's disciples, see Sack, *The Kabbalah of Moses Cordovero* (Heb.).
[23] Fine, *Physician of the Soul, Healer of the Cosmos*, 150.

All the leading kabbalists of Safed were experts in contacting the divine realms, ecstatic voyages, and spiritual healing. Those treated were mostly women, and the cures could involve dramatic events, such as during the expulsion of an invading spirit in a case of possession. They were communal events, attracting large number of spectators.[24]

The Lives of *Kedoshim*: The Public Image

The major figures in Safed attracted a great deal of interest. Their behaviour was believed to have a religious value, to be emulated in order to bring the presence of God into the lives of their disciples, and Vital relates how he followed Luria's every move no matter how small or trivial-seeming.[25] The need to internalize the divine instructions required not only theoretical understanding but experience that could only be obtained through an apprenticeship with a living *kadosh*. Close relationships between masters and disciples have important precedents in the talmudic and post-talmudic literature, where they are referred to by the catchphrases 'the service of Torah scholars' (*shimush talmidei ḥakhamim*) or 'this too is Torah, and I must study it' (*torah hi velilmod ani tsarikh*); however, sixteenth-century kabbalists did not use these expressions. It is therefore not a continuation of a centuries-old pattern but a new type, of learning, much as the *kadosh* was a new source of creativity and legitimacy.

The stories of *kedoshim* reveal surprisingly intimate details of such things as their sexual lives, table manners and sleeping habits, and physical pains and illnesses.[26] The change in attitude is dramatic: from complete silence on the private lives of Jewish leaders to an at times embarrassing exposure of the most intimate details. This gave rise to another almost completely unprecedented genre in Jewish literature: autobiography.[27] Why Jews did not write

---

[24] Chajes, *Between Worlds*. On the importance of possession and its treatment in early modern religion in Europe, see Sluhovsky, *Believe Not Every Spirit*.

[25] See *Sefer toledot ha'ari*, 325; see also Vital, *Sha'ar hamitsvot*, 36*b*, 54, 55*a*, 56*b*, 78, 82*a*, 83*a*, 89, 109*b*, 128*b*; id., *Sha'ar hakavanot*, i. 323*a*, 333*b*; ii. 15, 24*b*–25*a*, 88*b*, 100*b*, 187, 206, 275, 298*b*.

[26] See Fine, *Physician of the Soul, Healer of the Cosmos*, 196–205; for an example, see *Sefer toledot ha'ari*, 322.

[27] Fine, *Physician of the Soul, Healer of the Cosmos*, 19, 111–12; see also Chajes, 'Accounting for the Self'.

autobiographies despite encountering fine examples from both Christianity and Islam remains an unanswered question, but 'ego documents' are quite rare in medieval Judaism and autobiographies even more so.[28] Again, an abrupt change took place in the kabbalistic milieu of sixteenth-century Safed. Three of the leading figures—Joseph Karo, Hayim Vital, and Eleazar Azikri—produced autobiographies, although of different types and extents, and, despite having no Jewish precedents to follow, all three are mature compositions. These writings were deeply concerned with sin and repentance (see Chapter 6) and contributed to the dissemination of the novel penitential practices of their authors. Azikri led a penitential confraternity in Safed and was intensely preoccupied with his own sins. He recorded them in fine detail as a preliminary stage to making reparations.[29] The awareness of God in every moment and every aspect of his daily life pervades the pages of his notes, provoking self-deprecation, ascetic limitation, and the constant need to repent and to impress upon others their own need to repent.

The *Kadosh*'s Self-Image

Another novel aspect of sixteenth-century *kedoshim* was how they saw themselves and their role in society. They did not think of themselves simply as individuals but as the latest link in an unbroken chain of earlier *kedoshim*, a conduit for sanctity that provided a new criterion for religious legitimacy. They sought to purify their own lives, those of their disciples, and ultimately those of the entire Jewish people. Although they stressed the need for modesty and condemned the quest for personal honour, they were often very sensitive about their own dignity in their personal writings, which are full of demands that they be shown respect in public and that their religious authority be accepted.[30] Many generations, so they claimed, had waited for their appearance. They considered themselves 'giants sitting on the shoulders of

---

[28] Dekker (ed.), *Egodocuments and History*. A special issue of the *Jewish Quarterly Review* was dedicated to Jewish autobiography (95/1 (2005)). According to Idel, the Expulsion from Spain and subsequent wanderings encouraged the preoccupation with collective identity in early modern kabbalistic writing (see 'On Mobility, Individuals and Groups').

[29] Azikri, *Yomano hamisti*, 135, 165–9.

[30] On the importance of the honour ethos in Mediterranean Jewish communities, see Weinstein, '"An Honourable Death is Better than a Shameful Life"' (Heb.); id., *Marriage Rituals Italian Style*, ch. 4.

dwarfs'. Hence the very personal tone of their interpretations of rabbinic literature and, especially, the Zohar. It seemed to them as if the entire Jewish canon was speaking about them in the most direct and urgent way. Their reading was not general or scholarly but concerned their own life course as the central event in the great drama of salvation. Yehuda Liebes stated:

> In recent years I have reached the conclusion that the claim that Lurianic kabbalah was mainly theoretical and ontological but not personal needs to be revisited. Luria and his group were not only the teachers but the subjects. It cannot be denied that Lurianic kabbalah offers a cosmic theory, but this is secondary to the personal aspect and derived from it, since—according to Luria—the souls of the righteous are the central feature of the divine realms (there are other phrases, such as the divine Faces are the senior brothers and sisters of human souls), and the myth about human souls is intended to elucidate the fate of Luria's soul and his circle.[31]

Their sense of their own superiority was a complete inversion of the traditional Jewish ethos of the 'degeneration of the generations' (*yeridat hadorot*). Luria and many of his contemporaries in Safed looked down on figures from the past with condescension: Luria is explicitly stated to be superior to Moses and Simeon bar Yohai.[32] Karo and Vital encounter figures from the past, including biblical ones, in visions and impose their own authority and mystical positions on them.[33] Vital also encounters the divine Faces and the Shekhinah, the feminine aspect of God,[34] and even sees and talks with God.[35]

Such a self-understanding is not solely the product of reflection and personal emotion but requires a theological underpinning, which was explicitly phrased for the first time in the Jewish context at Safed. The importance of the *kadosh* has clear antecedents in the zoharic literature, but he was now located in a well-structured system, affiliated with major elements of the kabbalistic world-view. This had started well before Luria arrived in Safed. Cordovero, a great systematizer, stressed the importance of Moses, who, as the source of every mystical revelation, encompassed the souls of all future sages.

---

[31] Liebes, '"Two Young Roes of a Doe"' (Heb.), 114–15.

[32] See Liebes, 'Earth Shaker' (Heb.); id., '"Two Young Roes of a Doe"' (Heb.); Huss, *Like the Radiance of the Sky* (Heb.), 11–42. Such claims have precedents in the Zohar, where the superiority of bar Yohai over Moses is asserted.

[33] Karo, *Magid meisharim*, 182, 193–4, 318, 343–4; Vital, *Sefer haḥezyonot*, 3: 63 (ed. Faierstein, 131).

[34] Vital, *Sefer haḥezyonot*, 2: 38; 3: 21, 38 (ed. Faierstein, 91–2, 110, 118); *Toledot ha'ari*, 229–30.   [35] Vital, *Sefer haḥezyonot*, 2: 5 (ed. Faierstein, 75–7).

The *kadosh* was different in essence from other Jews, and his ritual practice had far higher value. Luria took this position further and circumvented Moses. His acquaintance with the ceaseless divine machinery enabled him to reach the highest levels of the divine realms and hence of sanctity and to expound the secrets of Torah as had never been done before.

Despite the profound differences between the schools of Luria and Cordovero, they both agreed that *kedoshim* were distinct from the rest of Jewish population. To maintain their sense of being a separate community, Luria and his disciples signed a formal legal contract in which they bound themselves to share their fate even in the divine realms after their death.[36] Many *kedoshim* sought to found dynasties to pass on their teachings; however, these did not usually last beyond their death. They also related themselves to earlier *kedoshim*. Luria and his disciples felt connected to major historical Jewish figures, not only by continuing their work, but through personal mystical encounters in which they studied in the same heavenly school with them.

Another characteristic of early modern *kedoshim* was their missionary zeal. This was derived from their understanding of themselves as reformers of Judaism and from the intense messianic tension of the times.[37] Some of Vital's visions involve contemporary political events: in one, he rebukes the king of Spain for his treatment of the Conversos and threatens him with political disasters.[38] Yet Luria and his disciples did not hold classical messianic beliefs or have fervid eschatological expectations. They stressed the processes leading up to the eschaton and the need for religious reform as a precondition for the coming of the messiah, including the need to change Jewish life in all its aspects.

The influence of *kedoshim* in both public and private domains reflects the increase in control over individuals by both secular and religious authorities during the early modern period. As bearers of public authority, *kedoshim* were also involved in shaping the Jewish canon, which was printed in its entirety— the Bible with its main commentaries (*Mikraot gedolot*), the Mishnah, the Talmud, the midrashic literature, and the Zohar—in the sixteenth century.

---

[36] Scholem, 'The Bond of Fellowship of the Students of R. Isaac Luria' (Heb.).

[37] Goldish and Popkin (eds.), *Millenarianism and Messianism in Early Modern European Culture*; Goldish, *The Sabbatean Prophets*.

[38] Vital, *Sefer haḥezyonot*, 2: 22, 31, 34, 36, 39; 3: 26 (ed. Faierstein, 85, 89–92, 114).

This allowed them to censor any unwanted religious views.[39] There was also a struggle between the schools of Luria and Cordovero over the canonical status of mystical texts. It was an urgent matter for Vital, who encountered Cordovero, who had died several years earlier, in a mystical vision and asked him directly which school was superior—not only for the living but also for the erudite souls in heaven. Cordovero replied that both were true but the Lurianic took over where the Cordoverian ended, concluding: 'now I do not learn anything but the teachings of your master'.[40] Vital's seniority among Luria's disciples enabled him to confiscate all the alternative versions of Luria's sayings they had and maintain his own 'official' list. In his works he repeatedly emphasizes the authenticity and credibility of his version of the tradition.

Once the *kadosh* had arrived, he was there to stay as a focus of religious power and innovation, even after his death:

One day when they were studying, [Luria] said to his disciples: 'You should know that the rabbis have gathered, intending to cancel the feast over bar Yohai's grave, so that women do not go adorned to Meron [where the grave is located] but wearing ordinary clothes, and none will remain to sleep there but the old women. Should [the rabbis] do so, there will be a great plague and many will die, the good as well as the bad.' Luria was summoned and went to meet the rabbis and said: 'You are right [to fear immodest behaviour], yet what can we do, taking into consideration that bar Yohai is highly pleased with his veneration of recent years, and should it be cancelled he will be furious and strike the people with plague?' . . . Hearing his words they agreed to cancel their order.[41]

Reincarnation: Individual and Collective Aspects

The Safed kabbalists' claim to sanctity was not based solely on their personal characteristics and mission: they also claimed to have had previous incarna-

---

[39] On Jewish censorship during the early modern period, see Raz-Krakotzkin, *The Censor, the Editor, and the Text.*

[40] See the whole dream-vision in Vital, *Sefer ḥaḥezyonot*, 2: 17 (ed. Faierstein, 83–4); see also Faierstein, index (Heb.) to Vital, *Sefer ḥaḥezyonot*, s.v. 'Cordovero, Moses'; *Sefer toledot ha'ari*, 107, 158, 178, 220, 282.

[41] *Sefer toledot ha'ari*, 219. That a saint might become vengeful should his veneration be taken lightly is a common idea in medieval Catholicism.

tions.⁴² Reincarnation (*gilgul neshamot*) had a central role in Lurianic theology, but its main importance for the social reading of kabbalah lies in how it marked anew the lines between the personal and transpersonal, between the divine realms and human life, between body and soul, and between halakhic and mystical authority. The belief in reincarnation reflects the increased importance of individuality in early modern Europe. It acted as a bridge between the divine as the source of human souls and the individual personality and could explain character traits and inclinations. However, for the *kedoshim* of Safed, belief in previous incarnations was a useful tool in the construction of their holy auras. The possibility of having the learning and experience of a number of people from the past in a single human memory massively expanded the human capacity for knowledge and allowed the *kedoshim* to claim greater insights in a number of fields, especially halakhah.

The person who exploited this idea to the full was Hayim Vital. The last part of his four-part autobiography *Sefer haḥezyonot* (The Book of Visions) is devoted to meticulous descriptions of his previous incarnations, including as biblical prophets, kings, rabbinic sages, zoharic personages, geonim, and Spanish rabbis, most of them real historical figures.⁴³ The end result is quite remarkable: Vital was practically the flesh-and-blood embodiment of the entire Jewish tradition. This is probably the strongest claim a member of a traditional society—suspicious of novelty—could make. Jewish learning had achieved its culmination in Vital. Would not such a person be entitled, indeed obliged, to undertake any reform of Jewish culture and religion he deemed necessary?

This understanding of reincarnation made possible, for the first time in Jewish history, an explicit religious and social elitism. Differences did not depend on ability, commitment, or opportunity: they were innate. A rift opened up between the common people and the small elite group with higher souls and intimate relationships with God. The *tsadikim* and *kedoshim* formed

⁴² On transmigration of souls in early modern Judaism, see Elior, 'The Doctrine of Metempsychosis in *Galya raza*' (Heb.); for general background, see Ogren, *Renaissance and Rebirth*; Schwarz, 'Criticism of the Concept of Reincarnation' (Heb.); Helner-Eshed, 'Transmigration of Souls in the Kabbalistic Writings of R. David ibn Zimra' (Heb.).
⁴³ Vital, *Sefer haḥezyonot*, 4: 9–10 (ed. Faierstein, 139–41). The title of Part 4 is 'These Are the Things Told to Me by My Master, Regarding Me and the Source of My Soul' (ed. Faierstein, 134).

a 'professional guild' whose role was to mediate between the divine and human worlds. The similarity to the Catholic concept of divine grace and the special role of an elite priesthood is undeniable.

Luria created a historical narrative involving the activities and contributions of groups of *kedoshim* throughout Jewish history. The three most significant episodes in this narrative were Rabbi Akiva and the ten martyrs, the life of Simeon bar Yohai and his disciples as expounded in the Zohar, and the codification of Jewish law in the Mishnah, all of which occurred in the first two centuries CE. These mystics and sages all operated in the Land of Israel, where Luria and his disciples were based. The continuity of Luria's circle with earlier incarnations was theatrically demonstrated during one of their journeys outside Safed. Luria identified the exact place where bar Yohai and his disciples had had a special mystical revelation, and he seated each disciple in the exact place where he had sat in his previous incarnation.[44] The meticulous reconstruction of the event was important in the way in which it interwove physical location, myth, and ritual innovation, and in the effect it had on the participants' self-perceptions. Furthermore, it was not only a reconstruction of the revelation to bar Yohai and his disciples but also of the revelation of the Torah on Mount Sinai, and, as such, represents another moment of renovation and reform for the Jewish tradition, this time in its mystical aspect, for those worthy enough to experience it.

Kedoshim and Religious Innovation

In the classical midrash, the study of Torah and the creation of new interpretations of it were part of the ongoing Sinaitic revelation. The Safed kabbalists saw themselves as living at a time of divine revelation, when the Torah was being conferred anew in its mystically true and profound sense. As Luria and his disciples originated in the divine realms, they partook of the dynamic character of God, which gave them the freedom and inspiration to incorporate old elements of the tradition into new ritual practices:

Luria had a peculiar genius for ritual creativity to match his originality in the sphere of mythological thinking, and should be considered one of the preeminent

---

[44] *Sefer toledot ha'ari*, 179–81; see also Vital, *Sefer haḥezyonot*, 2: 37 (ed. Faierstein, 91) where he learns meditative prayers from zoharic figures.

innovators of ritual in the history of Judaism. In many cases, Luria adapted earlier kabbalistic rituals—from Safed and elsewhere—for his own purposes. But he went further by teaching his disciples a variety of ritual practices that had little or no precedent in Jewish tradition and were not tied to the performance of formal religious precepts.[45]

Kabbalists in general, and those of Safed in particular, were committed to the Jewish way of life. Their interest in speculative theology was secondary to their interest in religious practice. They did not alter ritual practices but charged them with new meaning. They did not consider themselves innovators but decipherers of the secret content of ordinary rituals.[46] For example, the daily prayer could have traditional and radical meanings at the same time. It was precisely their full acceptance of halakhah which allowed them to take it in new and surprising directions:

The dynamic processes within the organic life of the divine provide the template, or grid, to which the *mitsvot* are correlated. This correlation is constructed in the most thoroughgoing detail, each discrete component of any given *mitsvah* being interpreted in Lurianic terms. Lurianic Kabbalah also served to empower its practitioners by cultivating the theurgic art to an even greater degree than previous kabbalists had done. Each and every halakhic enactment presented one opportunity after another to transform both oneself and the cosmos.[47]

Religious practice was not only an expression of obedience to the divine will. For the kabbalists, it also provided the opportunity to contribute to the Reparation of the Worlds. This set their elite rituals apart from those of ordinary Jews. Yet for some of the Safed kabbalists it was also important to distinguish themselves from the *ba'alei halakhah*, the masters of halakhah. According to Cordovero, kabbalists could reach spiritual heights during their lifetime that halakhah scholars could reach only after their death.[48] Halakhah and kabbalah became two competing sources of religious authority and legitimacy (see Chapter 3 below).

There were three main mechanisms through which kabbalistic innovations spread to the general population. The first was printed books of *hanhagot* (rules of behaviour), providing clear guidance for members of the

---

[45] Fine, *Physician of the Soul, Healer of the Cosmos*, 259–60. [46] Ibid. 16–18.
[47] Ibid. 219. [48] Cited in Sack, *The Kabbalah of Moses Cordovero* (Heb.), 117.

public interested in kabbalah but lacking any deep acquaintance with it.[49]
The second was the personal habits of the *kedoshim* taken up by people
who wished to imitate their pious behaviour;[50] the third was the kabbalistic
confraternities (see Chapter 4).

Kedoshim, Saints, and Sufis

In the Middle Ages, the Jewish tradition differed from the other two monotheistic traditions in that it allocated a very minor role to holy people. The
cultural heroes of Judaism did not derive their authority and prestige from
charisma or divine revelations. Typical of this is Nahmanides (1194–1270),
leader of Spanish Jewry, halakhist, biblical exegete, and innovative kabbalist.[51] In none of his wide public activity is there any reference to his mystical
activity, which he kept a closely guarded secret. The rise of the *kadosh* was a
consequence of the Expulsion from Spain in 1492 and the cultural montage
that the Spanish Jewish diaspora pieced together out of the social patterns
of their place of origin—Catholic Spain—and those of their destination—
the Islamic Ottoman empire, then at its height throughout the eastern and
southern Mediterranean basin.

  Saints played a crucial role in the expansion of Christianity from the
beginning.[52] Their veneration and the veneration of their material remains,
or relics, contributed to the acceptance of Christianity in Europe and to the
solidarity of the earliest Christian communities. Stories about the incredible
courage and steadfastness of the early martyrs bolstered the new religion's
claim to be the true one. From the eleventh to the fifteenth centuries, their
cults expanded from the public into the private realm, mainly through attachment to local or personal saints.[53] Their presence in people's lives intensified,

---

[49] Gries, *Conduct Literature* (Heb.); Nabarro, 'Tikun' (Heb.); Hallamish, *Kabbalah in Liturgy,
Halakhah and Customs* (Heb.), 332–55. *Hanhagot* comes from the same Hebrew root as *min-
hagim* (customs). They were distinct from *takanot* and *halakhot*, which were derived directly or
indirectly from halakhic discourse.

[50] Liebes, 'New Directions in the Study of Kabbalah' (Heb.).

[51] Halbertal, *By the Way of Truth* (Heb.); Pedaya, *Nahmanides* (Heb.); on Nahmanides as a
leader, see Idel, 'Nahmanides', esp. 72–9.

[52] On medieval saints and the interaction between them and their followers, see Kleinberg,
Prophets in Their Own Country; on the variety of sainthood in Christianity, see id., *Flesh Made
Word*; on various models of the Christian saint in late antiquity, see Brown, *The Cult of the Saints*.

[53] Benvenuti, 'La civiltà urbana', 215–16.

and the gap between believers and saints diminished. Relationships with saints were characterized by personal devotions, pilgrimages to their graves, naming children after them, possession of artistic representations of them, celebrating their miracles with ex-voto offerings, or not working on their feast days. Saints gained increasing popularity throughout the Mediterranean basin, yet it is not only the social aspect which is of interest here but their place within the wider theological framework.

Christianity does not relate to God only as an infinite being, utterly distant from his creation, but also—through Jesus Christ, his son—as a human person. Christ, as God and man, stimulated sharp theological polemics which were finally resolved and officially accepted in the Creed. The agony and death of Christ—that is, of God—provided the model for future martyrs. Martyrs attempted to imitate Christ and thus create a mediating link between God and humanity in a very physical way. All the major elements of the future veneration of saints—their memorialization in liturgy and sermons, pilgrimages to their graves, hagiographical literature, commemorations on the anniversary of their death—existed for the first generation of martyrs and were passed on to medieval and later saints who continued their heritage not through physical death but through 'spiritual martyrdom'.[54] The identification of saints with Christ reached its apogee in St Francis of Assisi, who was one of the first to manifest the physical signs of crucifixion (stigmata) on his body.[55] His admirers described him as Christ-like, and after his death prayers were addressed to him alongside God. Lurianic kabbalah linked the vicissitudes of the divine realms—from their growth and revelation, to the great crisis of the Breaking of the Vessels, to their reparation—to the lives of the *tsadikim* and *kedoshim*. In this fundamental element, and others that follow from it, Lurianic theology stands close to the Christian tradition and in sharp contrast to Islam, where God remained utterly distinct and distant from humanity.

From the beginning, central figures of Christianity were enrolled among the saints: the Church Fathers (Augustine, Jerome); major theologians, 'the doctors of the faith' (Bernard of Clairvaux, Thomas Aquinas); the founders of monastic orders (Benedict, founder of the Benedictines; Ignatius of Loyola,

---

[54] Scorza Barcellona, 'Le origini'.
[55] Frugoni, *Francesco e l'invenzione delle stimmate*, esp. 8, 13, 22, 26–7, 103–10.

founder of the Jesuits); and mystics (Teresa of Ávila, Hildegard of Bingen). Clearly these hardly represent the full variety of Catholic saints, yet the 'sociology of saints' indicates that most came from a privileged background.[56] The *kedoshim* of Safed were never marginal figures either: they formed the mainstream religious establishment of the city, running yeshivas, courts of law, and confraternities.

Praying for saints was an important devotion in early Christianity. Augustine wrote that living believers prayed for dead saints in the hope that in return the saints would intervene on their behalf. Cycles of prayers and rituals over the graves of saints on the anniversary of their death developed, creating an annual liturgical rhythm.[57] Luria and his followers also made important changes to collective prayer, one of the most traditional aspects of Jewish culture. They transformed the regular synagogue prayers into a meditative and theurgical exercise, based on precise theological knowledge, and created another sequence of prayers with set times and places that ran alongside the synagogue one.

As already mentioned, the distinction between common Jews and the *tsadikim* and *kedoshim* as mediators between the divine realms and the rest of the Jewish community was in sharp contrast to the classical rabbinic ethos of the equality of all Jews before God, exemplified in the revelation of the Torah at Mount Sinai, which was witnessed by all the people. The new attitude of the Safed kabbalists was again close to the Catholic tradition, which distinguishes between lay believers and the small group of 'professional' church dignitaries with its monopoly on conferring divine grace.

As much as the Catholic background is constitutive, the historical construction of the *kadosh* took place in the town of Safed in Galilee, a small and relatively unimportant part of the Ottoman province of Syria. The local kabbalists, like the rest of the Jewish community, had close and daily contact with the Muslim population. Several *zawiyat* (Sufic lodges) were operating in Safed during the sixteenth and seventeenth centuries, and direct contact between kabbalists and Sufis is mentioned by Vital: 'In the aforementioned night, R. Tsadok the scribe dreamed that during the feast of Shavuot I was wearing a white *sawf* [Sufic robe] at home, and carried a Torah scroll deco-

[56] Burke, 'How to be a Counter-Reformation Saint'.
[57] Boesch Gajano, 'La strutturazione della cristianità occidentale'.

rated with a big crown [*keter torah*] and a wonderful cloth.'[58] His dreams repeatedly told of encounters with Muslim imams or those occupied with magic, for which he was sternly rebuked by Luria. Karo was criticized by his *magid*, the divine voice which directed his public path and judged his personal behaviour, for entering a *zawiya*.[59] Paul Fenton has listed some important Sufic elements in the religious practices of the Safed kabbalists: chanting outside synagogues, prostration over the tombs of *kedoshim*, the chain of transmission as the basis for religious authority and mystical truth, the hierarchy of the holy ones in heaven as necessary for the world's continued existence, the disciple's mystical rapport with his master through the visualization of his face.[60] Prayer patterns, solitude, reciting the names of God, and ethical writings such as *Ḥovot halevavot* (Duties of the Heart) could also be added to this list.

The Ottoman period witnessed a spread of Sufic activity and tight cooperation between the authorities and several of the Sufic orders. Extant places of Sufic worship were enlarged, and new ones constructed. Beside the similarity of folk beliefs and practices of Jews, Muslims, and Christians in Syria and Egypt, the basic tenets of Sufism were very compatible with those of Safed kabbalah. A striking example is the similarity of the mystical stature of the senior figures of the two religious traditions, Luria and Muhammad. They stood at the top of a hierarchy that always contained the same number of members, which was very different from Christian ideas. The Sufis developed the concept of the Nur Muhammad (the Light of Muhammad), an aspect of the godhead that pre-dated the Creation and shone through the great Sufic holy men and leaders; it was only surpassed by Muhammad himself.[61] Possessors of the Nur Muhammad were no longer subject to the regular process of Islamic law but were links in a parallel chain of mystical transmission. This led to radical positions in Sufism, such as intimacy with God, a state also sought by Luria and his followers. Unlike followers of Islam, where comparison with Muhammad is highly problematic, the Safed kabbalists did not hesitate to compare themselves with Moses, the founder of the

---

[58] Vital, *Sefer haḥezyonot*, 3: 30 (ed. Faierstein, 115).   [59] Karo, *Magid meisharim*, 279.

[60] Fenton, 'La Hiérarchie des saints dans la mystique juive et dans la mystique islamique'; id., 'Influences soufies sur le développement de la Qabbale à Safed'.

[61] I wish to express my thanks to Sara Sviri for drawing my attention to these elements of the Sufic tradition (see Sviri, *The Sufis* (Heb.)).

religion. A more fundamental difference is apparent in the kabbalistic claim that humanity is immersed in the divine world and can influence God. This is the truly radical aspect of Lurianic theology and theurgical activity. In Islam the distance between God and humans remains infinite, the will of God ever ineffable and beyond human influence.

Encounters between Sufis and Jews also occurred at a more mundane level. As the Sufis became more popular and powerful thanks to the support of the Ottoman authorities,[62] there was a slow infiltration of popular and folkloric elements from Sufic traditions into Jewish religious practices. Often, Jews, and at times Christians, visited the graves of the same holy people, as is clearly reflected for the entire Middle Ages in Muslim testimonies and the Jewish documents in the Cairo Genizah.[63]

Summary

The history of holy people is bound up with the history of the communities in which they live, which follow their ways, and which legitimize their acts and lives. Exceptional charismatic people with miraculous abilities have been part of the Jewish tradition since biblical times, yet their lives and deeds are only recorded in rabbinical and halakhic literature, which often took a dim view of their activities. The principle of direct contact between every believer and God and the study of the scriptures being open to everybody have minimized the role of the *kadosh* and the *tsadik* in the Jewish tradition.

Signs of change could be seen at the end of the Middle Ages in eastern Europe, with the German Pietists, and in Spain, with the stories of Simeon bar Yohai and his disciples in the Zohar. Tales of *tsadikim* began appearing in books such as *Shalshelet hakabalah* and *Mayse bukh* in the sixteenth century, demonstrating the new need for holy people, but they were not yet venerated

---

[62] For Ottoman state support of the Naqshbandi Sufic order, which spread throughout the empire from the sixteenth century onwards, see Le Gal, 'The Ottoman Naqshbandiyya in the Pre-Mujaddidi Phase' (my thanks to Guy Burak for drawing my attention to this work).

[63] Meri, *The Cult of Saints among Muslims and Jews in Medieval Syria*, 123–4, 200, 209–13, 224–5, 281–5; Talmon-Heller, *Islamic Piety in Medieval Syria*. A *genizah* (storehouse) is where all documents that mention the name of God are kept after use. Since most Hebrew documents opened with some kind of reference to God they contained all sorts of things. The Cairo Genizah, discovered in the late nineteenth century, is a treasure house of testimonies regarding every aspect of medieval Jewish life in the eastern Mediterranean. See Goitein, *A Mediterranean Society*.

as they were in Christianity and Islam. The dramatic change in this respect took place with Isaac Luria and to a lesser extent with other figures in Safed. Soon after his death, legends and miraculous stories about him began to spread throughout the Mediterranean and eastern Europe, gathered in books and collections of epistles dedicated entirely to him.

The sixteenth-century *kedoshim* saw themselves as entrusted with an unprecedented mission, to reform the entire Jewish religious heritage. They perceived their time as proper for such a change and themselves as pioneers, leading the rest of the Jewish people in new ways. Luria was seen as spiritually superior to both Moses and bar Yohai and as the culmination of Jewish learning and heritage. The list of incarnations claimed by Hayim Vital is a clear sign that this attitude was shared by his disciples. The preoccupation of Luria and his disciples with reincarnation underlined their self-perception as part of the long chain of transmission of Jewish learning and of Jewish mysticism. They saw themselves not only as inheritors of a past tradition but also as innovators and discoverers of new divine realms and secrets. In fact the *kedoshim* considered themselves the new religious elite of Judaism. At the same time Europe was witnessing a battle between innovators and conservatives which spilled over from the classical arena of the university. The pioneers of the new knowledge created alternative spaces for discussion and the dissemination of their views. They felt they were living in a period that offered new opportunities for the endless capacities of humanity to shape human life and nature, as if they were gods on the Earth.[64]

The kabbalists of Safed experimented in many areas—rituals, religious institutions, religious consciousness, confession and penitence, and sexuality—yet the driving force behind it all was the *kadosh*. As Yehuda Liebes points out, Luria's theological innovations reflected his own personal preoccupations and those of his disciples. The Lurianic God and the divine realms were in ceaseless motion; so was the life of the *kadosh*. Their intimate thoughts, internal struggles, physical failures, and spiritual victories are revealed in the mystical diaries that some of them left behind. Some of the experimentation mentioned in the diaries would later be deemed too bold and was discreetly stopped.

The *kadosh* was not only a source of religious reform but was also a central

[64] Rossi, *Philosophy, Technology and the Arts in the Early Modern Period*, esp. 9, 31, 65, 73–9, 95.

figure within the community. Both public and private spaces were tightly controlled in Spanish Jewish communities, and this continued after the Expulsion. The standards of sanctity, religious devotion, and pietism of the *kedoshim* gave them a great deal of power in such societies. However, positing themselves as new authorities led inevitably to a clash between kabbalah and halakhah, direct divine inspiration and the classical discourse of Jewish learning, spirit, and law. None of the *kedoshim* ever suggested rejecting the halakhah—on the contrary, most of them had profound halakhic knowledge —but the relationship between the two domains remained antagonistic. This tension was unavoidable in Safed, because the *kedoshim* were never marginal figures and took it upon themselves to mould public morality and behaviour. Lurianic hagiography tells of his public revelation while performing his duties in a quasi-legal court; Cordovero's *Tomer devorah* discusses complicated theology and human behaviour in a form suitable for the general reading public and inspired a new genre of kabbalistic ethical literature, including Elijah de Vidas's *Reshit ḥokhmah*, which became exceedingly popular.[65]

Finally, there is the question of why the *kedoshim* appeared in Safed in the sixteenth century. The answer lies in the encounter of the Sephardi diaspora with the religious ferment, often centred around holy people, in both Christianity and Islam. From their very beginnings the writings of the *kedoshim* showed signs of maturity and self-assurance, indicating how much development had taken place before their arrival in Safed. Lurianic theology had important similarities with Catholicism: the proximity of a god with human aspects (Christ, Ze'er Anpin) and a distance between regular believers and an elite group who could mediate between the divine realms and humanity and whose religious practices carried more weight. The rise of the *kadosh* echoed the rise of the Christian saint centuries earlier. There were also many features of the Safed kabbalists that were influenced by Sufic mysticism: the hierarchy of sanctity, the fixed number of holy people, and groups of disciples following a master. Intimate knowledge of both Catholic and Ottoman customs turned the *kadosh* not only into an agent of religious reform but also a truly global figure, whose perspective transcended local conditions.

---

[65] *Tomer devorah* was immensely popular from the moment of its publication and was printed three times in thirty-three years: by Zuan de Gara in Venice in 1588, by Isaac ben Aaron of Prostitz in Kraków in 1592, and by Moses Katz in Prague in 1621 (Bibliography of the Hebrew Book, <http://www.hebrew-bibliography.com> (Heb.)).

THREE

Kabbalah, Halakhah, and Ritual

T HE PRINTING of the Zohar in the sixteenth century, the spread of
hagiographical legends about Isaac Luria, debates over the kabbalists'
legitimacy as innovators of ritual, and the dissemination of ethical tracts with
concrete guidance on behaviour shifted interest in kabbalah from small
esoteric circles to the general public. Hardly any aspect of Jewish life was not
touched by these innovations: reading the Torah, praying, attitudes to sin,
deportment, table manners, pastimes, and especially sexual relations. The
intention to reshape Jewish daily life unavoidably led to confrontation with
the much more powerful element of the Jewish tradition charged with exactly
the same task: halakhah.

This chapter considers the interaction between early modern kabbalah
and traditional halakhah. Scholars generally equate halakhah either with the
rabbinic elite—as creators and preservers of the legal heritage, whose religious
instructions are followed by the rest of the Jewish population—or with their
writings—commentaries on the Talmud, juridical verdicts (*pesikot*), rulings
(*hora'ah*), books of commandments (*sifrei mitsvot*), community regulations
(*takanot*), and codes of law.[1] In this chapter I want to take a different starting
point: the written halakhah is a major component, but it is not the only, nor
necessarily the dominant, one in guiding the Jewish collective in its religious
and communal life.[2] Halakhah certainly has formalistic and legal aspects, yet
there are many other aspects as well, such as oral traditions, local customs,
family behaviour, non-Jewish normative practices, and informal methods of
conflict resolution.[3] Halakhah, as I consider it, shapes Jewish life in many
ways that are not monopolized by legal scholars.

---

[1] See e.g. Ta-Shma, *Creativity and Tradition*; Elon, *Jewish Law*.
[2] See Weinstein, 'Joseph K. (Karo) in Front of the Law'; id., 'Halakhic Research' (Heb.).
[3] Informal methods of conflict resolution have attracted a lot of interest from scholars of the
'anthropology of law' (see e.g. Falk-Moore *Law as Process*; ead. (ed.), *Law and Anthropology*).

Kabbalah and Religious Practice

The affinity between Safed kabbalah and Jewish ways of life and religious practice can be fully grasped when kabbalah is compared with another aspect of medieval Judaism: philosophy in its Aristotelian and Neoplatonist forms. Both kabbalah and philosophy were the products of esoteric circles which saw themselves as superior to the rest of the population, and both attempted to provide a radically new interpretation of the classical tradition and sacred canon. Yet the philosophers showed very little interest in the formal aspects of religious ritual and practice.[4] Safed kabbalah had a fascination with ritual as it appeared in the Zohar, and this was only intensified in Luria's theology. The kabbalists were very much at ease with the multiplicity of details in rabbinic literature, and their application to daily life was presented as parallel to the infinite reflections of divine lights in the world and in the lives of believers. Vital's *Ets ḥayim* is full of meticulous discussions of Jewish canonical texts, commandments, religious customs, and historical events. Common to all these discussions is the theoretical substratum supplied by the divine machinery, which relates to all aspects of Jewish heritage without hierarchical distinction.

In Lurianic kabbalah the metaphysical and the material are deeply entwined. The divine realms of Adam Kadmon and the *sefirot*, angels and demons, the four elements of physical matter, and the human body all reflect and influence each other. Reality is conceived in mystical and magical terms and interpreted through dreams and revelations. The world is full of mystical forces, and souls have physical qualities.[5] The dynamics of the divine are not only reflected on the human plane but have to be copied in detail. When Ze'er Anpin wished to expel the forces of evil he placed his hands on his thighs. The opposite movement, yet with a similar rationale, was to be used during ritual hand-washing: 'and this is the mystical secret, that during hand-washing one should actually [*mamash*] raise both hands to the head, especially on the sabbath, for it is most necessary to banish evil then'.[6] The link between

---

[4] Katz, 'The Interaction between Halakhah and Kabbalah' (Heb.), esp. 53–5.
[5] Elior, 'The Metaphorical Relation between God and Man' (Heb.).
[6] Vital, *Ets ḥayim*, ii. 113; see also i. 19–20, 126, 157, 160, 223–4, 227, 242, 245, 285, 299, 309, 310, 312–13, 331; ii. 14, 17, 139, 141, 174, 220, 266–8.

the divine and human is not symbolic or abstract: the human body should reflect the divine in a concrete and material way (*mamash*).

Chapter 1 demonstrated that the exploration of the divine dynamics was not inspired solely by a craving for divine knowledge but was also a way of communicating with God. Most Lurianic writings combine discussions of God with exegesis of the Jewish canon and interpretations of ritual practices. The link between the divine realms and human activity is evident in all of Vital's writings: 'Regarding the preoccupation with the Torah: as I have already written in *Sha'ar ruaḥ hakodesh* [The Gate of the Holy Spirit] . . . it is to link one's soul and attach it to its holy root through the Torah, in order to amend the tree of *sefirot* and Adam Kadmon.'[7] *Sha'ar hakavanot* (The Gate of Intentions) is a comprehensive commentary on the commandments and their reflection in the divine realms, practically a kabbalistic version of the classic Jewish book of commandments. However, it can also be read from the opposite perspective: the commandments provide co-ordinates for mapping the divine realms. The ceaseless rhythms of both are presented in infinite detail, and Vital implicitly claims that the divine machinery actually follows the annual cycle of Jewish festivals no less than the liturgical cycle reflects the divine realms. Like Spanish ethical literature and the great legal codes *Arba'ah turim* and *Beit yosef*, Vital's book is organized around the daily schedule; however, Vital also cites the personal habits of Luria as a justification for innovation and change without any other support, since he was the incarnation of sanctity and religious law. The theosophical descriptions, explanations of rituals, and guidance on ethical conduct and religious consciousness are woven together into a seamless cloth.

Rituals and their innovation were of great importance to the Safed kabbalists. Recent research has claimed that early modern kabbalah was not focused on systems or wide-ranging theories: these were created later, when the revolutionary ferment of the founding figures had subsided. In the beginning it was an organic component of the Jewish tradition and allocated a fundamental role to the performance of *mitsvot*; hence it was never too far from rabbinic Judaism. The major kabbalists were also halakhists and had undertaken long years of talmudic study.[8]

---

[7] Vital, *Sha'ar hamitsvot*, 78*b*; see also 12–15, 25*a*, 26*a*, 55*a*, 61*b*, 63*a*, 79, 144*a*; id., *Sha'ar hakavanot*, ii. 9*a*–10*a*, 125*b*–128*b*.

[8] Garb, *Manifestations of Power in Jewish Mysticism* (Heb.), esp. 114–15, 270. Garb remarks

Criticism of the Rabbinic Tradition

The kabbalists of Safed joined the long list of those who had changed the Jewish religion: the sages of the Second Temple period, who created the classical rabbinic heritage; the amoraim in Babylon and the Land of Israel, who created the two talmuds; the Babylonian geonim, whose encounter with nascent Islam introduced fundamental changes throughout the Middle Ages; and the Ashkenazi pietists and scholars, who created new theosophical and repentance patterns. Yet none of these had as much interest in recording their own thoughts and consciousness as the Safed kabbalists. As mentioned in Chapter 2, the kabbalists saw themselves as pioneers and vastly superior to any of their predecessors. The bluntest statements appear in Vital's introduction to *Ets ḥayim*, one of the fundamental documents for understanding early modern Jewish religiosity:

> The joy of the Holy One, blessed be he, is in his Torah. He created all the worlds, with [or through] the soul of Torah, called the mysteries of Torah. . . . Yet the mysteries of Torah are like an incomprehensible dream, and fathoming its secrets and riddles . . . is like interpreting a dream, as mysteriously revealed in the verse: 'I slept but my soul was awake' [S. of S. 5: 2]. The sages said: 'He hath made me to dwell in darkness, as those who have been long dead' [BT *San.* 24a]. This is the Babylonian Talmud, which is not enlightened by the Zohar concerning the Torah's secrets and riddles. . . . The Mishnah in relation to Torah's secrets is called the hay [the useless part of the wheat]. . . . The Mishnah is a servant, since it is studied in order to be rewarded [by God] . . . and so all those occupied with its external, corporeal, and advantageous instructions are rewarded with material benefits of honour and wealth, for their occupation is related to this world, concerning rulings of what is permitted and forbidden, defiled and pure. . . . When a person is occupied with the Mishnah and the Babylonian Talmud, and ignores the Torah's secrets, he is similar to a body sitting in darkness, soulless, disconnected from the source of life.[9]

The study of the formal rules of conduct has limited spiritual value: it is like the inedible hay compared with the grain and leads to spiritual darkness. The

---

that the literary genre *ta'amei mitsvot* (reasons for the commandments) was enriched by the kabbalistic analogy between the divine and human spheres and the idea of shaping God through theurgical activity. See also Fine, *Physician of the Soul, Healer of the Cosmos*, 8, 12, 113, 191, 219.

  [9] Vital, 'Author's Introduction', *Ets ḥayim*, i. 6–8.

truth is kept for the select few, not for those occupied with material benefits.[10] Unlike talmudic discourse, which is full of difficulties and controversies, the revelations of kabbalah are fluent and generous.[11] The talmudic Torah would eventually be replaced with the true and complete Torah, containing all the mystical revelations, the Torah of the messianic era: 'The Torah of this world is called the shell and is nothing compared with the messianic Torah.'[12]

The mystics accused the rabbinic elite of diverting the Jewish people from the right path through mistaken halakhic discourse and stringent legal attitudes.[13] Their critique included denouncing literal readings of the Bible —which had precedents in the Zohar—and presented the Mishnah as a deep sleep from which the people had to be awoken, the hard labour of the Israelites in Egypt, or the burial of Moses outside the Promised Land.[14] Similar criticisms had been made prior to the rise of the Safed kabbalists but were confined to a few marginal and anonymous figures and were not part of any comprehensive reform of the Jewish religion.

Much of the kabbalists' critique was similar to St Paul's censure of the Pharisees, as stated quite explicitly by Vital: 'For the literal sense of the Torah and its stories, rulings, and *mitsvot* there are hardly any signs of the knowledge [or proximity] of God. On the contrary there are *mitsvot* and rulings unbearable to the mind, and all Gentiles mock the Jewish people.'[15] Vital goes on to reiterate all the polemical arguments of St Paul and later patristic literature against Judaism: its legal formality, its carnal character, the blindness of the Jews, the role of the rabbinate in diverting them from the truth, the messianic disappointments, and the misreading of sacred texts.[16] Vital's words arose from his sense that reform was needed in two areas: textual and practical. The first concerned the study and exegesis of the scriptures, mainly in the light of the Zohar; the second concerned halakhah and its need for reinterpretation in the light of kabbalah.

---

[10] Elior, 'Messianic Expectations and Spiritualization of Religious Life in the Sixteenth Century'.   [11] Vital, 'Author's Introduction', *Ets ḥayim*, i. 6, 11.

[12] Ibid. 7.   [13] Ibid. 10, 12.

[14] Matt, '*Matnita dilan*' (Heb.).   [15] Vital, 'Author's Introduction', *Ets ḥayim*, i. 13.

[16] See Merchavia, *The Church versus Talmudic and Midrashic Literature* (Heb.).

Kabbalah and the Halakhic Establishment

The rivalry between the discursive study of legal texts and divine inspiration dates back to the period of the composition of the Mishnah and the Talmud.[17] Claims for legitimacy through prophetic revelation were made in all centres of Judaism during the Middle Ages and involved some of the leading halakhists,[18] yet it remained a marginal phenomenon and was rarely accepted officially.

Until the fifteenth century kabbalah and halakhah remained largely separate spheres.[19] There were a few cases of halakhic rulings being adopted from kabbalistic writings, such as by Menahem Recanati in Italy, Shem-Tov ibn Gaon in Spain, and Yohanan of Eucharide in Constantinople, but they were exceptions. The almost complete exclusion of kabbalah from medieval halakhah derives from the fact that most medieval kabbalists were not halakhists. Even those who were, such as Nahmanides, kept the two domains strictly separate. Kabbalists were secondary to halakhists as the carriers of Jewish tradition; however, the rediscovery of the Zohar tipped the balance.[20] Early in the sixteenth century several Sephardi rabbis (including Isaac Karo, uncle of Joseph Karo, and David ben Zimra) accepted the Zohar as a legitimate source of halakhah, on the condition that it did not contradict existing halakhic rulings.[21] They were following the tradition of the prestigious yeshiva of Isaac Canpanton of Castile, which set the pattern for halakhic and talmudic study throughout the Sephardi diaspora. Joseph Karo introduced zoharic notions into his *Shulḥan arukh*, and his standing within the legal field provided the Zohar with immense halakhic importance.[22] More and more halakhists became interested in the legal aspects of the Zohar, which proved significant for encounters between the Sephardi exiles and other Jews and sometimes led to heated confrontations.[23] Meir Kadosh, in a comprehensive examination of

---

[17] Urbach, 'Halakhah and Prophecy' (Heb.).

[18] See Heschel, 'The Holy Spirit in the Middle Ages until Maimonides' Time' (Heb.).

[19] This discussion relies on Pely, 'Lurianic Kabbalah' (Heb.), esp. 50–2, 336–40.

[20] On the effects of the Zohar on ethical and halakhic discussions prior to the Expulsion, see Kadosh, 'Kabbalistic Laws in Responsa' (Heb.), 114–15; Hallamish, *Kabbalah in Liturgy, Halakhah and Customs* (Heb.), 124–8.

[21] For Karo, see Pely, 'Kabbalah in R. Joseph Karo's Halakhic System' (Heb.); for Ben Zimra, see Kadosh, 'Kabbalistic Laws in Responsa' (Heb.), 237–8.

[22] Katz, 'The Interaction between Halakhah and Kabbalah' (Heb.).   [23] See esp. ibid. 61–2.

halakhic rulings and responsa, has established that the imprint of kabbalah on halakhah spread to exactly the same places as the Sephardi diaspora did during the sixteenth century: Italy, Turkey, the Land of Israel, Egypt, and Algiers.[24] As the Zohar reflected Sephardi traditions and halakhah, it was a useful tool to assert Sephardi primacy in the lands where they settled. Opposition to it was expressed by Ashkenazi and Romaniote halakhists, such as Solomon Luria in Poland, Azriel Diyana and Moses Provençalo in Italy, and Elijah Mizrahi in Istanbul. These heated polemics subsided in the early seventeenth century as a result of the spread of Vital's writings. Later seventeenth-century legal tracts introduced the Zohar and other kabbalistic writings into the decision-making process and often concluded in their favour.[25]

The interweaving of legal study and divine inspiration was an important part of Lurianic kabbalah. According to Vital, the yeshiva and direct contact with God were complementary sources of knowledge for Luria: 'Then, migrating from Egypt, [Luria] trusted me and enlightened my eyes with some fundamental and truthful revelations, conveyed to him by the supernal yeshiva and by God.'[26] There is no evidence that Luria considered himself, or was considered by his disciples, a great halakhic decisor. His genuine writings and those attributed to him contain hardly any legal discussions of the customary talmudic type nor was he ever asked to offer a legal judgment in public or write a book of halakhah. His instructions did not follow the ordinary Jewish juridical process but presented clear-cut conclusions derived from his general theological system. In the Lurianic hagiography, wrestling with talmudic problems was not seen as an essential component of mystical study but as a technique to combat evil.[27]

To the great halakhists of Safed, Luria was a decidedly marginal figure.[28] This was a direct consequence of his use of inspiration and intuition, methods which were completely unacceptable to the rabbinic elite. For them his emotional and intellectual commitment to mysticism and total immersion in the

[24] Kadosh, 'Kabbalistic Laws in Responsa' (Heb.), 263–5, 272–5.

[25] For an analysis of a confrontation between halakhah and kabbalah regarding correct behaviour when arriving late for morning prayer and its implications for social order and larger religious positions, see Goldish, 'Halakhah, Kabbalah, and Heresy'.

[26] Vital, *Ets ḥayim*, ii. 21; see Hallamish, 'Luria's Status as a Halakhic Authority' (Heb.).

[27] Hallamish, 'Luria's Status as a Halakhic Authority' (Heb.), 182–9; on Vital's involvement in halakhah, see Katz, 'Halakhah and Kabbalah as Competing Study Domains' (Heb.), esp. 92–6.   [28] See Pely, 'Lurianic Kabbalah' (Heb.), 113–35, 336–8.

divine rendered his halakhic judgments defective. Yet none of his writings
have anything to say against the rabbinic establishment or its halakhah.
Unlike the following generations, which attached much religious significance
to acts not defined as *mitsvot*, Luria persistently adhered to the principle that
mitsvot were channels to the divine. His nonconformist practices—inventing
new rituals, using revelation as a source of knowledge, reading *mitsvot* mystically—did not extend to constructing an alternative to the rabbinic establishment. However, his marginality in the field of halakhah did not prevent his
rulings from being accepted after his death: his followers claimed that even
when his halakhah seemed to contradict the existing halakhah, it was based on
some hidden mystical grounds.

Vital passed harsh judgments on his rabbinic contemporaries and their
work in the introduction to *Ets ḥayim*, yet even he had no intention of sub-
verting the rabbinic decision-making process or of presenting kabbalah as a
source of halakhic rulings. Kabbalah and halakhah were two parallel channels
with different purposes. Though his works are full of detailed references to
ritual practices, Vital did not propose an alternative to talmudic discussion or
to halakhah, as the Torah studied in heaven had minimal relevance to concrete regulations on earth. His legal conservatism is also apparent in his dis-
regarding reincarnation as a reason for enforcing certain *mitsvot* and his
abstention from focusing on specific *mitsvot* as a personal route to divinity.[29]

However, the kabbalists' sense of their own closeness to God led at least
some of them to see themselves as infallible. Menahem Azaryah da Fano
(1548–1620), an important talmudic scholar, kabbalist, and disseminator of
Luria's theology in Italy, took considerable liberties in reading his halakhic
sources, being assured that his truths needed no textual back-up or any of the
other justifications customary in rabbinic decision-making.[30]

The Spread of Kabbalistic Innovations

The renewal and invention of rituals in Lurianic kabbalah was related to the
dynamic nature of the divinity and its influence over human life (see Chapters
1 and 5). According to Vital, 'the first reflection [of the divine realms on the

---

[29] Pely, 'Lurianic Kabbalah' (Heb.), 135–79, 338–40.
[30] Bonfil, 'Halakha, Kabbala and Society'.

material world] is the spiritual powers of man. . . . The second is the body. The third is the clothes over the body. The fourth is the house within which dwells the man and his body and his clothes.'[31] Divine presence in the human world is far from abstract: the final reflection, 'the house', is not a mystical symbol but a very material one, familiar throughout the Mediterranean, with an internal courtyard, surrounded by a field near the desert.[32] The house has prosaic and sociological dimensions. These components would be pursued intensively by the following generations of kabbalists: practices of penitence ('spiritual powers'), deportment and etiquette ('the body'), dress ('the clothes'), sex and family life, communities and holy confraternities ('the house').

Despite many citations, anthologies, and appearances in the liturgy, the circulation of zoharic literature during the seventeenth century was limited to religious scholars and kabbalists. This changed abruptly at the end of the century,[33] coinciding with changes in how Lurianic kabbalah addressed the public. The first such change affected rituals by introducing kabbalah into halakhic tracts, such as *Shut ha'ari* (Lurianic Responsa), edited by Jacob Tsemah, or the famous halakhist Abraham Abeli Gombiner's *Magen avraham* (The Shield of Abraham). This allowed kabbalah to control halakhah and produce innovations in ritual. The second was the development of rules of etiquette (*hanhagot*), which lacked legal formality but came to be seen as utterly binding. The printing press was used to spread the message through the production of booklets, abridgements of kabbalistic treatises, and short guides to conduct at special events.[34] The popularity of this vast literature owed much to the spread of messianism by Shabetai Tsevi and his supporters.

It is surprising how quickly the new kabbalah left its imprint on the Jewish tradition and how little resistance it encountered. No less so is the extent of its innovations. There was hardly any aspect of Jewish ritual that kabbalah did not reinvent or reshape. Vital's writings are most often viewed as theological tracts, yet another reading would suggest they form a commentary on every facet of Jewish social and religious practice.

---

[31] Vital, *Ets hayim*, ii. 297.

[32] An alternative version has: '. . . The second is the body, including the brains, and the tendons, and the flesh. . . . The fourth is the house, and the courtyard, and the field, and the desert.'

[33] Huss, *Like the Radiance of the Sky* (Heb.), 254–5.

[34] Gries, *Conduct Literature* (Heb.), 44–5.

Non-Halakhic Kabbalistic Innovations

The Safed kabbalists confronted the halakhic elite using their own legalistic arguments and language, but they also had other strategies for reforming Judaism. Where formal halakhah played a minor role, they had a clear advantage. The human body had a central place in the Lurianic world-view, being seen as an analogy of the divine realms, and Luria and his followers sought to control it, especially through attitudes to cleanliness, deportment, speaking, clothing, eating, and sexuality.[35] Most of their interest centred on masturbation, which harmed not only the sinner but also the divine realms and future generations. The Zohar contains several strict injunctions against masturbation, which were taken very literally and inserted into halakhic works, making them obligatory for all adults, not just kabbalists. The elasticity of legal discussions was replaced by inflexible mystical admonitions which allowed no room for compromise or exception.[36] Early modern kabbalists were interested in people's consciences as well as in their behaviour. In Safed, a new form of personal confession and the remission of sins by an authoritative person was introduced (see Chapter 6). This led to rituals which were meant to produce habits of penitence outside the regular liturgy of the synagogue. They served as a bridge between the kabbalistic elite and those who accepted its authority, being Lurianic theurgical and meditative techniques couched in popular language.

Opportunities to perform some *mitsvot*, such as the obligation to free a fledgling when taking a nest, were rare, and, despite the biblical injunction that the obligation only arose when the situation occurred unintentionally, the kabbalists of Safed arranged things so that they could fulfil the *mitsvah*, because each *mitsvah* was believed to have its own function and leave its own imprint on the divine world.[37] Luria performed a rite not based on formal halakhah yet inspired by mythical thinking to reduce the gap between his

---

[35] See Weinstein, *Juvenile Sexuality, Kabbalah, and Catholic Religiosity among Jewish Italian Communities*.   [36] S. Pachter, 'Keeping the Covenant' (Heb.), 319–23.

[37] Fine, *Physician of the Soul, Healer of the Cosmos*, 191–2; on the *mitsvot* to perform in order to amend previous reincarnations, see Vital, *Sefer haḥezyonot*, 4: 48–50 (ed. Faierstein, 168, 174, 177); see also: 'A man should seek [the *mitsvot*] actively and perform them, because as long as he has not fulfilled all 613 *mitsvot*, analogous to his body members and to the tendons of his soul, his soul lacks some members and is therefore handicapped' (id., *Sha'ar hamitsvot*, 1a).

generation and the biblical period: he asked for thorns and thistles to be
brought to him so that he could eat them as Adam was ordered to do after his
expulsion from Eden (Gen. 3: 18).[38] Adam had a central place in Luria's theology, and, as in classical Jewish midrash, Luria ascribed exceptional spiritual
capacities to him prior to his sin. Other *mitsvot* were given new meanings,
sometimes radically different from those they had had previously. The Lurianic kabbalists, following the zoharic tradition, extracted the commandment
to give charity from its social context—help for the needy—to the sefirotic
context, where certain moments—during prayer, prior to copulation or confession—were considered propitious for charity in order to increase divine
abundance towards the material world.[39] The kabbalists were also concerned
with non-halakhic aspects of eating. According to Ronit Meroz, they were
afraid of consuming the divine sparks trapped in the material world, and their
belief in reincarnation, including the reincarnation of former human beings
as animals, gave rise to fears of cannibalism.[40] Other religious practices could
be turned into magical means to communicate with the divine and obtain
secrets of the Torah or for material gain. The danger of these practices did
not escape Vital, yet he continued with them.[41] Certain folk customs acquired
new meanings, such as eating fish on the sabbath[42] or placing the bride to the
left of the groom under the marriage canopy.[43] These practices, of no intrin-
sic halakhic value, were provided with metaphysical significance which further popularized and legitimized them.

Prayer in the synagogue, one of the most established practices in the Jewish tradition, became a form of meditation capable of affecting the divine
realms or a technique for achieving intimacy with God.[44] The kabbalists were
well aware that setting such high standards for daily prayer could alienate
people, and Ben Zimra forbade ordinary people to practise such techniques.
In other cases people were instructed to use a new formula prior to performing a ritual act—'I perform this *mitsvah* for the mystical unification of the
Holy One, blessed be he, and the Shekhinah'—so that unity and harmony

[38] *Sefer toledot ha'ari*, 318.
[39] Hallamish, *Kabbalah in Liturgy, Halakhah and Customs* (Heb.), 383–400.
[40] Meroz, 'Selections from Ephraim Penzieri' (Heb.).
[41] Vital, *Sefer hape'ulot*, 11, 14, 144, 202–3, 262, 274, 299, 300–1, 320, 325, 328.
[42] Hallamish, *Kabbalah in Liturgy, Halakhah and Customs* (Heb.), 486–506.
[43] Katz, 'The Interaction between Halakhah and Kabbalah' (Heb.), 65.
[44] Hallamish, *Kabbalah in Liturgy, Halakhah and Customs* (Heb.), 383–400.

would be achieved within the Godhead.[45] Following a halakhic ruling that made it obligatory, it became very popular and attracted many ordinary people to kabbalistic activity. They could feel that their everyday religious activity was now hallowed by mystical associations. Safed kabbalists used prayers distributed in cheap, accessible books to promulgate these practices.[46]

The Jews' exile from their homeland, one of the deepest and most central symbols of Jewish culture, was understood to reflect humanity's exile from itself and from God. In Safed the wanderings of the Shekhinah were ritualized in theatrical journeys outside the city by groups of kabbalists, especially Cordovero and his disciples, who documented his voyages and the mystical revelations in *Sefer hagerushin* (The Book of Peregrinations).[47] Many kabbalists entertained a desire for martyrdom, which was converted into a symbolic death during certain moments of prayer by the act of prostration.[48] It was a tense moment, which could lead to revelations of the divine. Ritual weeping could also lead to intimacy with God.[49]

Early modern kabbalah was also the inspiration behind an unprecedented expansion of music, chanting, and singing during the liturgy.[50] Many kabbalists composed *piyutim* which remain popular to this day. One of the major contributors was Israel Najara, who, like many of the Spanish exiles, lived a peripatetic existence, moving between Damascus, Aleppo, Tripoli, Bursa, and other cities, where he encountered many musical styles, including those of the Sufic Mevlevi order, the Ottoman high court, and Persian and Arabic traditions. His highly popular book of liturgy, *Zemirot yisra'el* (The Chanting of Israel), includes verses composed along Sufic lines. He also wrote poetry articulating the messianic expectations of his generation through its fusion of high and low writing styles.[51] The innovations of Najara and his followers

[45] Hallamish, *Kabbalah in Liturgy, Halakhah, and Customs* (Heb.), 45–70.
[46] Giller, 'Between Poland and Jerusalem', esp. 227–9.
[47] Pedaya, *Walking through Trauma* (Heb.).   [48] Fishbane, *The Kiss of God*.
[49] Wolfson considers this state to have been erotically charged (see Wolfson, 'Weeping, Death, and Spiritual Ascent in Sixteenth Century Jewish Mysticism'; see also Fine, *Physician of the Soul, Healer of the Cosmos*, 246–7).
[50] Seroussi, 'From Court and *Tarikat* to Synagogue'; id., 'R. Israel Najara' (Heb); Yayama, 'The Singing of Bakashot in the Aleppo Jewish Tradition in Jerusalem' (Heb.); Benayahu, 'R. Israel Najara' (Heb.); Beeri, 'Israel Najara's "Monthly Sacrifice"' (Heb.); Regev, 'Israel Najara's "Lover's Wounds"' (Heb.); see also Pedaya (ed.), *The Piyut as a Cultural Prism* (Heb.).
[51] See Yahalom, 'R. Israel Najara and the Revival of Hebrew Poetry in the East after the Expulsion from Spain' (Heb.).

made it possible for Jews to appreciate music outside the regular synagogue cycle and legitimized the use of Islamic musical styles.

The central position of the Zohar in early modern kabbalah led to 'ritual reading', wherein the mere act of reading, without absorbing any of the content, achieved a sanctity of its own.[52] The practice was particularly popular in Jewish communities in North Africa in the sixteenth century and was promulgated by Lurianic kabbalists during the seventeenth century as a means to enhance the prestige of the Zohar and its followers. The rabbinic desire to minimize the influence of the Zohar (which was shared by some kabbalists) was only partly satisfied. Prohibitions against its systematic study could be circumvented by bibliographical tools such as indexes and anthologies, which were easy to come by after the development of printing.[53] The attachment of the general Jewish public to the Zohar was consolidated by sabbath and festival liturgies and songs of praise to its putative author, such as *Bar yohai, nimshahta ashreikha* ('Bar Yohai, the anointed one, be joyous').[54]

Kabbalah and halakhah were two different visions of Jewish life and religious practice, yet they influenced and changed one another. Thus Jacob Tsemah's *Shulḥan arukh ha'ari* (The *Shulḥan arukh* According to Luria), published fifteen years after Luria's death, used the format of Joseph Karo's *Shulḥan arukh*. Together with *Sidur ha'ari* (The Prayer Book According to Luria), conduct books, and moral tracts, *Shulḥan arukh ha'ari* reveals a tendency to anchor kabbalistic innovations in halakhic principles: typically kabblistic injunctions are described as *hora'ah*, a legal term meaning a talmudic ruling, and talmudic rulings are called *hanhagot*, a term used to refer to kabbalistic injunctions. The distinction between the two was not very clear to large parts of the Jewish population, however important it was to the rabbinic elite. The same was also true of Luria's standing as a halakhist: the legal experts considered him a marginal figure, but his popularity gave him great authority. In the seventeenth century Luria's legacy become so powerful that his followers' claims regarding specific halakhic and ritual points could no longer be rejected on the traditional grounds that 'the Torah is not regulated according to revelation' or the rule that legal rulings derived from kabbalah

---

[52] Huss, *Like the Radiance of the Sky* (Heb.), 251–5; see Hallamish, *The Kabbalah in North Africa* (Heb.), 96–104; on the ritual reading of other sacred texts, see id., 'The Ritual of Reading and Speaking and Its Kabbalistic Significance' (Heb.).

[53] Hallamish, *Kabbalah in Liturgy, Halakhah and Customs* (Heb.), 135–6.   [54] Ibid. 507–31.

could not contradict the existing halakhah. Other arguments were used to try to limit mystic interference in the halakhic process: appeals to the 'traditions of the fathers', warnings about the threat of internal strife, claims that Luria's doctrines were derived from Sephardi traditions and hence not applicable to other Jewish groups, allegations that his messages had been corrupted in transmission and were not halakhically credible.[55] However, opposition to Luria's theology as true Jewish tradition and a legitimate source of judicial argument waned during the seventeenth century, and the status of Luria and bar Yohai in the Jewish heritage was assured.[56]

The dissemination of kabbalah revealed certain inconsistencies within the movement. The wish to address the public and encourage the performance of kabbalistic *mitsvot* was countered by elitist currents that wanted to keep the 'mob' (*hamon*) from dangerous esoteric knowledge. The elite practised their own particular kabbalistic rituals which were not made available to the rest of the population, who performed traditional rituals with kabbalistic interpretations. Such a hierarchy in religious practice had precedents in the Jewish past, but the division was much wider in the early modern period. It was not confined to specific areas of halakhah (purity, agricultural tithes) or to levels of philosophical knowledge (regarding the nature of God) but attached to every religious act. Furthermore, the kabbalists claimed correct and detailed knowledge of religious practices and their impact on the divine realms. Never before in Jewish history had there been such a gap between religious 'professionals' and the rest of the lay population. Aware of the implications of the rift, the kabbalists attempted to narrow it by inventing more rituals, such as reciting the formula *yehi ratson she* . . . ('let it be considered that . . .') before performing a *mitsvah*, as if it would make the performance of the *mitsvah* into an entirely kabbalistic act.[57]

Summary

Luria's disciples kept certain theoretical aspects of his teaching within closed and esoteric circles. Those they made public were focused on practical

---

[55] Hallamish, *Kabbalah in Liturgy, Halakhah, and Customs* (Heb.), 271–84.
[56] Katz, *Halakhah and Kabbalah* (Heb.), 66–7; Kadosh, 'Kabbalistic Laws in Responsa' (Heb.), pp. iii–iv, 129, 263–5, 372–5.
[57] Hallamish, *Kabbalah in Liturgy, Halakhah and Customs* (Heb.), 71–105.

behaviour and reinterpreting *mitsvot*. Practical guides, such as *Sefer hahan-hagah* (The Book of Guidance) were available 160 years before any of the theological writings were printed.[58] In their drive to change Jewish lifestyle and religion, the kabbalists were often strongly critical of the Jewish past and its leaders. This criticism was all the more pointed when it came from a member of the rabbinic elite, such as Vital.

As Boaz Huss has shown, the theology of early modern kabbalah owes much to the spread of the Zohar. The various stages of this centuries-long process reflect the spread of Sephardi dominance through the Mediterranean basin after the Expulsion. The flashpoints between kabbalists and halakhists follow the foundations of new Sephardi settlements: in Algiers, Egypt, Italy, and Turkey. However, as the Sephardim achieved hegemony in these places, opposition to the use of kabbalistic reasoning in halakhic decision-making subsided. The Sephardim were well aware of the power of economics and politics in society, as well as religion—such ideas were part of the Europewide discourse on the advantages of practical knowledge over abstract thought —and the kabbalists were also interested in power and its imprint on the material world through divine revelations, in language, in the relationships between the sexes, and in physical acts during rituals.[59] Nevertheless, their innovations focused on issues within the Jewish milieu, such as family and community life. Kabbalah turned its back on the world of real politics, economics, science, and the dramatic confrontation between the Ottoman empire and Europe.

Following the Council of Trent the church played a more active role in society as it revitalized old institutions and established new ones. Clear and unambiguous messages regarding the Catholic faith were now held to be more important than abstruse theological arguments, although there was no noticeable change to deep-rooted traditions until the end of seventeenth century.[60] Members of the clergy became distinguished from the lay population as an elite that could provide instruction and examples of piety and devotion. This was similar to the development of the distinction between kabbalistic

---

[58] Hallamish, 'Luria's Status as a Halakhic Authority' (Heb.).

[59] Garb, *Manifestations of Power in Jewish Mysticism* (Heb.), 174–5, 185.

[60] For changes in family and marriage habits, see Menchi and Quaglioni (eds.), *I processi matrimoniali degli archivi ecclesiastici italiani*.

mitsvot for the few and traditional *mitsvot* with a kabbalistic interpretation for the many in Judaism. This fractured the classical rabbinic ethos of all Jews standing equally before God performing the same *mitsvot* and could lead to scorn for the traditional practice of *mitsvot* as insufficient, shallow, and not leading to intimacy with God.[61] The rabbinic elite saw the kabbalists' appeal to direct heavenly revelation as a threat to their authority which could not be refuted by any legal counter-argument. In practice, however, kabbalists bowed to rabbinic power as it was greater than theirs. The kabbalistic sense of superiority eventually led to fissures within kabbalism itself, with many kabbalists insisting that theirs was the only true kabbalah. The tolerance characteristic of much Jewish erudition ('the Torah has seventy faces' (BT *San.* 34*a*)), was replaced by absolute truth claims. This reflects similar changes in the Catholic world and stricter distinctions between the customary and the strange, faith and heresy, orthodoxy and heterodoxy.

The public turn of kabbalah led to an unavoidable encounter with halakhah, and it is an open question to what extent these two domains influenced and modernized each other. Joseph Karo, the greatest halakhist of his time and a mystic full of divine inspiration, represents this polarity most clearly.[62] His legal activity was intimately linked to his mystical insights, and he attempted to construct a homogeneous and unified structure straddling both domains. The Safed kabbalists never managed to resolve the conflict between their missionary campaigns to promote kabbalistic practices and the unbridgeable gap they saw between themselves and the rest of the Jewish population, including the rabbinic elite. This tension was to explode during the messianic movement of Shabetai Tsevi.

[61] See Vital, *Sha'ar hamitsvot*, 2*b*.   [62] See Raz-Krakotzkin, 'Law and Censure' (Heb.).

Religious Confraternities

T HE SIXTEENTH CENTURY witnessed a shift in interest in kabbalah
from elite, esoteric circles to the general public. In what they said and
wrote, the kabbalists of Safed repeatedly stressed the need to educate more
people about their reforms, although the more complicated aspects of their
theology, and especially the 'dangerous' elements, were still meticulously
hidden from the public eye.[1] Their new spiritual messages led to the establishment of a new kabbalistic institution: the religious confraternity (*ḥavurat
mitsvah*). These confraternities spread, slowly at first, throughout the Mediterranean and eastern Europe. They became the most important instrument
for the dissemination of kabbalistic doctrines, ritual innovations, and ethical
literature.

The kabbalistic confraternity was a stable, self-regulating institution.
Preconditions were set for entry, and members could be expelled for mis-
behaviour, lack of community spirit, or dissent. Confraternities often produced their own liturgical or pious literature to serve their particular needs.
They acted as bridges between the leading kabbalists and the public at large,
which often had very little acquaintance with kabbalah; between Judaism and
Catholicism, especially in Italy; and between Judaism and Islam, especially
through the Sufic brotherhoods.

Community and Congregation in Religious Practice

Jewish religious life has always had a markedly collective character, beginning
with the revelation at Mount Sinai in the presence of the entire people. Jews
are encouraged to perform their daily prayers—one of the fundamental

---

[1] On the distinction between 'open' and 'closed' knowledge in early modern Europe, see
Ginzburg, 'High and Low'.

elements of their religious practice—in the synagogue, not in a private space. This trait became ever more prevalent during the Middle Ages when Jews lived as part of a religious minority. In a world of religious competition and polemic between faiths there was no neutral zone. Jewish communities nurtured a sense of shared destiny, in part through the re-enactment of the Israelites' journey from Egypt to the Promised Land in the annual liturgical cycle, and maintained a constant network of intercommunal communications. However, the voluntaristic element of community involvement proved a source of weakness, as it limited the community's ability to impose discipline and to finance communal projects. For example, in Salonica, one of the leading Sephardi communities of the sixteenth century, 'every ethnic group, with its own language, stands by itself: descendants from Apulia, Sicily, Catalonia, and Ashkenaz. There might exist twenty-two separate courts of law, especially as every ethnic group is entered separately in the register of the Ottoman sultan.'[2] The Cairo Genizah provides invaluable insights into how community needs were met in the Jewish communities of the Mediterranean during the early Middle Ages.[3] What was beyond the community's capabilities was met by private individuals, who would often leave part of their real estate to charity, following the Muslim *waqf* system of setting aside some of the revenue from real estate for various charitable purposes. In the equivalent Jewish *hekdesh* system, the property was managed independently of the community, and the practice did not acquire any air of sanctity or established rules.[4]

The first evidence for confraternities with their own regulations comes from Spain and southern France and dates to the end of the thirteenth century.[5] The economic and demographic crisis of Spanish Jewry at the end of the fourteenth century led to increased tensions, sometimes breaking out into

[2] Cited in Hacker, 'Communal Organization among the Jewish Communities of the Ottoman Empire' (Heb.), 294.

[3] Goitein, *A Mediterranean Society*; see also Ben-Sasson, *The Emergence of the Local Jewish Community in the Muslim World* (Heb.); Frenkel, *The 'Compassionate and Benevolent'* (Heb.).

[4] Gil, *Documents of the Jewish Pious Foundations from the Cairo Geniza*; on the adoption of this practice by Jewish communities in Catholic Spain, see Galinsky, 'Jewish Charitable Bequests and the Hekdesh Trust in Thirteenth-Century Spain'.

[5] Assis, 'Welfare and Mutual Aid in the Spanish Jewish Community' (Heb.); Stuber, 'Charity in Sephardi Communities' (Heb.); see also Ben-Shalom, 'The Jewish Community in Arles and Its Institutions' (Heb.).

violence, between the rich and poor, and many confraternities were established partly in response to these tensions. They were mostly founded by private individuals, and their names (Almosna de la Aljama (Community Charity),[6] Confraria del Cahal (Confraternity of the Community)) testified to the unresolved tension between community control and the desire for autonomy. The first religious confraternity appeared in Saragossa in 1378 with the establishment of the Confradia de la Maytinal or Confadia d'Azmuro (Confraternity for Morning Vigils),[7] whose members committed themselves to rise at dawn and pray. Later confraternities provided sacred and liturgical books for the synagogue where they held their meetings. These activities were stimulated by the spirit of repentance and piety that arose in Spanish communities following the massacres of 1391.[8] Nevertheless, most Spanish Jewish confraternities were devoted to material needs, not liturgy or prayer, and were not conceived as sacred organizations.

The Spanish model spread throughout the Mediterranean following the Expulsion, although the practice seems to have declined in Spanish communities in the sixteenth century and there is little evidence of it in the Ottoman empire during this period.[9] At the start of the century confraternities needed a persuasive justification for their activities so as not to be thought of as hotbeds of dissent by community leaders, and this could often only be supplied by citing religious motivations. The foundation documents of most confraternities expound apologetically the social and economic needs to which they were a response. Their main period of activity in the Ottoman empire was the middle of the seventeenth century in the wake of Shabetai Tsevi's messianic movement.

Confraternal Activity at Safed

In the early sixteenth century a Jewish confraternity in Jerusalem, initiated and headed by a Spanish exile, Abraham ben Eliezer Halevi, undertook prayer vigils, but this only lasted a short time and ceased once the messianic

---

[6] *Aljama* was the name for the Jewish communities of Muslim Iberia.

[7] *Azmuro* is a corruption of Hebrew *ashmurot boker*, 'early dawn'.

[8] This spirit also inspired the halakhic *summa* of Jacob ben Asher, *Arba'ah turim* (see Galinsky, 'The *Arba'ah turim* and the Halakhic Literature of 14th-Century Spain' (Heb.)).

[9] Ben-Naeh, *Jews in the Realm of the Sultans*, 270–88.

hopes that had encouraged it subsided.[10] The significant religious development in confraternities took place at Safed.[11] There they functioned outside
the liturgical rhythm of the synagogue and were well organized, with formal
rules (*hanhagot*) set by the founders and binding on all members governing
many aspects of behaviour, piety, and thought. For example, the *hanhagot* of
Joseph Karo do not include any complicated kabbalistic theology or esoteric
meditative techniques but focus on daily religious practice and personal and
group morality, although they do end with the unprecedented promise that
following them will ensure a place in paradise:

[1] Not to swear even regarding truthful matters. [2] Not to become angry or be
vengeful. . . . [4] To associate daily with [at least] one companion [of the confrater-
nity] in order to instil fear of God. [5] To fast every Thursday and recite the midday
prayer in the synagogue with others who are fasting. [6] To ensure that every sub-
group [of the confraternity] recites the pre-sabbatical prayer at its proper time, in
preparation for the coming of Queen Sabbath. . . . [13] To beware of obscene
words, malicious tongues, and speaking trivialities. [14] To avoid as much as possible any trivial conversation. . . . [18] To avoid looking at women as much as
possible, even when they are dressed [and more so when they are naked]. . . . [21] To
confess prior to sleeping and eating. . . . [23] To speak Hebrew with [confraternity]
members, as well as with regular scholars on the sabbath, as long as there are no
strangers present [who might mock them]. [24] To confess any sin or transgression
of these regulations on the eve of the new moon before all the other [confraternity]
members, or most of them. Whoever adheres to these regulations is promised to
inherit a place in the World to Come, as long as he acts out of perfect love.[12]

Like the *hanhagot* of other Safed confraternities they introduced new religious practices, such as personal confession before other members of the
group.

The most prestigious confraternities in Safed were founded and led by
major kabbalists. Solomon Alkabets (*c*.1505–*c*.1584), Cordovero's teacher,
arrived in Safed in 1535. Before that he had led a mystical group in Edirne
whose religious devotion inspired some ecstatic revelations of the secrets of
the Torah in the zoharic tradition. Karo was a member and started his mysti-

---

[10] Robinson, 'Messianic Prayer Vigils in Jerusalem in the Early Sixteenth Century' (my
thanks to Jonathan Garb for drawing my attention to this work).
[11] See Fine, *Safed Spirituality*, esp. 10–16, 42, 58, 61–5, 83–90.
[12] Toledano, '*Tikunim* and Customs of Safed Kabbalists' (Heb.).

cal career during a famous session at Shavuot in which the Shekhinah told the group to move to the Land of Israel.[13] For Alkabets, the basis for collective mystical activity lay in the shared source of Jewish souls in the divine realms, as it created a collective solidarity and made each member responsible for the destiny of the whole Jewish people. He declared, following the Zohar, that 'if the leaders or one [Jewish] community would repent entirely, this would benefit the redemption of all diasporas'.[14]

Prior to the arrival of Isaac Luria, Moses Cordovero (1522–70) was the leading kabbalist of Safed. He compiled the most comprehensive synthesis of kabbalistic positions and wrote a comprehensive commentary on the Zohar.[15] As mentioned in Chapter 3, Cordovero's confraternity practised mystical walks outside the city known as *gerushim*, symbolizing the exile of the Shekhinah. Intimacy with the Shekhinah led to divine revelations, which were eventually collected and put into writing as *Sefer hagerushin*. Several of the novel aspects of this first Safed confraternity would be adopted by later ones: collective mystical activity, the dominant role of *tsadikim* and *kedoshim*, and the inspiration drawn from Simeon bar Yohai and his disciples.

Eleazar Azikri (1533–1600) represents the ascetic and pietistic trend at Safed, especially in his mystical diary and later in *Sefer haredim* (The Book of the God-Fearers),[16] one of the most fascinating products of the Safed kabbalists. It opens the door to his most intimate thoughts, personal motives, and the unresolved conflict between his wish for seclusion and individual devotion and his commitment to the life of his community. At some points in Azikri's life the second was dominant and he established a religious confraternity whose members practised collective confession:

On the sabbath eve, 26 Tamuz, [all the confraternity members] gathered to perform the commandment 'form a friendship', so that each one would help the other not to leave God's Torah. . . . And we agreed to provide regular accounts of gain and

---

[13] Alkabets, *Derashat haperedah*, esp. 19–21; Sack, 'The Land of Israel, the Zohar, and the Kabbalah of Safed' (Heb.).

[14] Cited in Sack, 'The Land of Israel, the Zohar, and the Kabbalah of Safed' (Heb.), 53.

[15] Sack, *The Kabbalah of Moses Cordovero* (Heb.), esp. 17, 28–9, 228; see also Huss, 'The Zoharic Communities of Safed' (Heb.); Zohar, *Decoding the Dogma within the Enigma*; for Cordovero's *hanhagot*, see Schechter, *Studies in Judaism*, 292–4.

[16] Azikri, *Yomano hamisti*; see also M. Pachter, 'The Life and Personality of R. Eleazar Azikri' (Heb.).

loss . . . and not to conceal anything from each other and to pray for the benefit of each other and that whatever we had would be shared, for the good of the Torah and worship, with great fear and love and devotion to God, may he be blessed, and to his people of Israel, for all of them are saints and we are despicable. All sound and valid [a formula for concluding legal contracts].[17]

It is unclear if 'whatever we had would be shared' is merely a ritual declaration of solidarity or if they did share everything. A set of *hanhagot* provided the structure of the group, and it was read aloud daily by all the members. The main occupation of Azikri and his group was repentance (see Chapter 6).

The confraternity of Moses ben Makhir left a detailed set of *hanhagot*, outlining an elitist mode of life not available to the general public.[18] The group was dedicated to the study of classical Jewish texts, including the Mishnah—a Safed innovation—the Zohar, and halakhic texts by Maimonides and Isaac Alfasi, in the Sephardi manner. They also maintained the unbroken recitation of sacred texts, with one shift (*mishmeret*) replacing another in imitation of the ceaseless angelic chanting in the presence of God and the ritual rhythm of the Temple, during which they wore phylacteries and prayer shawls 'to instil humility and seriousness'. Ben Makhir's confraternity met outside Safed near the grave of a third-century sage.

Abraham Barukhim represents the kabbalistic tradition of North Africa, which he brought with him from Morocco. Religious practice was used as a tool of social discipline: Barukhim loudly proclaimed the approach of the sabbath all over Safed, which put pressure on those slow to close their shops or businesses. He would take people to synagogues or the meeting place of his confraternity where he would initiate them into his practices. Night vigils provided another opportunity to enforce conformity. Repentance was seen to require a public act rather than to be a personal accounting with God.[19] This was all held to be necessary for a community considering itself sacred, where prophets, or their later reincarnations, walked in their midst: 'And Luria testified that [Barukhim] was a reincarnation of the prophet Jeremiah' who relentlessly rebuked the people of Israel for their sins with his sharp tongue.[20]

---

[17] Azikri, *Milei dishemaya*, 134.

[18] Meroz, 'The Circle of R. Moses ben Makhir and Its Regulations' (Heb.).

[19] On Barukhim's attitude to sabbath regulations and public repentance, see Benayahu, 'The Confraternity Shomerim Laboker' (Heb.).   [20] *Sefer toledot ha'ari*, 225–8.

Several other confraternities were active in Safed prior to Luria's arrival. They were primarily devoted to repentance, but they also practised Sephardi traditions of morning vigils, regulated hours, and liturgical chanting, which they charged with cosmic and theurgical significance.[21]

The Safed Confraternities: A Cosmic Move

The new confraternities established at Safed did not continue the Sephardi confraternal tradition from before the Expulsion, but sought to encourage piety, repentance, intimacy with God, and physical asceticism. Currents of religious piety were not a new phenomenon in the Jewish tradition. There were precedents in the German Pietists and others who were influenced by Sufic practices. Yet the extent of the phenomenon at Safed, the involvement of wide sections of the public, the theurgical activity, the theoretical substratum provided by Lurianic theology, the messianic expectations of the times, and the belief that they were actually the reincarnation of the zoharic confraternity of Simeon bar Yohai, all turned the Safed confraternities into something new. Isaac Luria's confraternity had a cosmic aspect far beyond any of the others. In Lurianic kabbalah, the divine Faces interact with each other incessantly and emanate their lights beyond the divine realms into the human plane. There are five kinds of interaction among the lower Faces, and these are manifested in Jewish history through five confraternities: Joseph and his brothers in the biblical period, the group around Judah Hanasi during the period of the sages, the ten martyrs including Rabbi Akiva, Simeon bar Yohai's zoharic confraternity, and, finally, the most important one, the kabbalistic confraternity of Isaac Luria.[22]

Moses Cordovero and his disciples used zoharic traditions as the inspiration for their activities, lives, and writings. Luria went a step further and presented himself as the reincarnation of bar Yohai. Luria's disciples were united in confraternal solidarity, because their souls were derived from the same

---

[21] Benayahu, 'The Confraternity Shomerim Laboker' (Heb.). Benayahu claims that after the Expulsion Sephardi prayer books included extra-liturgical components. These reveal their pre-Expulsion origins and their later elaboration in Safed.

[22] Liebes, '"Two Young Roes of a Doe"' (Heb.), esp. 114; id., 'Zohar and Eros' (Heb.); Huss, 'The Zoharic Communities of Safed' (Heb.); Fine, *Physician of the Soul, Healer of the Cosmos*, 307–14.

conglomeration of divine lights[23] and they were all conceived following the same divine interaction and were bound to each other from before birth. The unity of the confraternity was important, because, in Luria's mind, salvation could only be achieved by mutual endeavour, not by individual action, and an elite group such as theirs could further the salvation of the entire Jewish people:[24] the rabbinic injunction to 'love the other as oneself' became a ritual formula recited and meditated upon prior to any religious activity.[25] The erotic metaphors for their religious activity are reminiscent of similar intensely homosociable groups. Many confraternal writings contain expressions of misogyny and describe the members' wives as a competing for the members' affection with their true beloved, the Shekhinah.[26] Members were instructed to love one another as a precondition of being 'perfected in piety', and co-operation both reflected and fashioned harmony in the divine realms. Another formula used to express their mutual commitment after Luria's death was a written contract signed by all the confraternity's members recognizing Hayim Vital as the master and sole exegete of the Lurianic heritage. Salvation depended on collective effort, not the achievements of individuals, even exceptional *kedoshim*. Thus the confraternity members under Vital were required to develop close emotional ties and to increase their moral integrity:

Those ten persons should love one another as much as possible, and be perfected in their pietism . . . for salvation depends on these ten, once their ethical virtues are amended. This is the reason why we [the angelic voices who spoke to Vital] cannot inform you of the exact date of salvation, as it depends on their deeds and reparations.[27]

Luria spent a lot of time with his disciples. Before he arrived in Safed most of his attention was dedicated to decoding the secrets of the Zohar; afterwards he was concerned with reincarnation and the links between his confraternity and bar Yohai's.[28] Luria took his responsibilities as a spiritual guide very seri-

[23] Vital, *Sefer ḥaḥezyonot*, 4: 52 (ed. Faierstein, 179–82). Reincarnation could equally provide the reasoning behind 'holy' quarrels over God's name, as well as the basis for personal and neighbourhood disputes (see ibid. 4: 50 (ed. Faierstein, 177); *Sefer toledot ha'ari*, 188–9).
[24] Vital, *Sefer ḥaḥezyonot*, 4: 54–8 (ed. Faierstein, 184–91).
[25] See ibid. 4: 21 (ed. Faierstein, 149); *Sefer toledot ha'ari*, 316. On the spread of this new custom, see Hallamish, *Kabbalah in Liturgy, Halakhah and Customs* (Heb.), 356–82.
[26] See Scholem, 'The Bond of Fellowship of the Students of R. Isaac Luria' (Heb.).
[27] Vital, *Sefer ḥaḥezyonot*, 1: 54–8, 63 (ed. Faierstein, 53–4).
[28] Liebes, '"Two Young Roes of a Doe"' (Heb.).

ously. His disciples benefited from his knowledge of their previous incarnations and any reparations that needed to be made for failings in their religious obligations due to imperfections in their earlier lives. Luria also composed *hanhagot* regarding personal ethics and group etiquette. Anger was considered especially serious, as it damaged the spirit of solidarity of the confraternity, and confession in front of others was encouraged, as an individual's sin damaged all the other members and confession reunited them.[29] Even in the last moments of his life Luria left specific instructions and blessings for each of his disciples, depending upon their unique souls, and promised to maintain contact with them through mystical modes, such as dreams and visions.

As Luria's death approached, his disciples attempted to prevent it by constructing a 'sacred neighbourhood', which they called Hesger after the Sephardi institution involving mystical and liturgical activity away from inhabited areas. The whole confraternity and all their families were to move there.[30] The attempt to advance salvation through a social institution intended only for the elite is close to the Catholic tradition, in which monasteries were seen as privileged spaces where monks lived holy lives and prayed for the sinful world. The Lurianic neighbourhood was conceived on a similar pattern: a distinct elite leading the way for the rest of the believers, a conception which has precedents in the zoharic literature but was never part of mainstream rabbinic Judaism. According to the hagiography, feminine jealousy and quarrels caused the disintegration of the sacred neighbourhood and consequently Luria's death. Afterwards his confraternity, now headed by Vital, was rent by quarrels and dissension and eventually disintegrated. A competing confraternity was formed by another former disciple, Moses ibn Tabul, who constructed his own version of Lurianic theology.

Safed Confraternities after Luria

One problem with the elitist model of the *kadosh* and his disciples was also faced by Christian monasteries: the spiritual elite were supposed to inspire imitation; however, they were often perceived as being too far above the

---

[29] *Sefer toledot ha'ari*, 314–19; Fine, *Physician of the Soul, Healer of the Cosmos*, 61–5.
[30] *Sefer toledot ha'ari*, 201; for a slightly different version, see Solomon Shlomiel of Dresnitz, *Sefer ha'ari vegurav*, 55–6; see also Fine, *Physician of the Soul, Healer of the Cosmos*, 351.

rest of the populace, which could lead to despair and indifference. To combat this, kabbalistic confraternities undertook missionary activities and, like their Catholic counterparts, developed a new role as instructional institutions. They were instrumental in educating former Conversos in their 'new' ancestral religion and in the establishment of the pedagogical institutions of *hesger* (separation) and *mishmarot* (shifts).

Safed contained a large number of former Conversos, most of whom had had minimal acquaintance with the Jewish tradition prior to their return to full Jewish life. Abraham Barukhim was especially active in forming confraternities for initiating them into the practical and theological aspects of Judaism.[31] The wider context for his involvement was described by a Spanish rabbi living in Venice, Samuel Aboab:

Concerning our brothers, sons of Israel, coming from various lands. . . . It is necessary to provide teachers to instruct them in the truth and the path to follow and what they should do. . . . Each and every city should construct a special confraternity [*hevrah meyuhedet badavar*] for such a matter, as there are many confraternities for various sacred goals, and this confraternity would be the fundamental one.[32]

Aboab's programme was similar—in its confraternal aspect as well as in others—to those followed in Counter-Reformation Catholicism, and the common background of Jewish and Christian confraternities is apparent in the presentation of theological truth as the basis for any significant religious activity. Connections between Italy and Safed played an important role in the spread of kabbalistic confraternities.

The institutions of *hesger* and *mishmarot* were established in Spanish Jewish communities before the Expulsion. *Hesger* sought to create an isolated space for study, either outside the city or behind closed doors within it. *Mishmarot* involved the continuous recitation of holy texts by scholars working in shifts, reflecting the sacred rhythms of the Temple in Jerusalem. Each participant was required to evacuate his body prior to study, so that no harm came to the sacred succession of learning and liturgy. The ten regulations (inspired by the Ten Commandments) required ceaseless Torah study and liturgy as a means to create an intensified atmosphere of sanctity. Solidarity

---

[31] *Sefer toledot ha'ari*, 225–7; see also Fine, *Physician of the Soul, Healer of the Cosmos*, 67. For the importance of former Conversos for Lurianic kabbalists, see Magid, *From Metaphysics to Midrash*, esp. ch. 2.   [32] Samuel Aboab, *Sefer hazikhronot*, 258–9.

between the members was bolstered by shared meals on special occasions. The regulations of the most famous *hesger*, near Safed, were printed in order to raise funds.[33]

Safed confraternities did not usually survive long after the death of their founder; however, they left a model that was followed by future generations, including the *kadosh* as the centre of the group, the cosmic link between members based on their previous incarnations, the importance of religious consciousness, and kabbalistic rituals and theurgical activities aimed at the Reparation of the Worlds.

Italian Confraternities

Jewish confraternities were active throughout the Mediterranean before they appeared in Safed. They existed in various cultural settings and served different purposes. In Italy, they were generally an urban phenomenon. The charitable confraternity Gemilut Hasadim established at Ferrara in 1515 was typical.[34] It had no hierarchy—disputes were settled by internal arbitration—and no sacral character, although its regulations were engraved on the synagogue wall. The late sixteenth century saw a sharp increase in the activities of confraternities in Catholic society, and this was true of Jewish society as well.[35] There is no documentary evidence of Jewish confraternal activity in Venice prior to 1570; by the early seventeenth century the local rabbi Judah Aryeh of Modena could boast of more confraternities than any other community in northern Italy.

Inspired by their Catholic equivalents, Italian Jewish confraternities became an integral part of the urban fabric and reflected the heterogeneous character of society, embracing Italian, Sephardi, and Ashkenazi traditions. Their goals were diverse: education, charity, furnishing dowries, burial and spiritual assistance before death, providing food for the poor, ransoming captives, and assisting the communities in the Land of Israel. However, their

---

[33] Benayahu, 'The Epistle of R. Moses ben Makhir to the Turkish Communities' (Heb.).

[34] Ruderman, 'The Founding of a "Gemilut Hasadim" Society in Ferrara in 1515'.

[35] E. Horowitz, '*Yeshiva* and *Hevra*'; id., 'Jewish Confraternal Piety in Sixteenth-Century Ferrara'; id., 'Coffee, Coffeehouses, and Nocturnal Rituals in Early Modern Jewry'. For documentation of Jewish confraternities in early modern Italy, see Rivlin, *Mutual Responsibility in the Italian Ghetto* (Heb.).

character changed during the sixteenth century, as can be seen from the regulations of Gemilut Hasadim.[36] The regulations of 1515 are very similar to those of confraternities in Spain and southern France, which were brought to Italy by immigrants. In 1552 a distinction between rich and poor members becomes apparent. The rich avoided the more laborious and less honourable tasks, such as digging graves, by paying others to do them. The religiosity that arose in Catholic circles in response to the Council of Trent also made its way into Jewish practices and is reflected in the requirement that each member confess in front of the group and in the writing of wills. The regulations of 1583 excluded women, who had previously participated as active members but were now considered a threat to the sanctity of the group. Discipline and obedience were stressed, and the fine for leaving the confraternity increased significantly. The regulations of 1603 posited Gemilut Hasadim as the archconfraternity, supervising the activities of other smaller groups, and increased the standards required of new members.

The sixteenth century also saw the rise of kabbalistic confraternities in Italy. This was due to the activity of Menahem Azaryah da Fano, who had close connections with the Safed kabbalists[37] and was one of the first people to spread their teachings in Europe. He established a 'Confraternity of the Italians' in Venice devoted to morning vigils and *seliḥot* prayers. He also set the precedent of teaching publicly the secrets of Cordovero's *Pardes rimonim* in the local yeshiva. His senior disciple, Aaron Berakhyah of Modena, was ordained as a rabbi by a special envoy from Safed and established another confraternity in Modena. His *Seder ashmurot haboker* was the first popular version of kabbalistic instructions on mystical prayers and theurgical reparations.[38]

Berakhyah established the paradigm for the new kabbalistic confraternities, and his great innovations were in whom he considered suitable members—not just those adept in kabbalah or those of great piety but anyone who was interested—and in pilgrimage practices—it was no longer obligatory to make the long journey to the Land of Israel; pilgrimages to the tombs of local Italian *kedoshim* would suffice. This greatly facilitated the spread of the Safed

[36] E. Horowitz, 'Jewish Confraternal Piety in Sixteenth-Century Ferrara'.
[37] Bonfil, 'New Information on R. Menahem Azaryah da Fano' (Heb.).
[38] Bar-Levav, 'R. Aaron Berakhyah of Modena and R. Naftali Katz' (Heb.).

mystical tradition among the general public. The *hanhagot* also repeatedly stressed the importance of educating the young. This reflects a change in attitude to education in the Jewish population more generally, and also in Catholicism. Previously, religious institutions had shown little interest in the education of the young; now they were passionately involved in establishing new educational institutions and producing books for them.[39] As kabbalistic confraternities were typically masculine organizations, they provided an ideal model for the new pedagogical institutions for educating young men appearing in Italian communities.[40] Teachers and students described their shared pedagogical venture as a confraternity and themselves as *haverim*, confraternity members. Teachers were ordered not to bring their wives to the cities where they worked, as a feminine presence was seen as a menace to the sacred order of the school. Long hours together nurtured strong personal attachments between masters and students, who might be of much the same age, although strict hierarchy and discipline were still maintained. Masters and students not only spent the daytime together but were supposed to sleep in the same dormitories, so that the young were kept away from 'the street', a code-word for all sorts of harmful influences beyond the school's control. The study schedule was long and left very little free time, which was also considered dangerous. Besides the study of canonical texts, these new schools aimed to shape the religious piety and everyday behaviour of the students, instilling in them regular prayer habits and good table manners and teaching them to avoid idle talk, discussing Torah while eating, and kitchens (a distinctly female area). Such a school was established in the middle of the seventeenth century in Conegliano, Veneto, far enough away from Venice. The school took it upon itself to supply all the pupils' material needs so that they could dedicate their entire time to study and would have no reason to leave the school building. Staying indoors was seen as a sign of contempt for the mundane world and its temptations and of dedication to religious piety.[41] The programme underlined the pietistic component, as well as the constant surveillance of the students. The similarities to Catholic schools of monastic origin are obvious.

The need to control unmarried young men also led to their organization

---

[39] Weinstein, 'What Did Little Samuel Read in His Notebook?' (Heb.).

[40] E. Horowitz, '*Yeshiva* and *Hevra*'.   [41] See Benayahu, 'The Conegliano Yeshiva' (Heb.).

into their own groups, in which the older ones initiated the younger ones into aspects of adult life, such as work and courting. These groups, which only developed in Italy, were self-managed and served the community interests, although at times they could get out of control.[42] The increasing concentration of Jews in ghettos in the early seventeenth century raised new challenges for social institutions, and confraternities of various types (charitable, burial, educational) served as agents of control and discipline: alms were made conditional on the proper behaviour of those who received them; deathbed confessions were encouraged as a precondition for divine pardon; the poor were forced to attend Torah lessons or have their names published on the synagogue walls; limits were put on how long strangers, beggars, and vagabonds could stay and receive hospitality.[43] A typical change took place in the night vigil prior to circumcision.[44] The long night hours were usually filled with games and gambling. To the kabbalists this was sacrilegious, and they gradually took over these events, so that the time was spent in study and meditation.

The kabbalistic confraternities were not conservative institutions but agents of religious change. Their disciplinarian role was new to Italian Jewish confraternities and was ultimately derived from the innovative and reforming Safed tradition. The prayer books and liturgies they used for both traditional rituals, such as those relating to death and burial, and their new ritual practices of fasts and reparations reflected the theurgical and meditative techniques of Safed. These popular booklets were typically modern in content, organization, production, and circulation and differed markedly from earlier liturgical literature, which mainly repeated older material.[45] Like Catholic liturgical publications and non-religious literature of the period, they were mainly the work of contemporaries and, in many cases, of a single author, which gave them an individual character. The production and publication of this literature were closely controlled by the confraternities, as it had to serve their needs.

[42] Weinstein, *Marriage Rituals Italian Style*, ch. 6; id., 'Mock and Clandestine Marriages, Deceits, and Games in Jewish Italian Communities during the Early Modern Period'; id., '"Thus will *giovani* do"'; id., 'Rituel du mariage et culture des jeunes dans la société judéo-italienne 16e–17e siècles'.   [43] Rivlin, *Mutual Responsibility in the Italian Ghetto* (Heb.).
[44] E. Horowitz, 'The Eve of the Circumcision'.
[45] Andreatta, *Poesia religiosa ebraica di età barocca*, esp. 10–13, 43–4, 47–51, 71–4, 95–101; ead., 'Libri di Preghiera della confraternità "Le sentinelle del mattino"'.

Italian confraternities sought to attract those of little or no kabbalistic knowledge, as they saw this as an opportunity to spread their ideas of reform. They did not promote a strict ascetic lifestyle but sought to combine piety with lay activities, such as theatre and music. Chanting could not only serve religious purposes but was also used at social events. Influenced by similar developments in Christianity, Jewish liturgy witnessed a florescence during the seventeenth and eighteenth centuries, which provided the background for the composition of polyphonic music by Salamone de' Rossi and other Jewish composers for non-synagogue settings. The spread of baroque music was part of the overall aestheticization of religious activity and reflects similar concerns in both traditions: mystical experience, anxiety about death and sin, and religious consciousness.

Contemporary Catholic Confraternities in Italy

Confraternities were a success in Italy during the thirteenth and fourteenth centuries and into the Renaissance.[46] They were strongly influenced by the Spanish military and political presence in Italy since the late fifteenth century.[47] Their popularity was in part due to the fact that they fitted into the urban social and cultural networks so well, although there were also some in the countryside. They combined lay and sacred activities and reflected local traditions. In a society that saw class distinction as a natural fact, they were relatively egalitarian: members from very different social backgrounds referred to each other as 'brother', 'son', or 'friend', and personal differences were resolved by arbitration. Acceptance of new confraternity members required the forgoing of status symbols and the temporary suspension of class distinctions, as demonstrated by Christ when he washed his disciples' feet (John 13: 1–17). Confraternities undertook certain religious obligations under the auspices of the church. Each had its own patron saint to whom it addressed special devotion, they took part in religious processions, and some

---

[46] On earlier pre-Tridentine confraternities in Italy, see Zardin, 'Il rilancio delle confraternite nell'Europa cattolica cinque-seicentesca', esp. 119–29; Weissman, 'Cults and Contexts'; id., *Ritual Brotherhood in Renaissance Florence*, 52–103.

[47] Vismara, *Settecento religioso in Lombardia*, 19–21. On the common traits of Italian and Spanish confraternities, see Poska, *Regulating the People*, 70–6; on the impact of the Spanish occupation on Italian confraternities, see Dandelet, *Spanish Rome, 1500–1700*, 109–59.

had their own private chapel. Catholic confraternities left their stamp on Protestants and religious minorities in Europe, including Orthodox Greeks in Italy and Jews and Muslims throughout the Mediterranean and in the New World.[48]

The profound changes that occurred during the Counter-Reformation also affected the confraternities. They became more elitist: new candidates for membership tended to be wealthier, and senior members managed to obtain more privileges.[49] As confraternities weakened the old social cohesion based on geographical location or profession, the church and city authorities co-operated to increase their control over them using spies and informers. Juvenile confraternities often lost their independence to adult or religious organizations.[50] The change was especially felt in cities like Milan, where determined and energetic individuals, such as Carlo and Federico Borromeo, were employed by the church to incite members to watch their neighbours and report any scandalous behaviour.[51]

Religious confraternities were also important agents for the dissemination of the decisions of the Council of Trent,[52] and, since many people were involved in confraternal activity, they could target specific audiences such as women, particular groups of workers, juveniles, or inhabitants of certain parts of a city. The Jesuits had a key role in this, and their confraternities gained considerable popularity. Members were inspired to view traditional rituals such as the Eucharist in a new light and to accept new practices such as the Feast of Corpus Christi, Marian brotherhoods, the rosary, and the Adoration of the Sacred Heart. Often, the sacred and secular activities of the confraternities could not be easily distinguished. Many of them were involved in theatrical and musical productions, with wealthy patrons and employing the best artistes. They were also well aware of the benefits of the new printing presses for the promulgation of religious propaganda. Reams of pious literature were written at the request of confraternities, especially pedagogical

[48] Terpstra, 'Ignatius, Confratello', 163–82.

[49] Weissman, 'Cults and Contexts'; id., *Ritual Brotherhood in Renaissance Florence*.

[50] On the fate of one confraternity for the young, see Eisenbichler, *The Boys of the Archangel Raphael*.

[51] Zardin, 'Relaunching Confraternties in the Tridentine Era', esp. 196–209; on similar control in small Italian cities, see Brambila, 'Il Concilio di Trento e i mutamenti nella legittimità'.

[52] Zardin, 'Riforma e confraternite nella Milano di Carlo Borromeo'; Terpstra, 'Confraternities and Public Charity'; Pullan, '"Difettosi, impotenti, inabili"'.

material intended to instruct the young in theology, morality, and 'civilized' behaviour.

Education of the young was a major concern for the church, and most of its pedagogical institutions—such as the Jesuit colleges—were based on the confraternal model, with regulations reminiscent of those of monasteries.[53] The students' activities were constantly monitored, including their modesty, deportment, devotion, and respectfulness as well as their attendance at church and the performance of their religious duties. As in adult confraternities, the social aspects were shot through with religious consciousness and a deep sense of divine immanence.

Summary

Confraternities were active for several centuries before Isaac Luria established his confraternity in Safed. They first appeared in Spain, in response to community welfare needs and class tensions. A small number were dedicated to religious devotions outside the regular synagogue liturgy. The Zohar revolves around a mystical confraternity headed by bar Yohai, and this centuries-old tradition stood behind the early modern confraternities. The confraternities established in Safed were a novelty. They had profound theological underpinnings and were suffused with a mystical spirit; however, they did not concentrate on esoteric secrets but on manifesting those ideas through ethical behaviour, religious practices, and personal conscience. Some of them inspired deep personal relationships between masters and disciples and encouraged and sanctified their interactions.

The Jewish confraternities of Safed had several traits in common with Sufic brotherhoods, which were very successful as they were encouraged and supported by the Ottoman authorities. They both stressed the importance of the master for the spiritual growth of his disciples, the regulation of personal interaction in order to maintain unity and sanctity, and ethical lifestyles as a precondition of true mystical experiences. The Safed confraternities rarely outlived their founders, but the confraternities they inspired throughout Europe and especially Italy played a major role in the advancement of kabbalistic tenets. Alongside traditional charitable and pedagogical activities,

---

[53] Turrini and Valenti, 'L'educazione religiosa'.

they promoted religious practices outside the synagogue and provided lessons on kabbalistic doctrines. Yet they were different from the confraternities of Safed in that ordinary people with little kabbalistic knowledge could join without being required to live an ascetic life or change their daily routine. In many cases, these were the target audience of the confraternities, as they facilitated the spread of kabbalistic reforms.

Italy played another important role in the spread of kabbalistic doctrines. It was where many of the Spanish exiles ended up, and it already had a number of strong Jewish communities. The Spanish Jews maintained contact with other members of the Spanish diaspora throughout the Mediterranean, including those in Safed. As Moshe Idel has noted, the spread of kabbalah in the early modern period should not be seen as radiating out from one centre, Safed, but from many.[54] The new mystical message was absorbed and passed on with a local inflection, as Spanish and Italian connections introduced Catholic ideas, especially those of the Council of Trent. Both the Safed and Italian confraternity models persisted over the next few centuries and influenced various aspects of religious life. The Italian model, with its Catholic influences, was prevalent among Jewish communities in Europe, whereas the Safed model, with its Sufic influences, left its imprint on Jews living in the Ottoman empire. The descendants of the Safed confraternities tended to be elitist mystical groups, who studied intensely and often had a decidedly messianic character. Most important of these was the group around Shalom Sharabi in Jerusalem, the mystical fraternity of Moses Hayim Luzzatto in eighteenth-century Italy, and the religious school in seventeenth-century Brody in Poland.[55] These groups had a profound effect on the cells of adherents of Shabetai Tsevi and the hasidic movement in eastern Europe.

[54] Idel, 'Italy in Safed, Safed in Italy'.
[55] Giller, *Shalom Shar'abi and the Kabbalists of Beit El*; Tishby, 'R. Moses David Valle and His Status within the Circle of R. Moses Hayim Luzzatto' (Heb.); Reiner, 'Wealth, Social Position and the Study of Torah'.

FIVE

'From my body I shall envision God'
The Body and Sexuality

ELEAZAR AZIKRI's *Sefer ḥaredim* is a typical example of popular kabbalis-tic ethical writing,[1] continuing a literary tradition of books of command-ments that went back to the geonic period. However, in one fundamental respect it differed markedly from previous works in the genre: each *mitsvah* was associated with a part of the human body. Both Jewish and Catholic tradi-tions had similar, almost obsessive, attitudes to the body and its close connec-tion to sexuality and sin as an obstacle to approaching God.[2] *Sefer ḥaredim* rejected these attitudes and embraced the body as an essential component of any religious activity. In the sixteenth century the human body became a focus for fundamental cultural, mental, and political changes. The new polit-ical and professional elites that arose wished to control the body through civil norms and religious rituals: control of the body was seen as another means of controlling society.

The Body and Early Modern Kabbalah: Ze'er Anpin

Sefer ḥaredim contains many of the central themes of Safed religiosity. It was written as a result of Azikri's experience as head of a confraternity which saw penitence as a necessary stage on the path to constant intimacy with God.

---

[1] See M. Pachter, 'Homiletic and Ethical Literature of Safed in the 16th Century' (Heb.), 382–97. It was first printed in Venice by Daniel Zanetti in 1601, it was nearly two centuries before its second printing (Zholkva, 1778), and most later printings were in the nineteenth cen-tury (Bibliography of the Hebrew Book, <http://www.hebrew-bibliography.com/> (Heb.)).

[2] Weinstein, 'The Rise of the Body in Early Modern Jewish Society'. On the growing inter-est in sexuality, see id., *Juvenile Sexuality, Kabbalah, and Catholic Religiosity among Jewish Italian Communities*; Idel, *Kabbalah and Eros*, esp. 143–50, 163, 202–9, 214, 231, 235, 239–40, 243, 247; see also Garb, *Manifestations of Power in Jewish Mysticism* (Heb.); Wolfson, *Language, Eros, Being*.

Entire sections of Azikri's spiritual diary were copied into it, turning his most personal experiences into normative standards. There is no system, and the prescribed behaviour is simply presented through didactic stories. The book's concern with the body, and especially sexuality, is its main contribution: the body is proposed as a tool for religious and cultural reform.

The basis for this reform was Lurianic theology, which described God and his interaction with the world in vivid corporeal terms. Rachel Elior has claimed that this was easily accepted in sixteenth-century Europe, where the physical and the metaphysical were fully integrated in a continuum of divine realms, angels and demons, humanity, and the material world with its four elements.[3] Lurianic discourse is full of analogies between Adam Kadmon and humanity. Human experiences appear in all aspects of the divine: birth, growth, copulation, parenthood, breastfeeding, jealousy, violence, sickness, and death recur again and again.

Within the divine realms there is a constant oscillation between what Vital called *katnut* and *gadlut* (smallness and greatness), especially in relation to Ze'er Anpin. His growth through the stages of foetus, baby, adolescent, and youth are described, and he is noted as reaching various ages which mark increased levels of halakhic responsibility: 4, 6, 9, 13, 15, 18, and 20 years. When he reaches maturity, *katnut* and *gadlut* cease to indicate the processes of growth and reflect the entire divine and cosmic rhythms. On Earth these rhythms are reflected in the regular appearances of *tsadikim*, starting with the biblical characters Moses, Joseph, Elijah, and Samuel and ending with the *kedoshim* of Safed. The rhythms are repeated at a lower level within the lives of individual *tsadikim* and *kedoshim*. The *gadlut* of the *kadosh* connected him to aspects of God and allowed him access to divine knowledge, while his *katnut* linked him to the Jewish people.[4] The oscillation of *kedoshim* between *gadlut* —marked by openness, creativity, and innovation—and *katnut*—marked by closure, aridity, and melancholy—reflects the highs and lows, the triumphs and sufferings, of the Jewish people.

Attributing physical traits to God did not start with Safed kabbalah. It can be traced back to the Bible. Such descriptions were subjected to harsh criti-

---

[3] Elior, 'The Metaphorical Relation between God and Man' (Heb.); Liebes, 'Myth and Symbol in the Zohar and Lurianic Kabbalah' (Heb.).

[4] M. Pachter, 'Smallness and Greatness in Lurianic Kabbalah' (Heb.).

cism in later philosophical traditions, but that did not prevent the appearance of daring anthropomorphism in zoharic literature, mainly in *Idra zuta* and *Idra raba*. These were the parts that most interested Luria and his disciples. Luria's innovation can be seen quite clearly in his focus on Ze'er Anpin rather than the more elevated figure of Adam Kadmon or the *sefirot* of the zoharic tradition. The five divine Faces exist in a family relationship below the supreme Face Atik Yomin: Abba (Father) and Imma (Mother), Ze'er Anpin (their son), and Nukba Deze'er Anpin (his consort). As the firstborn son, Ze'er Anpin attracts the most attention:

First was the creation of Ze'er Anpin and his consort. They were conceived in the womb of Binah [the supernal mother], and then came their time of birth, they descended to the world of creation . . . and suckled during the time of breast-feeding . . . then they grew up and ascended to NHY [the *sefirot* Netsah, Hod, and Yesod], like a [human] mother lifting her baby, so that he can suckle, embraced in her arms. . . . You should know that this suckling is real [*mamash*], as mentioned often in our writings.[5]

Like many religious symbols, Ze'er Anpin is multifaceted, and his various aspects cannot be organized into a coherent system. One of his most important features is his human character, which is presented through the phases of the course of his life. On several occasions Vital stresses that the physical human body is the bridge between God and humanity.[6] Knowing the bodily secrets of Ze'er Anpin provides a key methodological advantage, as aspects of his nature recur in the other Faces and in the divine realms, as Torah, world, human, and body. Ze'er Anpin was more affected by religious practices than were the other divine Faces, but they could be influenced through him. Ze'er Anpin and Nukba Deze'er Anpin rise towards Abba and Imma and descend into the physical world, where their descendants, the *kedoshim*, exist in corporeal form. According to Vital, all human beings are younger brothers of Ze'er Anpin,[7] and in later Lurianic literature, such as Naftali Bacharach's *Emek hamelekh*, the Jewish people were explicitly described as the children of Ze'er Anpin and Nukba Deze'er Anpin. In Lurianic kabbalah, Ze'er Anpin

---

[5] Vital, *Ets ḥayim*, i. 244, 250, 283–317.

[6] Ibid. i. 40, 52–3, 64, 84–5, 103–6, 111–12, 138–9, 231, 242–3; ii. 41, 156, 282–3, 291, 325, 379–80.

[7] Vital, *Sha'ar hamitsvot*, 35*a*; on the father and son metaphor in Jewish mysticism, see Idel, *Ben*, 446–54.

takes on the role played by the Shekhinah—the last and feminine *sefirah*, in the zoharic tradition—as the main mediator between God and the material world. He is the Son of God, the Firstborn Son, and the Superior Israel. It is hard to exaggerate, *pace* Moshe Idel, the importance of Ze'er Anpin and Nukba Deze'er Anpin in Lurianic thinking as generative and controlling forces, as the bridge between God and humanity, and as the inspiration for religious practice.[8] Ze'er Anpin is the divine Face most relevant to human life, with its doubts and faults, sin, evil, and even death and resurrection. Having both human and divine aspects, he performs many of the same functions as Christ in the Christian tradition,[9] and Imma is described as a virgin and has the ability to intercede with her son, like Mary the mother of Jesus.[10]

In traditional Jewish thought, the human body is believed to reflect the divine (Gen. 1: 27), but in Lurianic theology the relationship is reversed: 'everything is derived from the human body'.[11] This was nothing less than a Copernican revolution in theology. This new insight led to a 'sacred biology' informed by recent medical advances, especially in surgery,[12] which involved detailed and minute analogies between the human body and God. All three elements of the new theology were encapsulated in the verse 'From my body I shall envision God' (Job 19: 26): concern with human flesh and blood ('my body'), the close inspection and visualization of the body ('envision'), and the acquaintance with divine secrets ('God'). The physical human body was the vehicle to reach divine realms. The verse was often cited by Vital, who was well aware of how easily metaphorical expressions could slide into assertions of fact. In several places he hints that his anthropomorphic model is 'real' (*mamash*).[13]

For early modern Europeans, there was no distinction between the physiological body and the cognitive mind. The body and mind of Ze'er Anpin, like those of human beings, were one:

This is the mystical sense of the verse 'and he breathed into his nose a breath of life' [Gen. 2: 7], as an artisan breathing into ashes and matter. So the spirit from the

---

[8] Vital, *Sha'ar hakavanot*, i. 75*a*; ii. 21*a*, 207*b*, 216*b*, 325*b*; id., *Ets ḥayim*, i. 52, 68, 89, 113, 117, 121, 138, 149–51, 153–4, 156–7, 168, 224–5, 235, 262, 267, 279, 280, 296, 316; ii. 42–3, 169, 220, 256, 279, 282–3, 307.

[9] Gélis, 'Le Corps, l'Église et le sacré'.   [10] Vital, *Ets ḥayim*, ii. 246.

[11] Ibid. i. 46. This position is reflected in Vital's ethical guide for attaining prophecy: see *Sha'arei kedushah*, 29.   [12] Vital, *Ets ḥayim*, ii. 379–80.   [13] Ibid. i. 248, 253; ii. 245.

moment of seeding never separates from the matter [body], even after death, which causes her grief, until the final resurrection.[14]

There was a great deal of interest in the human body among the Safed kabbalists, and Luria attempted to neutralize its magical aspects in favour of theological ones. A person's face revealed their soul and their previous incarnations, and Luria could discern the spiritual condition of the people addressing him and choose which ones could become his disciples or suggest to them the proper reparations.

The Body: From Divine Secrets to Religious Praxis

The kabbalists' interest in the body—both human and divine—was not confined to their theological writings. It was present in their spiritual diaries, hagiography, and ethical literature. However, the ethical literature produced in Safed differed from the homiletic literature of the same period, which was plainly based on Sephardi traditions going back to before the Expulsion, and from the ethical literature of other communities of the Sephardi diaspora.[15] By its very nature, ethical literature was intended for a wide audience that did not necessarily have much knowledge of the intricacies of kabbalah, and it became one of the primary methods by which the Safed kabbalists hoped their esoteric knowledge would influence the lives and behaviour of ordinary Jews. This is the impact of the Safed kabbalists' Copernican revolution: it shifted the centre of interest from the divine recesses of God to reforming human life.

Both Eleazar Azikri and Elijah de Vidas discussed the body, its needs, its dangers, and its role in worship.[16] As they were writing for the general public, they wrote emotively as well as rationally, including frightening stories and dire threats. De Vidas included the story of a *kadosh*, whose corpse—like those of other *kedoshim* and Christian saints—did not decompose, except for his leg, which had been responsible for dishonouring another person.[17]

---

[14] Ibid. i. 68; see also i. 33, 55–6, 71, 292; ii. 44, 49–50, 89, 234–6, 268–9, 280–1, 285; Vital, *Sha'ar hakavanot*, i. 268a. There are 248 spiritual powers, corresponding to the 248 positive commandments of the halakhic tradition, and they are disseminated into 248 bodily members.

[15] See M. Pachter, 'Homiletic and Ethical Literature of Safed in the 16th Century' (Heb.), esp. 319–22.   [16] Azikri, *Sefer haredim*; De Vidas, *Reshit hokhmah*.

[17] See De Vidas, *Reshit hokhmah*, 71c–d.

According to De Vidas, the human body stores sanctity, and thus it is the body, rather than the mind, which unites the physical, human, and divine realms.[18] He further stated that it was the body, rather than the spiritual element in humanity, that emanates from the divinity and unites all the worlds.[19] The human body is, therefore, central to the Reparation of the Worlds. From being a hindrance to sanctity, as it was in medieval Jewish moral and philosophical thought,[20] it became the central driving feature of religious life and devotion. The immense positive potential of the body did not, however, obliterate the dangers. It was the scene of the struggle between good and evil, and, as it stored sanctity, it also stored sin, which became tangible and left physical traces on the body, forcing the Shekhinah to withdraw from the sinner.[21] The contemporary hagiographical literature also reveals a deep interest in the physical aspects of saints' lives as evidence of their sanctity, but also of their vulnerability to evil.[22] For example, every stage of Hayim Vital's spiritual life story was reflected in his body, as temporary or permanent disabilities.[23] The kabbalists were also interested in magic and its possible effects on the body. Vital himself collected many magical recipes, some of which he put to the practical test.[24]

The Safed kabbalists consciously attempted to sanctify certain bodily functions previously considered religiously neutral.[25] Azikri introduced new religious elements to eating, sleeping, speaking and keeping silent, and sexual behaviour through the classic hermeneutic technique of charging traditional expressions with new meaning, going far beyond the usual halakhic assertions about human deportment and its religious value. Luria instructed his disciples on various aspects of bodily well-being alongside moral virtues, spiritual intentions (*kavanot*) during prayer, and confraternal behaviour.[26] He reinterpreted walking *pesi'ah gasah* ('with long strides', prohibited on

---

[18] See De Vidas, *Reshit ḥokhmah*, 71c–d.   [19] Ibid. 140b–c.

[20] See e.g. *Menorat hamaor* in its two versions by Isaac Aboab and Israel al-Nakawa.

[21] De Vidas, *Reshit ḥokhmah*, 168a, 201d.

[22] *Sefer toledot ha'ari*, 50, 101–5, 110–11, 156, 160, 167, 177, 184, 189, 197, 224–5, 236, 251, 293, 315–34, 347.

[23] Vital, *Sefer haḥezyonot*, 1: 17, 19; 2: 5, 23–4, 26, 49; 4: 6–7, 14, 32 (ed. Faierstein, 52–3, 73, 85–6, 96, 136–8, 143, 158–9).

[24] See Vital, *Sefer hape'ulot*, esp. 9–10, 75, 148, 172, 184, 192, 194, 211, 200, 229, 237, 283, 296, 320.   [25] Azikri, *Sefer ḥaredim*, 207; id., *Milei dishemaya*, 117, 181, 185.

[26] Vital, *Sefer haḥezyonot*, 4: 59 (ed. Faierstein, 193).

the sabbath) much more broadly and directed that not only walking but all demeanour should be refined. Classical Jewish literature, such as *Masekhet derekh erets*, geonic and later responsa, and medieval ethical books, dealt with refinement in personal behaviour, but the shortcomings of this literature were that it merely presented a list of unconnected instructions that were not anchored in any pedagogical system or implemented through any formal institutions. This changed at Safed, where a vast body of instructive literature developed for the use of confraternities and wider parts of the Jewish public, containing directions for controlling both the body and the mind (see Chapter 6). The new rules of conduct were intimately connected with mystical and pietistic concepts.

An increased sensibility to all kinds of bodily secretions is reflected in De Vidas's instruction not to spit on the floor of the synagogue but to use a small cloth, so as not to desecrate the synagogue.[27] This is probably the first Jewish reference to a handkerchief. He also discusses how to behave at mealtimes.[28] The table was seen a classic area in which to put personal refinement to the test, and most books of etiquette discussed eating, socializing at the table, and making the experience agreeable for all. De Vidas tailored his instructions to different sections of the population—religious scholars, the elderly, women —as was common in contemporary European guides to etiquette.[29]

Sexuality in Safed

Perhaps the most significant aspect of the human body in the writings of the Safed kabbalists is sexuality. The entire theological plane has a highly erotic tone, as if the internal dynamics of divine Faces and *sefirot* are motivated by mutual desire. This is even true of many of the technical terms: *kelim* (tools), *penim* and *ḥuts* (inside and outside), *mekif* and *sovev* (enclosing and enclosed), *yetsiat ha'orot* (the departure of the lights).[30] The entire cosmos is filled with passion. Speaking, breathing, and eating are all used as metaphors for erotic excitement.[31] The eroticized divine realm radiates out into human sexuality,

---

[27] De Vidas, *Reshit ḥokhmah*, 47a; see also Vital, *Sha'ar hakavanot*, i. 2b, 23a.
[28] See De Vidas, *Reshit ḥokhmah*, 259a–261a.
[29] Ibid. 262d–283a.   [30] Vital, *Ets ḥayim*, i. 47b.
[31] Ibid. i. 111a–112a, 204a, 234a, 235a, 240a–243a; ii. 23a, 133a, 220b, 228b–229a, 239b–240b, 245a–247a.

and human intimacy is a reflection of and a way to intimacy with God. According to the kabbalists, classical halakhah only partially governed sexual behaviour, since it reflected this link between God and humanity incompletely, and the mission of the *kadosh* gave him special authority in this area. The *kadosh* was often torn between his passion for his human wife and his desire for the Shekhinah. A constant battle was waged between the wife and the divine feminine, and the Shekhinah would always avenge her temporary abandonment for the human wife, especially as scholars were instructed to abstain from sexual intercourse during regular days and dedicate the sabbath to human intimacy, the same day when the divine presence was welcomed into every house.[32]

The private lives of Luria and Vital are exposed in their spiritual diaries, and the stories told about them include intimate details of uncontrolled semen emissions and Vital's temporary impotence on his wedding night:

I need to amend for both these sins, the first of wasting seed when I was under [a magical spell that hindered virility] and the second of arrogance as an adolescent.... In respect to wasting seed, I need to avoid copulation until midnight and to stay on [my wife's] belly until all the seed drops have ended so they are not spilled outside, and I need to not speak with her during copulation and fast for eighty-four consecutive days.[33]

The wedding-day trauma remained with Vital for many years. His diary was an important tool in the expiation process and satisfied his constant need for confession (see Chapter 6). Nothing of this kind was ever recorded about earlier Jewish sages. The details might seem scandalous and voyeuristic, but the *kedoshim* of Safed were seen as models of new religious and ethical behaviour to be followed by their disciples and the general public, and nothing they did was trivial or insignificant. These paradigmatic stories were elaborated on in guidance books and ethical tracts and later became popular in abridged versions adapted to local Jewish vernaculars.

An important inspiration was the analogy between the *sefirot* and human virtues drawn by Moses Cordovero in *Tomer devorah*.[34] Many of his assertions

---

[32] Vital, *Sha'ar hakavanot*, i. 27a.

[33] Vital, *Sefer haḥezyonot*, 4: 6 (ed. Faierstein, 137); see also *Sefer toledot ha'ari*, 189–90.

[34] M. Pachter, 'Homiletic and Ethical Literature of Safed in the 16th Century' (Heb.), 356–62.

were developed in other ethical and normative works: the need for moderation in sexual activity, the importance of not seeking enjoyment but the reparation of the Shekhinah in the sexual act, the anxiety over unintended emissions of semen, and the link between sexual desire and the evil inclination (*yetser hara*): 'The evil inclination should be tied and chained, lest it incite the body to all kinds of acts, such as sexual passion, coveting money, anger, or desire for honour.'[35] Sexual activity was only permissible within marriage with the intention of procreation, and any deviation was severely criticized. Religious scholars were prohibited from sexual activity during the week, and it was limited it to the night hours of the only permitted day— the sabbath.[36] These restrictions were later extended to all Jews as part of a general ascetic trend that aimed to restrict sexual activity even within marriage much more than was required by halakhah.[37] These instructions were derived from the sexual rhythms of the divine Faces and their reflection in human life.

Azikri's *Sefer ḥaredim* and other kabbalistic tracts presented unregulated sexuality as a major sin and source of other sins.[38] Many Safed kabbalists were obsessed with masturbation, or *hotsa'at zera levatalah* ('wasting the seed').[39] The term was extended to include all kinds of sexual deviations, even including what people thought about during sexual activity, and became a means of social control.

The godly kabbalist Isaac Ashkenazi [Luria], inspired by the holy spirit, amended the sins of many, since he told them of harm to the *sefirot* caused by each sin . . . and this sin [*hotsa'at zera levatalah*] has various levels: the first level, when a man has fantasies of a certain man or woman and unwillingly spills his seed during the day or while dreaming during the night . . . the second level, more grave, when he copulates with his wife properly, but spills his seed outside; the third level, even more grave, when he copulates with his wife in an unpermitted position as mentioned in the Zohar, and the Babylonian Talmud, tractate *Yevamot* . . . and the fourth level, even more grave, touching his genital member with his hands or feet and spilling seed by rubbing, which was the sin of the generation of the Flood.[40]

---

[35] M. Cordovero, *Tomer devorah*, esp. 163–4, 185–7.
[36] See Vital, *Sha'ar hakavanot*, ii. 13*b*–14*a*, 88*b*–89*a*.
[37] On this issue I concur with Wolfson (see *Language, Eros, Being*, 42, 107, 118, 264–7, 296, 307–21, 363–4).   [38] Abraham Tsahalon, *Marpe lanefesh*, esp. 8*a*.
[39] See S. Pachter, 'Keeping the Covenant' (Heb.).   [40] Azikri, *Sefer ḥaredim*, 199.

Azikri suggested an analogy between masturbation, outbursts of anger, and slander: all three equally pollute the person.[41] Marking uncontrolled personal thoughts and emotions as being as dangerous as sexual deviations was a common technique in contemporary Europe for increasing social control. The 1593 edition of Tsahalon's *Marpe lanefesh* includes a tract entitled '*Tikunim* for the Soul Composed by Luria', which includes discussions of masturbation, lustful homosexual thoughts, homosexual acts, sex with non-Jewish women, adultery with Jewish women, and sex with unpurified women. Similar attitudes are found in the writings of Jacob Tsemah and Meir Poppers, two of the leading missionaries of Lurianic kabbalah. Within a few decades these concepts had been accepted throughout the Jewish world. The Safed kabbalists based their utterances on the Zohar's statements on masturbation, yet they elaborated on and extended them and inserted them into the halakhic discourse, so that their rigorous positions would be legally binding.[42] The prohibition on masturbation acquired a mythical dimension, and fear of *hotsa'at zera levatalah* appeared in contemporary autobiographical writings, such as the mystical diaries of Joseph Karo and Eleazar Azikri. Every emission of semen outside the female body, especially within marriage, became problematic and created anxiety. Such an act was effectively coition with a female demon which would lead to the birth of polluted souls. The possibility, accompanying every legitimate sexual act, that some semen might not reach its proper destination created the need for constant vigilance.

Anxiety over the destructive consequences of masturbation was prevalent in contemporary discourse in both Protestant and Catholic regions of Europe.[43] According to Thomas Laqueur, modern ideas about masturbation arose only in the eighteenth century.[44] In contrast to the Middle Ages—when very little about masturbation appeared in canon law, confessors' books, public sermons, or normative literature—the seventeenth century witnessed an

[41] Azikri, *Milei dishemaya*, 179; id., *Sefer ḥaredim*, 207.

[42] S. Pachter, 'Keeping the Covenant' (Heb.), 203–4.

[43] On Protestant preoccupation with masturbation from the early eighteenth century, see Roper, '"Evil Imaginings and Fantasies"'; Mentzer, 'Notions of Sin and Penitence within the French Reformed Community'.

[44] Laqueur, *Solitary Sex*, esp. 83–183; see also Stengers and Van Neck, *Masturbation*; Bennett and Rosario (eds.), *Solitary Pleasures*. On the link between the European and Safedian obsession with masturbation, see Weinstein, *Juvenile Sexuality, Kabbalah, and Catholic Religiosity among Jewish Italian Communities*, 223–30.

increased interest by church, lay, and pedagogical authorities in controlling juvenile sexuality and minimizing the opportunities for masturbation. This was accompanied by a campaign of threats, linking masturbation at a young age with mental degeneration and damage to fertility and the soul. Educational institutions, such as the Jesuit colleges, controlled the social contacts of their disciples and their bodily habits in order to suppress it.

In Safed, the demonization of masturbation was only one attitude to sexuality. As with many aspects of Safed kabbalah, Ze'er Anpin was central. His daring and wild moments reveal suppressed aspects of human sexuality—masturbation; prohibited sexual positions; close examination of genitalia, especially the vulva; homosexuality; sexual contact with demonic entities; incest within the divine realms[45]—and raise troubling issues regarding sexual drives and their harnessing to religious activity and community life. In a way that would not be possible in a later period, the boldness of the Safed kabbalists was not confined to mystical writing, for they legitimized the transgression of sexual borders in certain cases. Vital and others accepted sexuality as a powerful magical cure, including techniques such as the insertion into a baby's or woman's mouth of a penis (not necessarily her husband's) in order to heal them.

Beware of the witch killing babies. . . . Another means to combat her, the moment the baby is born, put the masculine member of his father in his mouth. . . . [To cure] an epileptic, take a young lad, who has never spilled his semen, and force him to ejaculate, and use the emission to anoint the lips of the epileptic, so that the illness will never return.[46]

Contemporary kabbalah offered a liberating discourse on sexuality and its fundamental role in human life and religious intimacy alongside a repressive one aimed at previously unheard of restrictions. The liberating and experimental attitude would not continue in later periods, and any vestiges of it were bluntly censored in later rabbinic literature.

---

[45] Vital, *Ets ḥayim*, i. 11, 16, 64, 95, 111–12, 204, 226, 234, 242, 264, 311–12; ii. 114, 127, 132–3, 134, 176, 185–6, 193, 210, 226, 308, 320–2, 360; for more on detailed descriptions of female sexual organs, see Abrams, *The Female Body of God in Kabbalistic Literature* (Heb.); Garb, 'Gender and Power in Kabbalah'.

[46] Vital, *Sefer hape'ulot*, 216, 325; *Sefer toledot ha'ari*, 224–5.

The Body in Early Modern Europe

Interest in the human body increased during the early modern period, most influentially for the lives of the whole population and the religious authorities.[47] The church continued its centuries-long tradition of viewing the body as a major source of sin and emphasizing the need for ascetic behaviour, but it also explored other avenues in response to the new religious circumstances after the Council of Trent. The story of the life and death of Christ was told in mystery plays at Christmas and Easter and put forward as a model for human behaviour. The seventeenth century saw a growing fascination with the stigmata—Christ's wounds on the cross—and their appearance on the bodies of holy people, especially female mystics. The preoccupation with Christ's suffering was accompanied by interest in the instruments of his torture. The church also emphasized the real physical presence of God in the Eucharist, which led to the establishment of numerous confraternities focusing on the communion wafer as their main object of veneration. This was not an innovation so much as an intensification of late medieval patterns of group and individual piety centred on the body of Christ and the Eucharist, which led to a rise in popularity of Corpus Christi processions.[48]

Christ's agonies were central to mystics such as Teresa of Ávila and John of the Cross. Their writings repeatedly touch on the issue of human suffering. Pain and illness were seen as gifts from God, as opportunities to create a closer intimacy with Christ. Death was one of the central concerns of contemporary religiosity, aestheticized in sermons, paintings, and theatres. Sermons were accompanied by highly realistic statues of decaying corpses, representing the futility of human vanity; real bones were displayed in religious buildings; and entire bodies were preserved in open graves for the edification of the public.

Scientific advances in anatomy and the circulation of the blood and the development of the microscope increased knowledge of the human body. Surgical operations were performed in anatomical theatres observed by medical students and members of the public, and magnificent books with highly

---

[47] Gélis, 'Le Corps, l'Église et le sacré'; Feher, Naddaff, and Tazi (eds.), *Fragments for a History of the Human Body*; Hanafi, *The Monster in the Machine*.

[48] M. Rubin, *The Eucharist in Late Medieval Culture*.

detailed illustrations of dissected limbs and body tissues were published.[49] Adriano Prosperi has described the discovery that the cell was the basic element of the body as no less significant to European culture than the discovery of the New World or the astronomical findings of Copernicus and Galileo.[50] The fact that the human body was known to consist of basic units allowed it to be understood using contemporary mechanistic or mathematical models. In philosophy, Descartes explored the distinction between the body and the soul: while the soul represented the rational and individual aspects, the body was a mechanical system very much like a clock.

In the sixteenth century physiognomy, the study of human inclinations and character according to external signs, especially on the face, became very popular. Physiognomists believed that the body could provide an exhaustive narrative of a person's life and inclinations if it were deciphered correctly. This found practical applications in manuals of rhetoric, which explained how to use body language to emphasize verbal messages; in guides to etiquette, conversation, sociability, and self-control; in directions on how to decipher the body language of others; in lists of visible symptoms and their internal causes for doctors; and in tracts for artists who wanted to use the correct gestures to represent emotions and attitudes.[51]

Blood, always associated with Christ's death on the cross for Christians, acquired new significance. On the one hand, with the rise of the modern nation state, ideas of nationality became prominent, most noticeably in the Spanish concern with *limpieza de sangre* (pure blood), which established that the possessor had no Jewish or Muslim ancestors.[52] On the other, half-human monsters or hybrid creatures were a common topic of conversation among the educated classes, and they appeared in freak-shows, where they elicited fascination and fear. They straddled the line between the natural and the miraculous, the known and the unknown, the normative and the marginal.

The nude is usually understood to have been part of Western art from the beginning, yet, according to Daniel Arras, the fully erotic presentation of the human body began in the early sixteenth century: for example, Titian's

[49] Mandressi, 'Dissections et anatomie'.
[50] Prosperi, 'Scienza e immaginazione teologica nel seicento', 187.
[51] Courtine, 'Le Miroir de l'âme'; Margolin, 'Physiognomy and Chiromancy' (Heb.).
[52] Sicroff, *Les Controverses des statuts de 'pureté de sang'*; on the medieval roots of this discrimination, see Nirenberg, *Communities of Violence*, 149–50.

rendering of Mary Magdalene completely naked and erotically charged is very different from her depiction in medieval art.[53] Renaissance nude paintings were largely private affairs—on dowry chests or bedchamber walls—or part of mythological scenes, while in the sixteenth century the naked female was represented out of narrative context and attention was focused on her body.[54] The erotic emphasis was noticed by contemporary manuals for confessors, which underlined the sin of lust instead of those of avarice or disobedience, which had been more prevalent in medieval manuals.

Discourse on the Body in Italy

Two literary works dealing with the fate of the dead written in Italy 150 years apart reveal the increasing concern with the body and sexuality. The first is *Tofet ve'eden* (Hell and Paradise) by the fifteenth-century poet Manuele Romano. Like Dante, he presented examples of sinners who ended up in hell; however, very few of them had committed sexual sins or infringed bodily taboos. The second is a play written in the middle of the seventeenth century by the rabbi and kabbalist Moses Zacuto, *Tofteh arukh* (Hell Exposed). Some sections of hell are specifically reserved for young men who have committed sexual sins or abused their bodies.[55] A society's view of hell is generally more revealing of its fears and taboos than its vision of paradise, and there is no doubt that the human body occupied a central position among these.

The change is also obvious in the content of sermons, which can be taken to reflect the common ground of the preacher and his congregation. Two of the most popular preachers of the period were Judah Moscato and the rabbi and kabbalist Azariya Figo. Moscato denounced the body as a hindrance to personal and religious perfection in *Nefutsot yehudah* (Spreading [the Word] of Judah). He was following in the Aristotelian philosophical tradition, but his innovation lay in relating the education of the young to bodily themes.[56] Figo used similar techniques to those in Catholic sermons, such as including detailed analogies between heavenly and earthly justice and technological and scientific discoveries—including the eye-glass and the telescope—which

---

[53] See Ginzburg, 'Titian, Ovid and Sixteenth-Century Codes for Erotic Illustration'.
[54] Arras, 'La Chair, la grâce, le sublime'.
[55] Romano, *Tofet ve'eden*; Zacuto, *Tofteh arukh*, esp. 141–6, 172.
[56] See Moscato, *Nefutsot yehudah*, sermon 17, 79a-80a.

extend human vision, as means for examining and perfecting the soul, in *Binah le'itim* (Understanding the Times), one of the most insightful books of Jewish baroque religiosity:

Following our arguments, we shall refer to Elul [the month preceding the Day of Atonement, dedicated to repentance]. For when taking medicaments and drugs, if the patient is not punctilious about their order and proper management in general, not only will he not get better, and achieve his goal, but risks dying. . . . So is the Torah, a medicament for your flesh, which empties the belly of sickening phlegms . . . and by analogy for the other regulations.[57]

In contrast to the practice in medieval sermons, here the analogy between the corruption of the body and of the soul, expressed by vices and disobedience to God, is worked into a detailed and extensive system.[58]

In the second half of the sixteenth century discourse about the body occurred in many areas of Italian Jewish culture:[59] in medicine, the classical tradition began to absorb the discoveries being made in Italian universities; in philosophy, the mainly male, educated elite discovered the ascetic life and repressed the body and sexuality; in magic, the body was used for material gain or to reveal divine secrets; and in literature, sexual restraint became a major theme of poetry, prose, and plays.[60] Personal writings, such as love-letters, could include bold and direct references to sex.[61] The destructive potential of unrestrained sexuality as well as its contribution to religious sensibility is reflected in exegesis of the Song of Songs. In both Jewish and Christian traditions this book was understood as an allegory of the relationship between the soul and God or between the chosen people (Jews or Christians) and God. In the hands of early modern Italian Jews, it became a fascinating story of courtship and love between a young man and a woman leading to carnal intimacy. Many of these commentaries offer fascinating insights

[57] Figo, *Sefer binah le'itim*, ii. 223; see also i. 72–3; Dato, *Perush nevi'im*, fo. 18*b*; id., *Derekh emunah*, fos. 2*a*, 3*a*, 5*b*; Jacob ben Isaac Tsahalon, *Otsar hashamayim*, fos. 175*a*–180*a*; Jacob Pojetti, *Divrei ya'akov*, fos. 19*b*–24*b*.

[58] Figo, *Sefer binah le'itim*, i. 90–2, 106–9, 133; ii. 16–17, 19, 114–15, 163–8, 178, 196–7, 222–4, 232–3, 269, 361–2, 388–9.

[59] See Weinstein, *Juvenile Sexuality, Kabbalah, and Catholic Religiosity among Jewish Italian Communities*, ch. 7.

[60] Sommo, *Zahut bediḥuta dekidushin*; see also Belkin (ed.), *Leone de' Sommi and the Performing Arts*.   [61] See e.g. *Sefer ha'igeron*, fo. 26.

into urban life in the late Renaissance and Jewish juvenile subculture prior to marriage.[62]

A large contribution to this discussion was made by Italian kabbalists, including Moses Zacuto, whose letters to his disciples contained meticulous instructions regarding their sexual life as married men,[63] and Mordecai Dato, who discussed physical desire and daily behaviour in the context of intimacy with God.[64] However, the major tract was Aaron Berakhyah of Modena's *Ma'avar yabok*, an encyclopedic work which covers all the major issues of interest to European Jewry under the pretence of a discussion of death and mourning rituals in the medieval tradition of a 'good death' (*ars bene moriendi*) —family, sin and repentance, conscience and emotion, religious reform, intimacy with God, and new rituals and new interpretations of old ones—all linked in one way or another to the human body.[65] It is a typically baroque work, in which death and the afterlife hold a prominent place. The corporeal and the spiritual are intimately connected, and one cannot exist without the other: the spiritual may confer sanctity on any corporeal act; the body is essential in any human activity.

How can a man be sure to serve his king [God] well? Only by knowing that material deeds all have their roots in the spiritual world, and their culmination is reached by linking the material and the spiritual act, so that the hidden spiritual root would be awakened. . . . This fundamental issue was taught to us by Cordovero in his sublime sermons. . . . He who controls his mouth and tongue from any sinful eating or talking will keep his soul from troubles, as is said in the Zohar section *Mishpatim*, regarding the prohibition on meat and dairy. . . . On these matters my family were following the orders and admonitions of my pious grandmother, the mother of my mother, Signora Fioretta . . . and my household and kin were so accustomed to them that they did not want to change these rulings.[66]

The regulations combine halakhic formalities, mystical innovations, and popular traditions, in this case passed on from one generation of females to the next.

[62] Provenzalo (attrib.), *Perush leshir hashirim*; Gallico, *Kav venaki*; Alatrino, *Kenaf renanim*; Shemaryah Ha'ikriti of Negroponte, *Perush leshir hashirim*; Joseph ben David ibn Yahya, *Perush hamesh megilot*; Provenzali, *She'ar yashuv*.

[63] Zacuto, *Igerot haremez*, esp. epistles 22, 31, 65, 74–5, 81, 89, 90, 119, 121, 123–4, 127, 130, 133.   [64] See Dato, *Perush nevi'im*, fo. 18*b*.

[65] Aaron Berakhyah of Modena, *Sefer ma'avar yabok*, esp. 'Siftei emet', 23: 23, 34; 'Sefat emet', 4: 35; 'Siftei renanot', 1: 39.   [66] Ibid., 'Siftei tsedek', 24: 171.

Ma'avar yabok was a major work, but the kabbalistic message was more often circulated among small circles of acquaintances in abridged versions. One late seventeenth-century manuscript contains kabbalistic instructions alongside magic, popular medicine, guidance for confession, prayers for women, sermons, and sexual advice.[67] Abraham Yagel-Gallico is typical of the writers of such tracts. He knew all the leading Italian kabbalists personally and absorbed local culture and material life in order to facilitate the promulgation of his kabbalistic reforms.[68] He popularized kabbalah through various literary genres, including a description of a voyage to the other world, a treatise on plagues, a medical encyclopedia, and a tract on running a household based on the exegesis of Proverbs 31: 10–31.

Other channels of dissemination included public sermons, short ethical tracts, personal letters, and halakhic discussions dealing mainly with intimate issues. Yet the area in which Italian kabbalah left its deepest impression was the education of the young. Teachers composed small books of guidance or reworked earlier ethical tracts for their students and included sections on the healthy development of bodies and seemly behaviour.[69] The author of one such tract used very simple language and instructed his readers to divide it into sections and repeat one a day for thirty days before beginning the cycle again:

This booklet of small quantity but great value . . . briefly instructs a man in human and heavenly matters, in ethics, virtues, and social interaction, not as a burden but with directions that everyone can follow. . . . I divided it into thirty sections to ease its reading for the reader, so that he could read it at least once a month, and so he would consider more carefully and implement the instructions that he reads. . . . I copied it for the sake of my uncle, the honoured David son of the honourable Moses Portaleone of Mantua.[70]

It contains a list of sins with the reparation necessary for each; instructions on

---

[67] Brotherton Library, Leeds, MS Roth 711, fos. 1*a*–6*a*, 8*b*, 11*a*, 14*a*, 20*a*, 28*b*, 30*b*, 35, 36*a*, 37, 38*b*, 39*a*.

[68] Yagel-Gallico, *A Valley of Vision*; see also id., *Moshia ḥosim*; id., *Perush eshet ḥayil* (where the contribution of kabbalah to shaping Jewish life is clear); Weinstein, 'Abraham Yagel Galico's Commentary on "Woman of Valour"'.

[69] *Sefer hadokterinah*, esp. fos. 10, 12, 21, 409; Weinstein, 'What Did Little Samuel Read in His Notebook?' (Heb.). [70] Brotherton Library, Leeds, MS Roth 405, esp., fos. 1*b*, 81*b*.

controlling the body and personal piety;[71] and—the longest section—sexual guidance for young men prior to and during marriage.[72]

Such material was aimed at younger and younger audiences. The public barmitzvah celebration, marking the passage from child to adult at the age of 13, was invented at this time in Italy, and barmitzvah sermons composed by adults for delivery by the barmitzvah boy proclaimed the danger of early sexual activity or excessive eroticism.[73] The use of dialogues and catechisms as didactic tools was adopted from Catholic pedagogical literature.[74] One such tract links the section on sanctity with the following and longest on civility and good manners.[75] There were also works addressed specifically to women, including their religious obligations, intimate issues, and practical and daily matters.[76] Female sexuality was presented as secondary to male sexuality, something to be mobilized only in co-operation with the husband during sexual intercourse.[77]

As in contemporary Christianity, fear and threats were ever present. The body was seen as the arena of combat between the good and evil inclinations. The evil inclination and the impurity it produced acquired corporeal properties, and their presence in the human body could be smelt.

The place of sin is defiled and absorbs bad smell, so the bricks of his house testify to his deeds without words, and every sin carries a different smell. . . . For this reason R. Shila said that two angels accompany man, which are good and bad inclinations, and they testify to the time, place, and kind of sin he committed. . . . R. Zerika said that his soul testifies [about a man's sins]. . . . The sages said that a man's members testify, for the member related to the sin was damaged, since the light of the soul does shine on it, though it does not show to the human eye. And so one should

[71] Ibid., fos. 3, 4*a*, 5*a*, 9*a*, 10*b*, 11*b*, 13*b*, 15*b*, 38*b*, 39*a*, 43*a*.

[72] Ibid., fos. 22*a*–24*a*, 31*b*, 48*a*, 71*a*–73*a*.

[73] Ibid., esp., fos. 27–31; see Weinstein, 'Childhood, Adolescence, and Growing Up in the Jewish Community in Italy during the Late Middle Ages' (Heb.).

[74] Gedalyah ben Joseph ibn Yahya, *Sefer hamaskil*. For a discussion between a rabbi and his disciples presented as a catechism, see Yagel-Gallico, *Sefer be'er sheva*, fos. 113*a*–121*a*.

[75] Yagel-Gallico, *Sefer be'er sheva*, fos. 135*b*, 137*b*.

[76] Modena Mayer, 'Il "Sefer miswot" della biblioteca di Casale Monferrato'; Brotherton Library, Leeds, MS Roth 711, fos. 2*b*, 6*a*. On guidance literature for women in Italy composed in Yiddish, see Turniansky and Timm, *Yiddish in Italia*, 43, 59, 62, 64, 66, 74, 79, 96, 120; Turniansky, 'Special Traits of Yiddish Literature in Italy'.

[77] Weinstein, *Juvenile Sexuality, Kabbalah, and Catholic Religiosity among Jewish Italian Communities*, 82–6.

beware of letting the evil inclination have any place, for it acts on the human being as a worm within a fruit: to the outside observer it looks fine, yet inside is all worms.[78]

Combating the evil inclination was seen as similar to combating illness, requiring the use of medicaments, or to combating a distinct personality, which often called for trickery. Control of the body was a precondition to approaching God in the material world. The centrality of the body was also revealed in discussions of its fate after death and its resurrection.[79] It became vital to maintain the eternal identity of the body, no less than that of the soul.

Sexual Control in Italian Communities

The work that deals most comprehensively with control over erotic and sexual norms was Pinhas Barukh ben Pelatiyah Monselice's *Tiferet baḥurim* (Glory of Youth).[80] It is actually the first Jewish tract containing advice for young unmarried men, preparing them for marriage and sexual life. It is full of kabbalistic directions, presented not as a pious exercise for the few but as norms to be followed by all. As such it is part of the massive missionary effort to spread the kabbalistic message about the body, as is Monselice's other composition, *Magen ḥayim* (Shield of Life), a series of rituals to be performed before sleeping.[81]

Monselice discussed the sexual mores of Italian Jews as prescribed by halakhah, but very selectively and mostly in order to marginalize them and put forward his kabbalistic ideas. Sexual activity was presented as a holy act, but one that required an abstemious and ascetic attitude. The thoughts and feelings accompanying it needed to be controlled, and it should be limited even within marriage. His advice was directed especially to men, but women were expected to follow his guidance as well, as a necessary condition for producing praiseworthy children. Lurianic and Cordovean doctrines tend to overwhelm the halakhic norms: for instance, the obligation to procreate

[78] Foa, *Sefer ma'amarim me'inyan hateshuvah*, 9; see also 1, 4.

[79] Joseph ibn Shraga, *Teshuvot be'inyanei kabalah*, fo. 133*a*.

[80] Weinstein, *Juvenile Sexuality, Kabbalah, and Catholic Religiosity among Jewish Italian Communities*.

[81] Monselice, *Magen ḥayim* (Oriental Studies Institute, St Petersburg, MS A 21), fos. 1*a*–5*a*; for a parallel version, see Collegio Rabbinico Italiano, Rome, MS 122, esp. fos. 26*b*, 27*b*, 33, 34*b*, 36*a*, 40–9, 52–4, 79*b*, 164–75, 177*a*–189*a*.

(considered in the Jewish tradition as the first biblical commandment) was secondary to the higher theurgical intention of ensuring the copulation and fertility of Abba and Imma in the divine realms and the generation of Ze'er Anpin and Nukba Deze'er Anpin.

Summary

The human body had a central role in early modern kabbalistic literature, as a result of religious developments in Christian Europe. Christ and Ze'er Anpin both act as a bridge between God and humanity. Both traditions underlined the corporeal aspect of a God present and active in the material world, next to his hidden and transcendent aspects. Anthropomorphic descriptions of God have always been part of Jewish culture, but they became highly problematic in the context of other monotheistic religions and philosophical discourses. Lurianic kabbalah was a conscious defiance of current Jewish philosophical theology and a return to the mythological perspectives of the Bible and midrash.

One major change from zoharic to Safed kabbalah was the shift of emphasis from the *sefirot* to the divine Faces, especially to Ze'er Anpin. Luria's descriptions of him are quite unprecedented, containing references to bodily fluids and odours, birth and old age, and erotic moments. Some of these descriptions leave a clear sensation that, unlike in the zoharic literature, the divine not only imprints the human, but is in turn shaped by the human and corporeal. Sacred biology follows the processes of the human body in precise detail, and the body and its needs have a central place in theology. These were formative and daring years of blunt sayings about the divine body and sexuality. The frank portrayals of God's body had an impact in other areas as well, giving rise to a preoccupation with death and the afterlife, and new rituals preparing for death and burial developed. Death became a symbol of human frailty, and there were many vivid descriptions of paradise, hell, and the new Jewish equivalent of purgatory in ethical literature, dream reports, and ecstatic visions.[82]

[82] Vital, *Sefer haḥezyonot*, 1: 17, 23; 2: 24 (ed. Faierstein, 52–3, 64, 86); see also De Vidas, 'On Hell' (*Reshit ḥokhmah*, 36c–39d); for an extensive description of the structure of paradise and hell from a non-kabbalistic perspective, see Joseph ben David ibn Yahya, *Sefer torah or*.

Such daring sayings regarding the divine body and sexuality were possible as this was a time of experimentation, which would soon cease. Every taboo in the Jewish tradition was discussed in the Lurianic writings. This aspect had its counterpart in the Catholic world in discussions of erotic encounters between monks and female saints, between confessors and confessed, or in heretical religious concepts of the permissibility of complete sexual liberty to those who were beyond sin.[83]

As it always had in Christianity, visual imagery came to play an important role in knowing God. This was heightened by the discovery of new optical instruments—the telescope and the microscope—and the spread of emblem books containing allegorical illustrations, and iconological encyclopedias, including detailed diagrams of the divine mechanism, although this visual component was more important in books prepared for the general public than in theological tracts addressed to the intellectual elite.[84] There was a visual aspect to meditative techniques in which the mystic travelled through space in dreams, visions, and hypnogogic states.[85] The images, real or fanciful, of leading Jewish figures were printed and circulated as objects of veneration.[86] Tables with the name of God at their centre (*luḥot shiviti*) appeared in synagogues as an aid to prayer and meditation.[87]

The kabbalists' attitude to corporeal matters previously regarded as religiously neutral, such as sleeping, table manners, deportment, speaking and remaining silent, and personal hygiene, played a civilizing role and contributed to increased social control by community institutions over individual and family life. Sexuality was the domain where all this was most conspicuous and influential: discussions of the negative effects of masturbation have been obligatory in Jewish ethical literature ever since. The kabbalistic literature addressed to the young supplied an alternative non-halakhic substratum for religious practice and the Jewish way of life, providing halakhah with a different meaning to that offered by traditional Jewish legal literature.

The kabbalistic model progressively infiltrated the entire Jewish world, as revealed by popular books from eastern Europe and the Sephardi com-

---

[83] Canosa, *Sessualità e inquisizione in Italia tra cinquecento e seicento*; Romeo, *Esorcisti, confessori e sessualità nell'Italia della controriforma.*   [84] Busi, *Qabbalah visiva.*

[85] Weinstein, 'Kabbalah and Jewish Exorcism in Seventeenth-Century Italian Jewish Communities'; see also Chajes, *Between Worlds.*

[86] Cohen, *Jewish Icons.*   [87] Juhasz, 'The "Shiviti Menorah"' (Heb.).

munities of the Ottoman empire.[88] The Jews of Italy played a major role in spreading kabbalistic doctrines, and they have left an exceptionally rich trove of documentation, which records how the innovations coming out of Safed were absorbed into the European context, elaborated on, and interacted with the neighbouring Catholic religious traditions.

[88] Hakohen, *Sefer shevet musar*, esp. 19, 94–5, 187–90, 324–7, 352–6; Kaidanover, *Kav hayashar*; on the innovative aspects of this book, see Idel, 'On Rabbi Zvi Hirsch Koidanover's Sefer Qav ha-Yashar'. For another major tract from early modern Europe with long and detailed discussions of the body and sexuality, see N. Rubin, *Conqueror of Hearts* (Heb.).

SIX

Sin and Repentance
Jewish Confession

L URIANIC KABBALAH was two-sided: it had its esoteric secrets and its public doctrines; the *kadosh* moved between intimacy with God and activity in the community; knowledge of the reasons for religious practices separated the possessors of sanctified gnosis from those ignorant of it; Safed confraternities were originally open only to the initiated; and instructions on how to control the body and restrain the sexual urges were for those committed to the ascetic life, not the general public. In one domain, however, the hidden and the common converged: the concern with evil, sin, the need for constant self-examination, and repentance. This convergence is apparent in the similarity of the contents of the guides for reparation supplied by Luria to his close disciples as witnessed in the 'theological writings' and those in the stories preserved in the popular hagiographies.

Kabbalistic ethical books were printed long before the theological tracts and paved the way for their acceptance by the Jewish public. They represented a fascination with the presence of evil in the human soul and the world, where it was viewed very much as a motor of history. There was an urgent need to combat it as a precondition of personal and religious reform and of the Reparation of the Worlds, from the material up to the divine.

Law, Sin, and Conscience in Early Modern Europe

Following the Peace of Augsburg in 1555, the Holy Roman Empire was divided into Catholic and Lutheran parts, according to the principle of *cuius regio, eius religio* (literally, 'whose realm, his religion'), which allowed princes to decide the religion of their domains. What had often been bitter theological disagreements between Catholics and Lutherans over the previous thirty years practically ceased as both sides sought to establish themselves in their own spheres of influence. This process was known as confessionalization[1] and was a major part of the cultural, social, economic, and political changes occurring in contemporary Europe, especially the rise of the modern centralized nation state and its powerful forces of discipline and control.[2] The rulers of these new states held themselves responsible for the religious beliefs of their subjects, and the churches relied on the rulers' power to advance and enforce religious conformity. Extensive theological writings, guidance literature, and catechisms underlined the connection between religious and civic duties: Giovanni Botero, one of the leading Catholic political thinkers of the period, asserted that religion was a precious asset of the state. This alliance manifested itself in common pronouncements on authority and obedience, the persecution of marginal groups such as vagabonds, and the control of potential threats to social order, such as young men[3] and female mystics.[4]

While the first half of the sixteenth century was characterized by innovation and religious ferment, the second half saw a tightening of social control.[5] During the period of the Counter-Reformation it became ever more important to mark the line between legitimate theological and political opinions and heretical ones. Both Catholic and Protestant leaders felt called upon to enforce order from above at the expense of local traditions. There was very little restraint on either side, even though it threatened the precarious equilibrium achieved by the Peace of Augsburg. Interreligious confrontations acquired an apocalyptic character and provoked vast messianic movements alongside the civil disturbances caused by poverty and the expansion of state power. The number of pamphlets and polemical writings produced during this period testifies to how important the battle for public opinion was. Messages were spread through schools and universities, family life and marriage rituals were controlled, education was enforced, institutions of incarcer-

---

[1] Reinhard, 'Was ist katholische Konfessionalisierung?'; Schilling, *Religion, Political Culture and the Emergence of Early Modern Society*. On the 'general crisis of the seventeenth century', see Parker and Smith, 'Introduction'.

[2] Schilling, 'Die Konfessionalisierung von Kirche, Staat und Gesellschaft'.

[3] Schindler, 'I tutori del disordine'; Crouzet-Pavan, 'Un fiore del male'; Julia, '1650–1800'.

[4] Zarri, 'Dalla profezia alla disciplina'; Caffiero, 'Dall'esplosione mistica tardo-barocca all'apostolato sociale'.

[5] See Prodi, *The Papal Prince*; Jütte, *Poverty and Deviance in Early Modern Europe*; see also Maravall, *Culture of the Baroque*.

ation, religious confraternities, and charitable foundations sprang up. The intention was nothing less than the comprehensive reform of life and religious institutions, in which the theological coalesced with the social and political.

One of the consequences of the increasing co-operation between church and state was an increased interest in people's inner thoughts. On the Catholic side, the institution most concerned with the hearts and minds of the flock was the Inquisition.[6] The final breach with Protestantism instigated an uncompromising battle against heresy, defined very broadly to include anything that cast doubt on the position or doctrines of the Catholic Church. When the Lutheran threat waned, the Inquisition occupied itself with behaviour it considered incompatible with contemporary Christian life, such as folk traditions, magic and sorcery, blasphemous publications, false saints, and desecration of the sacraments. It became a force for social order, involving itself in family life, popular festivals and social occasions, and the observation of suspicious minorities, especially Jews and recent converts to Catholicism. During confession, people were encouraged not only to recount their own sins but to denounce others in order to obtain absolution. The Inquisition's wide-ranging new powers brought it into contact with vast numbers of people, and it came to view education and persuasion as more effective than threats and violence: the inquisitor was often presented as a guide and comforter, not just as a strict judge.[7]

One of the criticisms raised against the confessionalism thesis is that it stresses coercive mechanisms in the formation of modern states at the expense of others, such as religious confraternities, educational institutions, family ties, regional loyalties, and new religious rituals.[8] These responded differently to the new political environment, but each contributed to increased social control. They functioned by negotiation and compromise and adapted to their local contexts in order to achieve social consensus. Regional traditions maintained some power and could even on occasion resist pressure from the church and state. The subjugation of local heritages took centuries and rarely proceeded in a linear fashion. Religious confraternities tended to lose

[6] On the historical evolution of the Inquisition and its roles, see Del Col, *L'Inquisizione in Italia dal 12. al 21. secolo.*

[7] See Prosperi, *Tribunali della coscienza*; id., 'L'inquisitore come confessore'.

[8] Roodenburg, 'Reformierte Kirchenzucht und Ehrenhandel'.

their autonomy and become linked to the church hierarchy, their egalitarian principles collapsed, and they became the preserve of the cultural and political elite. There was less festive and ritual activity and more individual, internalized, and erudite piety.[9] Personal confession in front of the whole confraternity was encouraged, and members were expected to observe each other's behaviour and to report anything untoward.[10] In the Catholic world, they often assisted in the church's propaganda by printing tracts or displaying notices on their walls. Schools for the young adopted the patterns of adult confraternities, such as those dedicated to the Virgin Mary, which required students to practise constant self-examination and confession.

The Catholic Church, and especially the Jesuits, became much more involved in schools and education,[11] offering different courses of learning to different sections of the population. Counter-Reformation pedagogy was based on the assumption that children were inherently sinful and disobedient but that they could be reformed. To facilitate such reform, methods for diagnosing character and tendencies were devised. According to Luigi Secco, these methods tended to be more sensitive to the psychological effects of education in general.[12] An accurate knowledge of the child served as the starting point for a long pedagogical process aimed at minimizing spontaneous behaviour and promoting steady habits of mind and body. This required a full and well-ordered daily schedule, a total acceptance of discipline, and an incessant battle against sin, using methods derived from ancient Greek pedagogy, Jesuit humanism, and monastic discipline. Many tasks were repeated over and over again, not merely to instil good habits but also discipline and obedience. Education was not meant to distance the young from the world and its allurements but to prepare them to confront its challenges and dangers. One of the most popular books in Italy at the time was Lorenzo Scupola's *Combattimento spirituale* (The Spiritual Battle). Pupils were encouraged to observe their friends during and after school time, and parents were

---

[9] See Weismann, 'From Brotherhood to Congregation'; id., 'Cults and Contexts'.

[10] Zardin, 'Riforma e confraternite nella Milano di Carlo Borromeo'; id., 'Il rilancio delle confraternite nell'Europa cattolica cinque-seicentesca'.

[11] Niccoli, 'Éducation et discipline'; Julia, '1650–1800'; Frajese, *Il popolo fanciullo*, 44–56; Secco, *La pedagogia della controriforma*; Turrini and Valenti, 'L'educazione religiosa'.

[12] Secco, *La pedagogia della controriforma*, 117. On the wide theoretical writing on pedagogy, see Pancera, 'Educazione dei costumi e insegnamento delle virtù'.

required to report on their behaviour at home. Schools kept dossiers of their charges, which would accompany them throughout their education. Religious confraternities were established within schools as another form of control.

The church also intervened in family life. The family was charged with the salvation of the soul,[13] acting as the church in miniature, especially in its pristine and purified form.[14] Unlike the humanists, who limited the role of parents in the pedagogical process, the Counter-Reformation church mobilized them, especially mothers, in the cause of religious education during childhood. Many booklets were produced providing guidance for the family and encouraging parents to take more of a role in their children's religious development.[15] The holy family of Mary, Joseph, and Jesus was a common subject in the visual arts and held up as an ideal in popular preaching. The church significantly increased its control over marriage rituals: the various stages of courtship, engagement, and marriage now required formal registration with the clergy and courts of canon law.[16]

Sin, remorse, and penitence became standard topics for sermons. Preaching took place in churches or in public spaces during festivals, and sin and the consequent sufferings in hell were presented in highly visual and theatrical terms.[17] Life was depicted as a battle against evil based on the dichotomy between the soul and the body and its inclinations, which led to sin. Bodily inclinations were to be suppressed, earthly life to be held in contempt (in the medieval tradition of *contemptus mundi*), and the soul purified by ascetic practices. Life was lived under the long shadow of death and fear of the Last Judgement, purgatory, and hell.

[13] Frigo, *Il padre di famiglia*, esp. 38–41.

[14] On this rhetoric, see Zardin, 'Il rilancio delle confraternite nell'Europa cattolica cinque-seicentesca'.

[15] On contemporary guides to doctrine, see Grendler, 'The Schools of Christian Doctrine in Sixteenth-Century Italy'.

[16] Lombardi, 'Fidanzamento e matrimoni dal concilio di Trento alle riforme settecentesche; Zarri, 'Il matrimonio tridentino'; Frigo, *Il padre di famiglia*, esp. 38–41.

[17] On sacred preaching after the Council of Trent, see Weinstein, *Juvenile Sexuality, Kabbalah, and Catholic Religiosity among Jewish Italian Communities*, 186–8, 253–75.

Sin and Repentance among Safed Kabbalists

Most of the Safed kabbalists were concerned with identifying sins and offering means of reparation.[18] They believed that a sin, once committed, entered
the world and accompanied the sinner everywhere, inscribed on the sinner's
body—or bones, according to Cordovero[19]—very much like the memory-
signs left by the divine radiation of the Faces and *sefirot*. It could only be
removed by an intentional action: 'The obscenity of this verbal expression
would be imprinted in his body, actually in the physical body. And the body
being infected by this sin, the Shekhinah would withdraw from him.'[20]

Physiognomy has a long history in Judaism, being practised by the sects
from the Judaean desert who produced the Dead Sea Scrolls, Babylonian
geonim, and the owners of some of the documents found in the Cairo
Genizah. It is discussed in the Zohar with reservations about its magical and
astrological aspects and an emphasis on its use for curing the soul. Its techniques were developed further by Isaac Luria, who read the marks of sins
committed in previous incarnations on the foreheads of the people who came
to him, or detected the evil inclination in their pulses.[21] This knowledge,
combined with his profound acquaintance with the vast divine machinery,
allowed Luria to suggest the proper personal reparations, which were always
very specific to the sin, the sinner, and the time, and he introduced new techniques of personal and group repentance.[22] The reparations were an essential
part of Lurianic theology, as is clear from Vital's *Sha'ar ruaḥ hakodesh*, where
reparations for various sins are presented alongside descriptions of the relevant parts of the divine machinery. Lurianic reparations became very popular
and were recited as spiritual accompaniments to the daily prayers[23] and
during midnight vigils (*tikun ḥatsot*), sabbath vigils, and 'reparations of the

---

[18] Fine, *Physician of the Soul, Healer of the Cosmos*, 95.

[19] M. Cordovero, *Pardes rimonim*, Pt. I, 88; id., *Tomer devorah*, 31–2, 103, 156, 163–6,
191–202, 205–7.   [20] De Vidas, *Reshit ḥokhmah*, 168a.

[21] Fine, *Physician of the Soul, Healer of the Cosmos*, 66, 74, 96, 147–52, 155–60, 164–7.

[22] Vital, *Sefer haḥezyonot*, 4: 33, 40 (ed. Faierstein, 160, 166); for examples of the creative
reading of letters on the forehead, see *Sefer toledot ha'ari*, 189; Vital, *Sefer haḥezyonot*, 4: 28 (ed.
Faierstein, 155); Tsemaḥ, *Nagid umetsaveh*, 16, 42.

[23] For an elaborate discussion, which dates the rise in popularity of kabbalistic reparations to
the late sixteenth century, unlike Gries, who dates it to the middle of the seventeenth, see
Nabarro, 'Tikun' (Heb.), 9, 12, 32–5, 52–61, 96; see also Gries, *Conduct Literature* (Heb.).

mischievous' (*tikun shovavim*), which sought to undo the effects of masturbation. The practice of reparations spread from Safed to the entire eastern Mediterranean basin and would later play a crucial propagandistic role in the messianic movement of Shabetai Tsevi.[24]

The concern with exposing sin was prevalent in Safed before Luria's arrival. The threatening tone of public sermons, including depictions of hellish torments; the belief in reincarnation and the deeply felt need for repentance; and faith in the ability of *kedoshim* to assist in making reparations were all discussed in Judah Halewah's *Tsafenat pane'ah*.[25] Furthermore, the battle against sin was not simply a personal matter, but had support from the quasi-legal court, the *va'ad berurei averot*, which had operated outside the usual halakhic norms in Sephardi communities since before the Expulsion and which was the scene of the hagiographical story of Luria's revelation as a *kadosh*. With the arrival of Luria in Safed, fear over the fate of one's soul became more intense, and it was believed that he could influence what happened to people's souls after their death. A story from the Lurianic hagiography involves an extremely rich man who approached Luria seeking to make reparations. Luria refused to absolve him because the burden of his sins was too great. The rich man expressed his willingness to die by swallowing boiling metal in order for his soul to be saved (a mode of execution endorsed by the Talmud (BT *San.* 52*b*), analogous to the burning alive of heretics by the Inquisition). The man's face was covered, and, while listening to the prayers of the people, he opened his mouth for the boiling metal to be poured in. But the liquid Luria poured down his throat was not liquid metal but hot water. The mock execution generated genuine fear, remorse, and repentance, the rich man's sins were remitted, and he was eventually saved.[26]

In Lurianic theology, all the worlds are interconnected—the lower ones being derived from those above—including the evil ones,[27] and so the structure of the divine realms is reflected in the demonic domain. Humanity is the central link in this long chain and is the only thing binding all the worlds together before the eschatological Reparation of the Worlds. Therefore

See Elbaum, *Repentance and Self-Flagellation in the Writings of the Sages of Germany and Poland* (Heb.), esp. 90–3; Zucker and Plesser, introduction (Heb.) to Leib ben Ozer, *Sipur ma'asei shabetai tsevi*, pp. xxvii–xxviii; Leib ben Ozer, *Sipur ma'asei shabetai tsevi*, 39–43.

[25] Idel, 'R. Judah Halewah and His *Tsafenat pane'ah*' (Heb.).

[26] *Sefer toledot ha'ari*, 238–9.

[27] Ibid. 191–5.

human sin harms not only the sinners and those around them but the entire cosmos, and repentance has cosmic dimensions.[28] Human behaviour affects Ze'er Anpin most directly, and sin separates him from Nukba Deze'er Anpin.[29] In such a state of things, the divine flow of light is blocked, and Nukba Deze'er Anpin is forced into exile and under the influence of corrupting powers. Another model of the close relationship between the divine realms and the human world was suggested by Moses Cordovero. Each *sefirah* was associated with a human virtue: this made it incumbent upon humans to adapt their behaviour to the divine presence, for example by regulating male sexual desire not only according to the talmudic injunctions and the couple's needs but also, and principally, according to the divine copulations.

Cordovero's and Luria's theologies were different in many crucial respects, but they were both deeply concerned with repentance, both as a theological issue and as a practical concern, as were most of the sixteenth-century kabbalists. Joseph Karo is a key figure for understanding the change in Safed in relation to repentance, as he combined halakhah, mysticism, and piety, and his monumental legal codes are heavily coloured by his kabbalistic theology.[30] His mystical diary resembles a court transcript at times, as his *magid* constantly rebukes him for his sins and personal failings. Karo oscillated between his sense of self-esteem as a leader and a pioneer and his sense of being a great sinner. The constant presence of the evil inclination called for relentless vigilance and asceticism.[31] Karo was well aware of how similar his subtle distinctions between various kinds of evil and the means of confronting them were to Catholic doctrines.[32]

Cordovero's disciple Elijah de Vidas did not suggest any theological innovations, yet his *Reshit ḥokhmah*, an encyclopedic overview of Jewish ethics and techniques to tackle evil in daily life in which kabbalistic concepts are prominent, was immensely popular in the sixteenth century and later:

Here are the preconditions of prophecy, very succinctly. . . . He should fully repent of all sins or evil habits, never to return to them . . . be careful to fulfil all 248 posi-

---

[28] Vital, *Ets ḥayim*, i. 154, 160, 165, 253, 256–66; ii. 111, 210, 225, 317, 321–2, 371, 376; id., *Sha'arei kedushah*, 39–49, 95–6; id., *Sha'ar hagilgulim*, 26b–27b; see also Fine, *Physician of the Soul, Healer of the Cosmos*, 170–9. On the mutual mimetic interaction between God and man, see Sack, *The Kabbalah of Moses Cordovero* (Heb.), ch. 8.   [29] Vital, *Ets ḥayim*, ii. 382.
[30] On Karo and his internal world, see Werblowsky, *Joseph Karo*; see also Weinstein, 'Joseph K. (Karo) in Front of the Law'.   [31] Karo, *Magid meisharim*, 129.   [32] Ibid. 204–5.

tive commandments . . . to avoid transgressing all 365 negative commandments . . . and beware of all negative habits, for they defile the soul . . . and later be careful to study Torah with all his might, for study's sake, to please his creator. . . . The fundamental issue is to fear God at every moment, so as not to sin . . . by imagining God in front of him.[33]

Hayim Vital also composed a book on the long and arduous journey to sanctity, *Sha'arei kedushah*.[34] Vital explicitly declared that the kabbalistic practices of reparation and the struggle with the evil inclination were of greater significance than simply following the commandments, which is highly problematic in a Jewish context, especially from a prominent rabbi and community leader. As in Karo's mystical diary, Vital's *Sefer ḥaḥezyonot* radiates a constant sense of guilt and dissatisfaction,[35] extending even to guilt for sins committed in previous incarnations and the need to make reparation for the sins of his group after Luria's death.[36] Vital participated in several exorcisms and used them to publicize his messages of repentance as a precondition of the salvation of the Jewish people.[37] His dreams and visions often express his deep frustration at his failure to persuade everyone in Safed, and later in Damascus, to repent, as he saw this as his mission in life. He even rebuked the great liturgist Israel Najara for his dubious sexual behaviour.

Eleazar Azikri perhaps most fully represented the Safed obsession with repentance. He was haunted by it in his personal life, his dreams, and his writings. His *Milei dishemaya* is composed of small notes which recorded his most intimate spiritual moments and his keen sense of living a life exposed to the divine gaze: 'Enlightened by [God's] light constantly, I talk with him, walk with him, keep silent with him, sleep with him and wake up with him, and sit with him and stand with him, and all my movements are for him.'[38] He developed his own meditation techniques and new religious rituals and imposed strict restrictions on himself. At one point he even signed a legal contract with God, outlining his devotion, which he repeatedly read to himself. At the same time he was occupied with spreading the message of repentance to others: 'And a fine of one fiorino coin for every day during which I did not

[33] Vital, *Sha'arei kedushah*, 99–101.

[34] M. Pachter, 'Homiletic and Ethical Literature of Safed in the 16th Century' (Heb.), 398–408.   [35] Vital, *Sefer ḥaḥezyonot*, 3: 43 (ed. Faierstein, 120).

[36] Ibid. 4: 18 (ed. Faierstein, 143).   [37] Ibid. 4: 52–4 (ed. Faierstein, 179–84).

[38] Azikri, *Yomano ḥamisti*, 135.

write an account [of my deeds]. . . . In the year 1592 on the eleventh day of the
month of Tishrei I was committed to initiate repentance. . . . The fifth rule of
the repentance confraternity is to endure and persist with writing a book
recording our sins.'[39] The diary was both an extension of confession in front
of other confraternity members and part of his preparation for that confession. The diaries of other Safed kabbalists also record personal failings and
sins; doubts about their personal mission; self-remonstrations; and emotional
references to the miserable state of the Shekhinah, exiled as a result of the sins
of the Jewish people.[40]

Confession is effective when it brings conscious awareness to religious
activity, moulding the believer anew, and paving the way to intimacy with
God. Imagination is activated by this conscious awareness and becomes a creative force. It also heightens the sense of the all-pervasive presence of God,
one of the central themes of Karo's diary:

Be aware that God is watching you constantly and knows your thoughts. Had you
been standing in front of a king, you would be ashamed to do improper things . . .
for he watches you closely. And I [Karo's *magid*], as a messenger of God, constantly
accompany you, as you can see with your own eyes, and you should be ashamed
before me. . . . And I am the messenger sent by God to accompany you. Hence you
can reckon on the generosity and grace of God.[41]

A similar sentiment was expressed by Azikri: 'Even when I am among people,
there is none that sees the secrets of my heart but [God], and none intending
to confer good on me but him. . . . So the people cannot stop me, for they are
considered as nothing, and I and he alone are standing.'[42]

Safed kabbalah introduced several distinctive features into techniques of
repentance. Sin was linked to the sufferings of the Shekhinah—the divine
feminine, but also a symbol of the Jewish people—which aroused feelings of
guilt and shame, powerful emotions in early modern Mediterranean societies. Sinners were told to visualize themselves standing before royalty and
imagine the awe and fear of such an occasion and the need to be on their best
behaviour.[43] There was a physical aspect to repentance, since sin was seen as a

---

[39] Azikri, *Yomano hamisti*, 165–6.
[40] Fine, *Physician of the Soul, Healer of the Cosmos*, 59, 63, 74, 175, 200–5, 249–51, 295, 421.
[41] Karo, *Magid meisharim*, 198–9.   [42] Azikri, *Yomano hamisti*, 134.
[43] Azikri, *Milei dishemaya*, 131, 136, 142.

corporeal entity which could invade the human body, and some cures, especially for sexual sins, required divine names to be written on various parts of the body.[44] The main form of repentance was a rigorously ascetic attitude to the body and its needs. It even inspired several kabbalists to make the claim, very similar to the Catholic one, that the first sin stains the souls of all the succeeding generations until the messianic period beyond repair.[45]

The preoccupation with repentance existed alongside a deep fascination with the power of evil. The Safed kabbalists' view of reality as a great chain from the deepest demonic domain to the highest divine realm meant that reparation could only be properly achieved by connecting to the lowest abyss of evil. In humans this manifested itself in the role of the evil inclination in regular bodily functioning.[46] The Zohar describes the need to 'bribe' evil in order to obtain the divine secrets of God and thus expresses and the dependence of the righteous on the wicked.[47] While the power of evil was acknowledged, so was the need for vigilance against its trickery and cunning. In one revelation Karo is warned by his *magid*: 'even when you do a good deed, beware that you do not disqualify it by some base thought. You should always direct your thoughts to the fear of God and even when standing in wholesome places be reminded of your baseness and poverty and how much I assisted you.'[48] Using evil was a risky business, requiring constant vigilance, and Vital explicitly stated his personal anxiety that he might fail. This is consistent with the sixteenth-century concern—new in the Jewish context—with the control of sentiments such as melancholy, anger, and sadness resulting from sin: 'My master of blessed memory, told me that I had already started repairing the sin of Cain, and that I should follow the order of reparations suggested by my master, when the depths of the sea threatened to overcome me with melancholy and sin.'[49] The control of the emotions was achieved by

[44] Ibid. 80, 117, 178; Nabarro, 'Tikun' (Heb.), 38–41.

[45] Shalem, 'Thought and Ethics in the Commentaries of R. Moses Alsheich' (Heb.); for a similar Lurianic stand, see Magid, *From Metaphysics to Midrash*, ch. 1.

[46] Vital, *Ets ḥayim*, ii. 230, 291–3, 402–4.

[47] Karo, *Magid meisharim*, 214–15, 253–4. On the role of evil in Lurianic theology, see Tishby, *The Doctrine of Evil and the* Kelipah *in Lurianic Kabbalism* (Heb.); Meroz, 'Redemption in Lurianic Teaching' (Heb.), esp. 184–5, 203, 291–3, 328–35, 345–8, 361–2.

[48] Karo, *Magid meisharim*, 137–9; see also 129.

[49] See Werblowsky, *Joseph Karo*, ch. 7; see also Vital, *Sefer haḥezyonot*, 4: 28, 60 (ed. Faierstein, 155, 194); *Sefer toledot ha'ari*, 315, 336; Tsemaḥ, *Nagid umetsaveh*, 74; Karo, *Magid*

'guided imagination' marked by excess and exaggeration so as to shock the mind or arouse disgust. Kabbalistic writings describe the excremental stench of sin, and hagiographical tales often end with horrific deaths.[50] One of Vital's sermons resembles something from the Jesuit tradition in dwelling on every small and sensual particular of hellish torments, including minute visual details of deaths.[51]

Early Modern Catholic Confession

Confession has a long history in Catholicism.[52] In late antiquity the practice involved a one-off confession usually just prior to death; the early Middle Ages saw the development of lists of sins and their penances; and the Fourth Lateran Council (1215) prescribed annual confession for every believer, in preparation for the Eucharist.[53] Confession continued to assume greater and greater significance until the sixteenth century.[54] Rigorous control of the inner self was required, and the confessor functioned mainly as a judge putting the believer's conscience on trial.

The Council of Trent gave the church greater control over confession by insisting that confessors have professional training in religious institutions and obtain formal certificates of competence. The modern confessional closet was designed during this period by Italian bishops to facilitate secret confession and prevent any physical contact with the confessor or any sexual temptation.[55] Confession was not only a sacred duty but a sign of personal religious devotion and a necessary part of a life in which God was constantly present. When preparing themselves for their annual confession, people were instructed to imagine that God watched their every move and that their guardian angel remembered their every act.[56] The church also encouraged more fre-

meisharim, 5, 12, 18, 125, 197–8, 264, 324; Azikri, *Milei dishemaya*, 100, 115–16, 122, 128–9, 161. On ritual crying during prayer, see Fine, *Physician of the Soul, Healer of the Cosmos*, 228–9.

[50] De Vidas, *Reshit ḥokhmah*, 37a, 38a, 216b–d; *Sefer toledot ha'ari*, 237–8.

[51] Vital, *Sha'arei kedushah*, 36–8; see also M. Cordovero, *Pardes rimonim*, Pt. II, 416a, 426a, 428b; De Vidas, *Reshit ḥokhmah*, 35a–40a; Poppers, *Or hayashar*, ch. 1.

[52] Bossy, 'The Social History of Confession in the Age of the Reformation'.

[53] The most comprehensive and up-to-date synthesis on confession and penance is Rusconi, *L'ordine dei peccati*; see also Tentler, *Sin and Confession on the Eve of the Reformation*.

[54] See Rusconi, *L'ordine dei peccati*, 47–200.

[55] Ibid. 225–337; De Boer, *The Conquest of the Soul*; Prosperi, *Tribunali della coscienza*.

[56] Zarri, 'Christian Good Manners'.

quent and more detailed confessions. The control afforded by confession was tightened further, since in many places priests learnt the names of those who had confessed by collecting the tickets left near the altar after they had completed their penance. Missionary campaigns raised emotional tensions and often terminated in collective acts of confession, peace-making between rival factions, or the burning of 'frivolous' objects.

There were two images of the confessor prevalent in the sixteenth and seventeenth centuries: as guide and healer and as judge and chastiser. The rigorous aspect was related to the Inquisition's role in rooting out heresy. Under the influence of Spanish theologians and jurists, the Italian Inquisition put pressure on confessors to break the seal of confession and denounce people suspected of heresy. Adriano Prosperi has shown how the line between confessor and inquisitor became blurred, as the former was prevented from conferring the grace of pardon in many cases and told to refer the errant believer to the Inquisition.[57]

The confessor as comforter and guide is most clearly seen in the Jesuit order and its missionary and pedagogical activities.[58] The *Spiritual Exercises* of Ignatius Loyola and the practice of 'general confession' saw confession as the end point of a long process of reflection and soul-searching, a dramatic statement by the believer to themselves and God of their desire for spiritual renewal. This model was inconsistent with the Council of Trent's model of confession as judgement; instead, confession was a unique occasion for spiritual guidance with the confessor serving as counsellor and comforter. Under Loyola's direction, general confession changed from a rare practice into a habit adopted by aristocrats, students at Jesuit colleges, and even uneducated women in Jesuit almshouses. The *Spiritual Exercises* were circulated in abridged popular versions with minimal theological detail, and influenced the work of other monastic orders dedicated to education and mission, such as the Somascan Fathers and the Barnabites (Clerics Regular of St Paul).[59]

The attempt to control the thoughts of believers as well as their acts is especially clear in the instructions provided to confessors for dealing with

[57] Prosperi, 'L'inquisitore come confessore'; id., *Tribunali della coscienza*.
[58] O'Malley, *The First Jesuits*; Maher, 'Confession and Consolation'; Rusconi, *L'ordine dei peccati*, 323–6.
[59] On the application of the ecclesiastical messages to everyday life, see De Certeau, *The Practice of Everyday Life*; Turrini and Valenti, 'L'educazione religiosa'.

sexual transgressions.[60] The mere listing of sexual sins was considered insufficient, and emphasis was placed on the process that led to the actual commission of the sins. The physical act of sinning took second place to 'sins of the will': the thoughts that preceded the act, the failure to avoid or resist temptation, self-titillation with forbidden thoughts. Every small detail of sensual excitation was relevant to confession, and nothing was excluded as too trivial. This ocean of detail needed structure and classification: the wild domain of passion was brought into line for inspection and decipherment. This process is parallel to the civilizatory process described by Norbert Elias.[61] Elias presented the control of violent emotions and bodily gestures as a necessary accompaniment to the establishment of centralized states, inasmuch as it allowed people to live together in larger and more independent networks. Though he saw this change as taking place mostly in the French court at Versailles during the eighteenth century, he traced its roots back to the early modern period and the publication of popular etiquette books (such as Erasmus's *De civilitate morum puerilium*) and new pedagogical institutions.

Confession and its theological rationale were also a source of disagreement between Protestants and Catholics.[62] Luther denied the Catholic claim that the church had the power to absolve sins in the name of God, yet the reform movements did not abolish confession but brought it into the public domain, where it became a key tool for social control. Religious and lay authorities co-operated in condemning sins that harmed the fabric of society, such as violence, verbal abuse, gambling, and adultery. The sinner was required to confess in front of the community and had to perform a humiliating act of penance in order to be accepted back into the community. Many of the mechanics for dealing with sin and confession were common to both religious traditions: specialized experts to hear the confession (priests or pastors), lay authorities to impose the penalties, humiliation and contrition as the price for returning to the community, and complicated justifications. In both camps confession offered an efficient tool for social discipline and control.

---

[60] See Trombetta, *La confessione della lussuria*.
[61] Elias, *On Civilization, Power, and Knowledge*.
[62] Lualdi and Thayer (eds.), *Penitence in the Age of Reformations*.

Confession of Sin in Safed

Luria played a similar role to that of Catholic confessors. People distressed by guilt acknowledged his authority and came to him. He identified specific sins, prescribed an individual course of reparations, and pronounced the atonement for the sins. In the Jewish context, this process was unique to Luria.[63] Personal confession had comprised part of the Second Temple cult, as it was necessary before a sacrifice could be performed, and the execution of criminals was supposed to include confession of sin. Both were discussed in the Jewish ethical literature of the Middle Ages.[64] However, the implication was that a person was fully aware of all their sins, and their main task was to confront them and prevent their recurrence: there was no need to enumerate them to others. Even in Jonah Gerondi's guides to penitence, verbal confession of sin was merely a formal duty, of secondary importance in the repentance process to grief and remorse.[65] Jewish confession was typified by adherence to fixed formulae in specific parts of the daily prayers and the almost total lack of any individual element. On the rare occasions that Jews commented on Catholic confession they were highly critical, finding it most improbable that a person would honestly reveal their sins to anyone else and believing that no human being was qualified to pardon them. These positions were expounded in *Sefer ḥasidim*, alongside the partial adoption of the Catholic pattern by encouraging sinners to approach a sage for guidance on sins and proper repentance.[66] Yet in the halakhic literature confession was presented as a formal component of the penitential process, to be conducted privately while repeating a fixed verbal formula. Its main purpose was a commitment to oneself not to sin any further: it was geared to future intentions rather than past guilt. This also implied that there was no special difficulty in a person uncovering their past and their sins.[67] Luria shifted confession and penitence into the public domain as an encounter between a spiritual master and his 'patients'. However, in Safed there were more dramatic public

---

[63] E. Horowitz, 'The Jews and the Moment of Death in Medieval and Modern Times'.

[64] e.g. Isaac Aboab, *Menorat hamaor*; Al-Nakawa, *Sefer menorat hamaor*.

[65] See Gerondi, *Sefer sha'arei teshuvah*.

[66] *Sefer ḥasidim*, §§20–2, 181, 446, 596–7, 621, 692.

[67] Maimonides, *Mishneh torah*, 'Laws of Repentance', 1: 1; see also Jacob ben Asher, *Arba'ah turim*, 'Yoreh de'ah', 338.

revelations of sin: cases of possession.[68] In one example, Hayim Vital was called upon to exorcise an elderly widow whose sins concerned belief, not actual failure to perform the commandments: in Catholic terms, heresy.

Luria's innovations integrated perfectly with the local traditions prior to his arrival in Safed. Certain confraternities encouraged and practised confession in front of other members. Vital objected to this strongly, on the traditional Jewish grounds that it was unlikely someone would expose their secrets to others, but he acknowledged that he was unable to stop it.[69] The penitential confraternity headed by Azikri regulated the pattern of collective confession and considered it an important stage on the way to spiritual elevation.[70]

The importance of personal confession was enhanced by a change in religious outlook which underlined the new place of individual conscience.[71] This was a dramatic shift in Jewish thinking, which had previously considered praxis to be the central component of religious life. The new emphasis on conscience was paralleled by the rise in the sense of an omniscient, omnipresent God—or, in the Jewish context, the Shekhinah[72]—observing every individual wherever they went, whatever they did, and certainly whatever they thought.[73] Dreams were understood as the voice of the conscience and were described as an internal court of law.[74] The sense that 'a person is judged every day' was a source of constant anxiety,[75] as was guilt at failing to follow rules and fulfil commandments that were often too rigorous to be complied with in the first place.[76] Personal confession was supposed to be conducted several times a day—before eating, studying the Torah, praying, or, especially, sleeping—and extensively on the first day of every month, known in kabbalistic literature as Yom Kippur Katan (the Small Day of Atonement).[77] Falling asleep was understood as analogous to death, fear of encountering demons led to a concern with correct sleeping hours, and sleep was manipulated for spiri-

[68] *Sefer toledot ha'ari*, 191–6.

[69] Vital, *Sha'ar hakavanot*, i. 278a–279a, 332b, 355; ii. 210, 211a; id., *Sefer haḥezyonot*, 2: 10 (ed. Faierstein, 80–1); for further support for Vital's testimony, see *Sefer toledot ha'ari*, 316–17.

[70] Azikri, *Milei dishemaya*, 29, 165; see also the testimonies cited in Hallamish, *Kabbalah in Liturgy, Halakhah and Customs* (Heb.), 31.

[71] See Azikri, *Milei dishemaya*, 176.   [72] De Vidas, *Reshit ḥokhmah*, 30a.

[73] Karo, *Magid meisharim*, 198–9; Azikri, *Milei dishemaya*, 134.

[74] De Vidas, *Reshit ḥokhmah*, 70c.   [75] Azikri, *Milei dishemaya*, 103.

[76] De Vidas, *Reshit ḥokhmah*, 34b–d.

[77] Ibid. 126a, 192b; Poppers, *Or hayashar*, ch. 15; Benayahu, notes (Heb.) to *Sefer toledot ha'ari*, 347 n. 7; see also Hallamish, *Kabbalah in Liturgy, Halakhah and Customs* (Heb.), 537–66.

tual ends: 'no night would pass without thinking of what he had committed during the day, so that he confesses'.[78]

Summary

From the late fifteenth century waves of religious movements obsessed with sin, repentance, and atonement swept across Europe. They were accompanied by the circulation of apocryphal works, of secret messages originating from heaven, prophecies, and mysterious letters written by Mary the mother of Jesus. These movements were only partially under the church's control, and laymen played an important role in them.[79] They called for a radical reform of the Catholic Church and a deeper and more committed adherence by churchmen to their vocation. Some of the reform movements—such as Devotio Moderna—aspired to personal involvement in religious life rather than a passive role at religious rituals conducted by professionals. Their message was spread all over Europe through sermons, books, and new educational institutions. The Catholic Church in Italy established popular schools where catechisms were taught, extended the scope of theological discussions, and encouraged the pedagogical ambitions of the Jesuits and the religious confraternities in both city and countryside. The Inquisition was ever present, at times blunt and violent.

The Jews of western Europe were influenced by this religious ferment, and interest in individual penitence and remorse increased. However, the Safed kabbalists held the rabbinic canon to be deficient in this regard:

Like the German Pietists, Luria believed that the conventional ways in which individuals identified their transgressions and alleviated themselves of guilt were inadequate to the situation at hand. The various opportunities for self-acknowledgment of sin and repentance that rabbinic tradition made available failed to satisfy the need for the kind of rigorous and uncompromising self-improvement that Luria's approach called for.[80]

---

[78] Vital, 'Author's Introduction', *Ets ḥayim*, i. 23*b*; see also the regulations ascribed to Luria (*Sefer toledot ha'ari*, 335, 347).

[79] Prosperi, 'L'immacolata a Siviglia e la fondazione sacra della monarchia spagnola', 142; on a similar phenomenon in Spain, leading to the establishment of King Philip II's collection of relics, see Lazure, 'Possessing the Sacred'.

[80] Fine, *Physician of the Soul, Healer of the Cosmos*, 185–6.

This failure stood behind the rise of medieval Jewish repentance literature, which leaned only partially on the classical talmudic heritage, but predominantly on Aristotelianism and Neoplatonism. It struck a chord in the hearts of the Jewish public at the time, and more so in the early modern period. The impact of this literature has not been examined, but it could not have been wide since, until the rise of printing, it was distributed only in manuscript form.

The kabbalists of the early modern period provided repentance with a new dynamism, putting it at the centre of their teachings, ethical literature, and theological writings. This is clear in the tract composed by Vital, addressed to those aspiring to reach the *ruaḥ hakodesh* (holy spirit).[81] Ritual was presented as merely a precondition of reparation and atonement; Torah study was but a path to intimacy with God and the development of theurgical powers. Repentance pushed aside concerns with messianism and the salvation of the Jews as a people in both the Lurianic and Cordoveran schools of kabbalah: salvation became a personal issue, and messianism became a source of religious renewal. Repentance was an intense existential experience, because it brought the repentant into contact with saints and spiritual guides.

Lurianic theology had no great interest in the divine mechanisms, except as a means of interaction between God and humanity. The continuity between the divine and the human extended to the demonic domain as well. One of the clearest signs of modernity in Safed kabbalah is its dealing with evil not only as a separate demonic state but as a border zone, drawing all earlier lines of demarcation into question. Safed kabbalah provided one of the earliest comprehensive attempts to confront the challenge of individualism, and for the first time in Jewish history personal diaries were written in significant numbers.[82] These diaries not only focused on sin and remorse, but on the refinement and control of the emotions—especially melancholy and anger.[83] This fitted well with the general trend, mentioned in Chapter 5, of 'civilizing the self': taking great care over bodily comportment and a sense of disgust and shame in relation to basic needs. As in Christian Europe, melancholy and its link to sin was a common topic among contemporary Jewish mystics.

[81] Vital, *Sha'arei kedushah*, 99–101.   [82] Chajes, 'Accounting for the Self'.
[83] Idel, 'Saturn and Shabetai Tsevi' (Heb.); Gutwirth, 'Jewish Bodies and Renaissance Melancholy'.

The leading models of individualism were the *kedoshim* and *tsadikim*. They were often turbulent and inspiring personalities. They were not devoid of sin or failings, but this only strengthened their fascination for others. Sin was the primary locus for self-examination and personal progress. Their diaries often read like the transcripts of a law court or the contemporary guide books for Catholic confessors, listing every fault, even the most trivial.[84] It was not the act of sin as such that made them so anxious, but the circumstances leading to it, its gradual growth in the dark corners of the soul, and the lack of resolve to combat it.

These concerns did not remain confined to a narrow circle of kabbalists but spread to their disciples and penitential confraternities, and eventually to the wider public through ritual activity and liturgy. By the late sixteenth century they had transcended their local context and spread to the entire Jewish world through popular ethical literature, compendious tracts and their abridgements, hagiographical writings, and normative literature of all kinds. Another channel was the newly invented rituals of reparation performed several times a year, as well as music and *piyutim* that promoted devotion and the ascetic life. Spiritual masters, healers, and prophets would rise to prominence again during the messianic fervour surrounding Shabetai Tsevi, which also had at its core an obsession with sin, repentance, and reparation. An important link in the spread of the Safed model of confession was the Italian Jewish community. It was part of the regular procedure of confraternities, obligatory and necessary for a place in heaven. A story preserved in an Italian manuscript tells of a young girl whose life was destroyed by false rumours about sexual misconduct: on her deathbed she was required by the confraternity to confess and forgive her slanderers.[85]

[84] See Trombetta, *La confessione della lussuria*.
[85] Russian National Library, Moscow, MS Guenzburg 364 (National Library of Israel, Jerusalem, microfilm 47634), fos. 128*a*–138*b*.

SEVEN

Catholic Traditions in Safed Kabbalah
Sephardim and Conversos

L URIANIC HAGIOGRAPHY preserves a story about Luria's first encounter
with kabbalah.[1] The initiation did not entail heavenly revelations, a
chain of tradition, or study in a heavenly school or with the prophet Elijah—
all commonplaces of Jewish mysticism. Luria met a former Converso from
Spain who possessed a secret book—probably the Zohar—which he could
not read. The story has no historical basis, but it contains a grain of truth, significant for understanding early modern kabbalah: the pivotal role of Iberian
Jews and Conversos after the expulsions from Spain and Portugal. Unintentionally, the Conversos carried Catholic ideas into the heart of the Jewish
tradition, and it was kabbalah, more than any other area of Judaism, that
opened its doors to such ideas. Despite the trauma and sufferings of the
Iberian Jews, they maintained close ties with Spain and Portugal, primarily
through the Conversos, who moved between the two worlds physically and
culturally. The Conversos were one of the most significant components of
the mystical and religious innovations and reform of Safed kabbalah as it
created a Jewish counterpart to similar changes in the Christian world resulting from the Reformation and Counter-Reformation.

The Cultural Heritage of the Iberian Diaspora

The massacres of Spanish Jews in 1391 weakened many communities and led
to mass conversion, mostly by force. The establishment of the Spanish Inquisition in 1478 increased pressure on the descendants of those converts to give
up the Jewish practices they were not, as Christians, supposed to be following
anyway. It raised pressure on Jewish communities as well. In 1492 Ferdinand

---

[1] *Sefer toledot ha'ari*, 153–4.

and Isabella ordered the Jews of their kingdom to convert or leave; five years later they forced King Manuel of Portugal to expel the Jews from his kingdom. Most left, abandoning their fortunes and undertaking the long and difficult journey across the Mediterranean to seek refuge in the Ottoman empire.[2] Several decades later they had become established and regained much of their prestige. New communities were founded throughout Europe and the Mediterranean basin as well as in the New World, although when they arrived in places that already had Jewish populations, relationships were not always peaceful. In many places, such as the colonies of the Netherlands, Spain, and Portugal, there were no old Jewish communities, and the Sephardim were free to do as they pleased. Although some major changes also took place in Jewish communities in Germany at this time, their influence did not extend beyond the local context. East European Jewry was also increasing in importance, but it did not achieve the dominant position of the Sephardi diaspora. The sixteenth century can be considered the 'Spanish century' in Jewish history.[3]

There are indications that at the end of the fifteenth century the Iberian Jewish population was notably larger than the one in the rest of Europe. The Iberian refugees often had a numerical advantage over the native Jews of the places where they settled. Their strength was not confined to this, however; it was also derived from their political, economic, cultural, and religious heritage.[4] Spanish communities were ruled by a relatively small number of oligarchic families, whose relationships with the royal court had given them power and authority unheard of in any Jewish community in medieval Europe. Castile had a *rab de la corte*, who represented the Jews at the court and was their supreme judge. Under royal auspices, Spanish Jewish communities could impose penalties beyond those prescribed by rabbinic law, including corporal punishment and even death. Many communities considered themselves charged with controlling the religious and moral behaviour of their members and established their own police and quasi-legal courts, which collaborated with the local courts and community leaders and, in their zeal to control evildoers, did not always follow the halakhah. Rabbis and halakhists

---

[2] Hacker, 'Pride and Depression' (Heb.); on Spanish Jewry, see Baer, *A History of the Jews in Christian Spain*. [3] See Hundert (ed.), *Jews in Early Modern Poland*.

[4] See Beinart (ed.), *Moreshet Sepharad*; esp. id., 'The Jews in Castile'; Assis, 'Welfare and Mutual Aid in the Spanish Jewish Community'.

claimed to have the same authority as the Beit Din Hagadol (supreme court) in Jerusalem prior to the destruction of the Temple. Absolute halakhic truth would often be used by the Sephardim as a weapon in their struggles to assert their hegemony over the places they settled in after the Expulsion.

The Sephardim maintained their distinctive group identity throughout their wanderings, and it was only strengthened by memories of common suffering and resistance to the pressures to convert. They took with them their particular mode of life, halakhic traditions, the quasi-legal courts, methods of study, style of sermons, poetry and visual arts, and refined courtly style. One preacher, Joseph Garson, described them as *yedidei hashem* (friends of God) and *hayehudim hamegorashim* (the exiled Jews).[5] A few rich families continued to dominate the new communities, often through arranged marriages amongst themselves and the manipulation of the electoral processes.[6] Many sermons rejected not only the Catholic message but also the 'Averroism' of the elite Sephardi families, which saw the three monotheistic religions as being of equal value, viewed religious practices with contempt, and preferred a philosophical perspective which required no 'translation' into performative acts.[7] This attitude was seen as assimilationist and responsible for the enfeeblement of Judaism.[8]

The economic activity of Sephardi Jews and Conversos was conducted through international family networks linking the major economic centres of Europe and the Ottoman empire: Amsterdam and Cairo, Marseilles and Salonica, Venice and Istanbul. Families, such as the Mendes-Nassis, moved freely across religious and political borders, enjoying the protection of powerful figures, including the Ottoman sultan and the Venetian doge.[9] Many

---

[5] Garson, *Ben porat yosef*; see Hacker, 'The Sephardim in the Ottoman Empire in the Sixteenth Century'.

[6] See the responsa of Solomon Halevi discussed in Hacker, 'The Sephardim in the Ottoman Empire in the Sixteenth Century'.

[7] M. Pachter, 'Homiletic and Ethical Literature of Safed in the 16th Century' (Heb.); C. Horowitz, '*Darshanim*, *Derashot* and *Derashah* Literature in Medieval Spain'; Hallamish, 'Kabbalistic Ethical Literature before and after the 1492 Expulsion' (Heb.).

[8] For the spread of Averroism in Sephardi culture, see Kaplan, 'Foi et scepticisme dans la diaspora des nouveaux-chrétiens des débuts de l'Europe moderne'.

[9] Trivellato, *The Familiarity of Strangers*; Israel, 'The Sephardi Contribution to Economic Life and Colonization in Europe and the New World'; Swetschinski, *Reluctant Cosmopolitans*, ch. 3; Cesarani and Romain (eds.), *Jews and Port Cities*. On the Mendes-Nassi family, see Salomon, 'Mendes, Benveniste, De Luna, Micas, Nasci'.

Sephardi families continued trading with Spain and maintained contact with relatives living there as Conversos, occasionally travelling there themselves disguised as Christians. As well as trade, links were maintained through the exchange of books and responsa giving advice in halakhic matters and assistance to those returning to the Jewish faith. According to Yosef Kaplan, 'the history of one particular community can be understood only in relation to the general context of the entire western Sephardi diaspora'.[10]

They often arrived at their destination following political negotiations with the local authorities, sometimes by explicit invitation, and they certainly had no intention of taking a back seat in local Jewish politics. On the contrary, they contested the local traditions, often using violence or through their contacts with the authorities. Their attitude to Romaniot Jews, whose ancestors had lived under Byzantine rule, was often patronizing:

It is well known that the Sephardi people and the sages in the [Ottoman] empire are more numerous in comparison to other communities, the land is theirs, and they are its glory and brilliance . . . and the minority who previously occupied the land [the Romaniot Jews] need to follow the Sephardi traditions of Torah. . . . Glory to the creator, that the Sephardi are the clear majority in this land, both in quantity and in quality, and the Romaniot Jews are like two cresses at the top of the tree and two out of hundreds.[11]

Gradually the customs of the various communities of the empire were subsumed under Sephardi practice, partly as a result of Sephardi pressure and partly through absorption of the minorities into the majority. Similar processes occurred in Italy, Egypt, and the Maghreb, with various degrees of thoroughness. Throughout the sixteenth century the new immigrants conducted fierce battles over those domains they considered essential to their distinctive Sephardi identity: sexuality, courtship, marriage, and family life. They succeeded in breaking local taboos on polygamy and introduced their own custom which allowed a man to take a second wife if his first proved barren, a custom which weakened the legal position of women.[12]

---

[10] Kaplan, 'The Sephardim in North-Western Europe and the New World', 243.

[11] Moses Arokis of Salonica, cited in Hacker, 'The Sephardim in the Ottoman Empire in the Sixteenth Century', 115. Hacker also cites Elijah Mizrahi, chief rabbi of the Romaniot Jews, to the effect that the new immigrants outnumbered the local Jews by far. On Jewish communities in the Ottoman empire, see Ben-Naeh, *Jews in the Realm of the Sultans*, Pt. 2.

[12] On these clashes, see Rozen, *A History of the Jewish Community in Istanbul*, 133, 136, 148–

The most energetic and active Sephardi community in western Europe was in Amsterdam. The Amsterdam Sephardi described themselves as *hómens da nação* (men of the nation) or *benei ha'umah hasefaradit-portugezit* (sons of the Spanish Portuguese nation).[13] Theirs was a community founded on a separatist and elitist ethos, based on their refinement and civilization, very different from classical Jewish notions of solidarity and equality. This is of major importance for understanding their kabbalistic position. As Yosef Kaplan has observed, this ethos was actually an extension of the *limpieza de sangre*: in resisting Catholicism, the Sephardim adopted some of its most basic elements in their most baroque form and integrated them into Judaism. The Jewish community in Amsterdam was governed by elite families, who nominated their members to serve on the *ma'amad*, the council which established laws, punished those who broke them, appointed rabbis and other community officials, set tax rates, and even allocated seating in the synagogue. The *ma'amad* maintained tight control over social and moral behaviour. The poor and indigent were interned in houses of correction or expelled to the colonies.[14] Holding heterodox opinions, refusing to circumcise a son, or frequent journeys to the 'lands of idolatry' (Spain and Portugal) led to the imposition of the ban, or *ḥerem*. Amsterdam's Sephardim could not marry 'foreign' Jews or members of other ethnic traditions on pain of financial sanctions. No book could be published without the consent of the *ma'amad*.

Safed: A Sephardi Town

Safed's rise to the cultural forefront of sixteenth-century Judaism would not have been possible without the Sephardi diaspora. The Ottoman capture of Jerusalem in 1517 was a major benefit to Safed, which became one of the most important towns in the Land of Israel.[15] The Safed kabbalists saw Safed, not Jerusalem, as the centre of religious life.[16] At the same time Fray

---

51, 176–8; Rivlin, 'Major Lines of the History of Jewish Family in Greece' (Heb.); Westreich, '"Be Fruitful and Multiply"' (Heb.).

[13] On the Amsterdam community, see Kaplan, *From New Christians to New Jews* (Heb.); Bodian, *Hebrews of the Portuguese Nation*.

[14] Kaplan, *From New Christians to New Jews* (Heb.), 85–6.

[15] Fine, *Physician of the Soul, Healer of the Cosmos*, 47–8.

[16] See David, 'Safed as a Centre for Conversos Returning to Judaism in the Sixteenth Century' (Heb.).

Melchor, a Converso, prophesied that the church would be moved eastwards from Rome, either to Syria or Jerusalem, and Spanish visionaries anticipated the transference of the church from Rome to Toledo.[17] In all three cases the geographical change was a sign of religious renewal and held to be a necessary precondition for the descent of the Holy Spirit. According to Alain Milhou, this idea had its roots in Franciscan apocalypticism.[18]

Little is known about the Musta'arabi, the original Jewish population of the Land of Israel, but during the sixteenth century the number of Sephardi Jews increased until they became the majority, as attested by Ottoman tax registers, the names of rabbis signing local regulations, and the testimonies of Christian pilgrims.[19] This fundamental demographic change inflated the Sephardi sense of superiority. According to Moses ben Joseph Trani, 'since all the Sephardi people from the Spanish Expulsion are more numerous than any other [ethnic group] they should construct two synagogues [whereas the other groups should only have one each]'.[20] Sephardi discrimination against local Jews was also apparent in that charitable donations from Egypt, which had been sent to the poor of the Land of Israel for generations, were channelled to the Sephardi community.[21] The names of many of the halakhic and kabbalistic authorities reveal their Sephardi origin: Jacob Beirav, Joseph Karo, Moses ben Joseph Trani, Solomon Alkabets, Moses Cordovero, David ben Zimrah. Sephardi influence could be seen in sermons, especially Moses Albilada's *Olat tamid* and *Darash mosheh*, which were inspired by his master Isaac Aramah's *Akedat yitshak*.[22] The pre-Expulsion halakhic traditions were continued, most notably by Beirav, who followed Isaac Canpanton of Castile.[23] Karo, assured by his *magid* that he would rule 'all the Jewish diaspora of Arabistan',[24] inserted kabbalistic instructions into his halakhic codes to an unprecedented extent.[25] The halakhic courts of Istanbul and Edirne often turned to Safed for rulings. The scholars of Safed considered

[17] Pastore, *Un'eresia spagnola*, 80–2, 89.

[18] Milhou, *Colón y su metalidad mesiánica en el ambiente francicanista español*.

[19] David, 'The Spanish Exiles in the Holy Land'; Tamar, 'Safed before the Arrival of Karo' (Heb.); Ish-Shalom, 'Information Regarding Safed in the Books of Christian Travellers' (Heb.).

[20] David, 'The Spanish Exiles in the Holy Land', 96–7.   [21] Ibid.

[22] M. Pachter, 'Homiletic and Ethical Literature of Safed in the 16th Century' (Heb.), 4–5, 26, 45–6.   [23] Davidson, 'The Sages of Safed between 1540 and 1615' (Heb.).

[24] See Benayahu, 'The Revival of Ordination in Safed' (Heb.), 251–3.

[25] Katz, 'The Interaction between Halakhah and Kabbalah' (Heb.).

themselves further elevated because many of them had also undergone formal rabbinic ordination. Undoubtedly the profoundest influence of the Sephardi diaspora on Safed kabbalah was the spread of the zoharic literature beyond esoteric circles.[26] Before the expulsions non-Sephardi Jewish scholars knew very little of the Zohar and certainly did not accept it as authoritative.[27] Only at the start of the sixteenth century, with the spread of the Iberian diaspora, did it start to establish itself as a canonical book, alongside the Torah, the Talmud, and other texts.

The congruence of Safed kabbalah and Sephardi culture was already marked before Luria arrived, and it became even stronger during his time there. Luria's position in Safed was established not only by his saintly demeanour but also by his authoritative commentary on the Zohar. His disciples would later claim that they alone held the key to deciphering the mystical book and rejected any other readings. Hermeneutics became a method of defining orthodox opinions and, hence, a tool of power and authority. This attitude was entirely at odds with that of the fifteenth-century kabbalists, who noted the difficult, allusive character of the Zohar, but set no limits to how it should be read or understood.[28] As mentioned in Chapter 2, Luria's disciples considered his revelations and mystical secrets as higher and more esoteric than those of the Zohar.

The Iberian Space: Jews and Conversos

Between the outbreak of anti-Jewish violence in Spain in 1391 and the Expulsion in 1492, many Jews converted to Christianity, at least outwardly. The large number of Conversos posed a challenge to both Catholic and Jewish communities: the Catholics harboured doubts about the sincerity of the Conversos' new faith and took increasingly strong measures against them; the Jews considered the Conversos to be part of their society and did what they could to assist them. As a result of repeated persecutions by the state and the Inquisition, waves of Conversos left Spain for southern France, Italy, the Netherlands, Germany, and the cities of the Ottoman empire. Their

---

[26] Huss, *Like the Radiance of the Sky* (Heb.), 182.

[27] Ibid. 4, 8, 140, 142, 147, 149–50, 162–3, 165, 167; see also Abrams, 'The Cultural Reception of the Zohar'.   [28] Huss, *Like the Radiance of the Sky* (Heb.), ch. 6.

attachment to their lands of origin continued, and some even went to the New World in the wake of Spanish and Portuguese colonization.[29]

Previous historiography saw the Conversos in binary terms: they were either faithful to Catholicism or faithful to Judaism.[30] Either they saw themselves as part of the Jewish ethnic and religious tradition, which they could not express but sustained through messianic expectations and belief in a future shared with all other Jews; or the destruction of all the institutions responsible for transmitting the Jewish tradition—synagogues, communities, schools, books—and the prohibition of religious practices eventually caused an incurable breach with Judaism and, as time passed, an increased identification with the Catholic majority. The second alternative is supported by the fact that some Conversos held senior positions in the church and contributed to Catholic theology and missionary campaigns.

The collective identity of the Conversos was complicated and contradictory. Characterizing them as belonging more to one religious tradition than the other overlooks the deep problems that defined their existence. Theirs were lives of denial and concealment, even within families in some instances. Conversos' connections with family members who maintained an openly Jewish identity gave rise to doubts about their sincerity, and this was one of the motivations for the Expulsion. The two groups that laid claim to them saw them in very different lights: to the secular and ecclesiastical authorities, they were distressing evidence that universal Jewish acceptance of Jesus Christ as the messiah was still a long way off; from the Jewish perspective, the Conversos who remained in Iberia were an organic component of the Sephardi diaspora. This was explicitly stated by one of the leading intellectuals of the time, Isaac Abravanel, in his commentary on the book of Isaiah:

In the year 1492 God has inspired the kings of Spain to expel all three hundred thousand Jews, so that they left and [some] arrived in the Holy Land, not only the Jews, but converts as well, those who left the Torah, and so that all gather in the Holy Land.[31]

This resolute assertion joins a huge variety of contemporary rabbinic and halakhic discussion in the Sephardi diaspora regarding the legal status of the

---

[29] Swetschinski, *Reluctant Cosmopolitans*, chs. 2, 3; Wachtel, *La Foi du souvenir*.

[30] See Stuczynsky, 'A "Marrano Religion"?' (Heb.); id., 'New Christian Political Leadership in Times of Crisis'.   [31] Cited in David, 'The Spanish Exiles in the Holy Land', 437.

Conversos, their destiny, and their participation and share in the messianic process and future salvation, as well as more mundane issues such as the divorce of mixed couples, levirate marriage, and the inheritance of property. Communities of the Spanish diaspora established institutions for nurturing relationships, coping with common problems such as heresy, rejection of rabbinic authority, and poverty, and striving to draw the Conversos into Jewish life.[32] The Sephardi preference for people of the same origin, even if they did not live openly as Jews, over 'old' Jews of non-Iberian stock was clearly manifested in charitable confraternities in Amsterdam. They did not provide dowries to Ashkenazi women, but only to those of the 'nation', including those who openly lived as Catholics.[33]

Knowledge of the cultural and religious life of converts has been greatly enriched in recent years by research into the material in the Inquisition archives, which, since open Jewish life was totally prohibited to Conversos in the Iberian peninsula, is where the only records of the 'Judaizers' can be found. Claude Stuczynski has studied the faith and ritual practices of Judaizers in Portugal, especially in the city of Bragança, based on hundreds of Inquisition files. He describes Converso society as a polyphony of voices which created a new and distinct culture.[34] The Conversos' 'Jewish' beliefs were infiltrated by Catholic concepts and ideas, and paradoxically it was the competition with Catholicism that led them to adopt its culture and language. Even their polemics against Christians are suffused with expressions commonly used in anti-Jewish tracts, such as blindness, error, and drawing away from the path of salvation.[35] However, Stuczynski is more interested in their beliefs than their sociology—the role of the family in maintaining religious identity, the separate lifestyles of men and women, intermarriage, and substitutes for the lost Jewish community life. It was assumed that most Conversos established their own personal religious beliefs as a response to the Catholicism which refused to absorb them or as synthesis of what they learned from anti-Jewish literature or encounters with the Inquisition. Yet the Judaizers of Bragança repeatedly asserted the importance of knowing what to believe and what not to believe. They distinguished between Jewish

[32] Kaplan, 'The Sephardim in North-Western Europe and the New World'.
[33] Bodian, 'The "Portuguese" Dowry Societies in Venice and Amsterdam', 28.
[34] Stuczynski, 'A "Marrano Religion"?' (Heb.), 465–7.   [35] Ibid. 455.

and Catholic views of God and the messiah and were concerned that they had the correct Torah, the correct God, and the correct nation. They were not 'Jews without Judaism', to adopt Kolakowski's description of Christians who adhered to their religion out of habit with very little contact with or faith in its institutions.[36]

The Inquisition files reveal the deep gap between the Conversos' intentions to adhere to their forefathers' traditions and the reality.[37] There were several reasons for this: the need to keep their religious activity secret, the lack of any educational institutions, a heavy dependence on memory, the necessity of passing on what traditions they had orally following the Inquisition's ban on Hebrew books, and exposure to Christianity. Circumcision disappeared, and proficiency in Hebrew was lost. However, since not all Conversos were Judaizers, a rich variety of religious attitudes existed, from strict adherence to Jewish traditions to partial Judaizing, sincere Catholicism, syncretism, and complete indifference. Many of the migrants from Spain who arrived in Catholic countries, mainly France and Italy, maintained their Catholic identity, even though the inquisitorial threat was practically nil. A typical case of religious syncretism was the Suasso family: the father, a Converso, moved to southern France with his five children: two of them migrated further to Amsterdam and openly joined the Jewish community, two others worked as physicians in France and married Converso wives, and the fifth became a famous priest and a professor of theology at the University of Bordeaux.[38] As Conversos were often ignorant of Jewish practices, they adopted those of the surrounding Catholic society, such as celebrating the sabbath with musical instruments or giving alms, venerating icons, or addressing the Jewish patriarchs as saints—invoking 'St Moses' during childbirth for example. Relativistic positions, allocating equal importance to all religions or distinguishing them by technical ritualistic details, were common, as were deist, sceptical, and even materialistic ones.

Stefania Pastore claims that Conversos were deeply involved in religious life and made a profound contribution to the Reformation in Spain, and that

---

[36] Kolakowski, *Chrétiens sans église*.

[37] See Gitlitz, *Secrecy and Deceit*; Yovel, *The Other Within*, esp. chs. 4, 5.

[38] Swetschinski, *De familie Lopes Suasso*; for an analysis of the 'Marranic state of mind' of writers of Converso origins, such as Montaigne and Fernando da Rojas, see Wachtel, *Le Foi du souvenir*, 321–5.

they brought this body of knowledge and attitudes with them when they moved to Jewish communities outside the Iberian peninsula.[39] Spanish theologians sympathetic to the ideas of the Reformation stressed the need for gentleness and kindness in accepting the new converts into Christian society and rejected the use of violence and oppression. They criticized the popular construction of Catholicism as belonging solely to 'old Christians' and excluding those who did not have the correct genealogy, and objected to the *limpieza de sangre* regulations on the grounds that they produced dissension within the church and disrupted the channels of grace supposed to link all believers in Christ.

The new and reformed church reassessed its heritage in the Old Testament and the Jewish tradition. This inspired great biblical projects, such those of Jiménez de Cisneros and Arias Montano—projects in which Conversos played a prominent role. Hernando de Talavera, Alonso de Oropesa, Juan de Lucena, Pero López de Celain, Juan Gil, Costantino Ponce de la Fuente, and Juan Valdéz also made major contributions to the religious innovations in contemporary Spain. According to Catherine Swietlicki, the ideas of leading religious reformers of Converso origin, such as Teresa of Ávila, Fray Luis, and John of the Cross, were influenced by kabbalistic thought:

> Their use of Cabala is a very Christian and sixteenth-century version of the reformation of Judaic spirituality a century or more earlier in Spain, when Cabala provided the focus for the victory of pietistic Judaism over the rationalistic. In both cases, a deep-felt popular pietistic movement was underway.[40]

Leaning on both Catholic reformist and pre-Expulsion kabbalistic traditions they could bring their message closer to other Conversos. Conversos played an important role in the Spanish Christian mystic movement known as the Alumbrados, who believed that they could achieve such intimacy with God that it was impossible for them to sin, and that they could indulge in any behaviour they liked.[41] Some of the leading figures of Spanish reform move-

---

[39] See esp. Pastore, *Un'eresia spagnola* (including vast bibliographical resources); see also Olivari, 'La spiritualità spagnola nel primo Trentennio del Cinquecento'; Bataillon, *Erasme et l'Espagne*.

[40] Swietlicki, *Spanish Christian Cabala*, 190–1; see also 79–81, 105; for a critical review of these positions, see Idel's review of Swietlicki, *Spanish Christian Cabala*; id., 'Reflections on Kabbalah in Spain and Christian Kabbalah'.   [41] Ibid. 108–10.

ments, such as Fray Melchor and Talavera, had Converso origins.[42] Despite his lack of family or political connections, Melchor wandered all over Europe obtaining audiences with the rich and powerful and impressing them with his personal charisma, visions, and colourful prophecies of the corruption of the church and the coming era of the Holy Spirit. His prophecies left a deep impression on the Conversos. Talavera led an ascetic life completely devoted to intimacy with God, emphasizing conscience and emotion over external acts. He joined the Order of St Jerome, which was popular with erudite Conversos, and encouraged the use of the Bible as the basis for meditation and spiritual development. He led campaigns to Christianize both Jews and Muslims in and around Toledo and used biblical exegesis to criticize the religious institutions of his day as dry, scholastic, and stifling to the spirit. Talavera died at the instigation of the Inquisition, provoking an outpouring of Converso tracts on *kedoshim* martyred in the same way.

The Iberian Conversos considered themselves a distinct group within Christian society, on the basis of their shared heritage. They acted collectively to protect their interests, lobbying for more tolerance and immunity from the Inquisition through political contacts in Spain and the papal court.[43] For 150 years they negotiated with kings and popes regarding their interests, and their representatives were recognized as political envoys. Their leaders did what they could to persuade the local population to treat them more moderately. This activity, along with their tendency to marry other Conversos and to work in the same trades, strengthened their sense of their distinctive identity.[44] Fidelity to Jewish traditions was considered a sign of loyalty to parents and family.

The sense of difference between Conversos and those living openly as Jews was shared by rabbinical authorities and others who needed to confront the Conversos' ignorance in halakhic matters. Samuel Aboab, a leading Venetian rabbi whose writings were disseminated throughout the entire Sephardi diaspora in western Europe,[45] insisted on the need to instil former Conversos with knowledge not only of halakhah but also of correct theology through

---

[42] Pastore, *Un'eresia spagnola*, esp. 75–89.

[43] Stuczynski, 'A "Marrano Religion"?' (Heb.), 215–16; id., 'New Christian Political Leadership in Times of Crisis'. On similar political activity by Conversos in Sicily, see Zeldes, *'The Former Jews of This Kingdom'*, 267–76.   [44] Stuczynski, 'A "Marrano Religion"?', 205, 210.

[45] Samuel Aboab, *Sefer hazikhronot*, 258–9.

religious confraternities devoted to mission and education. This is very similar to what the Catholic Church was doing. Much propaganda and apologetic literature was produced to persuade the Conversos to return to Judaism, to educate them in its tenets, and to stress its advantages over Christianity. The authors of this literature—men such as Saul Levi Morteira, Moses Raphael D'Aguillar, Orobio de Castro, Abraham Gomez Silveira, Joseph Lopez, David Nieto, Elijah Monteiro, Benjamin Diaz Brandon, and Emmanuel Aboab—had extensive knowledge of Catholic theology, acquired at the best universities in Spain and Portugal. Jewish educational institutions throughout the Sephardi diaspora, especially the one in Amsterdam, continued this Hispanic literary and academic tradition, including the production of plays in Spanish, prose and poetry in Castilian, and religious literature inspired by major Spanish figures such as Pedro Calderón de la Barca, Louis de Góngora, Francisco de Quevedo, and even the Jesuit theologian António Vieira.[46] Such literature could also serve in the battle against heretics, deists, sceptics, followers of Spinoza, and those who chose to return, occasionally or permanently, to the 'lands of idolatry' after their return to open Jewish life.[47] This battle reached its peak in the late sixteenth century, during the height of Safed mysticism.

The community of Amsterdam was often beset by heretics, who challenged the authority of rabbinic and community leaders.[48] Some Conversos had developed their own theological positions, which they found hard to surrender, and often could not fully accept the normative halakhah: the Averroists viewed religious practice and observance of commandments as less important than mental attitude; others had no intention of disconnecting themselves entirely from their Catholic past, and their poor knowledge of Judaism made the absorption of Catholic attitudes, often hostile to Jewish culture, easier; others maintained that internal adherence to the Jewish nation and its heritage was of greater importance than ritual acts. The more resolute

---

[46] See Kaplan, 'The Sephardim in North-Western Europe and the New World'; id., 'The Intellectual Ferment in the Spanish-Portuguese Community of Seventeenth Century Amsterdam'; Swetschinski, *Reluctant Cosmopolitans*, 85–95.

[47] Graizboard, *Souls in Dispute*, 1–11, 57–8, 64–5, 71–8, 91–104, 129, 136–9, 171–8; Kaplan, 'The Struggle Against Travellers to Spain and Portugal' (Heb.).

[48] Kaplan, *From New Christians to New Jews* (Heb.), 137–9, 169, 182–6, 199, 204–8, 257–91; id., 'The Sephardim in North-Western Europe and the New World'; id., 'The Intellectual Ferment in the Spanish-Portuguese Community of Seventeenth Century Amsterdam'.

among them even produced strong theological arguments against the Jewish faith and ethos on crucial issues such as salvation, religious practice, the uniqueness of the Jewish people, and the exegesis of scripture.

Conversos in Safed

In the sixteenth century Yom Tov Tsahalon observed that 'Conversos have come to [Safed] in order to repent in the Islamic zone [out of the reach of the Inquisition]'.[49] The city became an important centre for former Conversos, mainly of Portuguese origin,[50] as witnessed by Ottoman tax records, which have almost seven times more entries for Conversos in the second half of the century as they do for the first. The Conversos set up a separate synagogue and court of law and established their own confraternity for the atonement for transgressions during their life as Christians. They became the second largest group in the city, surpassed only by the Castilians. Accounts of Christian pilgrimages to Galilee also include references to increased numbers of Conversos.[51]

Many major kabbalists had Converso connections, including Solomon Alkabets, Jacob Tsemah, and Judah Albotini.[52] Alkabets composed a special prayer praising the Conversos for settling in the Land of Israel;[53] Cordovero was involved in the Converso penitential confraternity; Isaac Karo dedicated elaborate legal and theological discussions to their status according to halakhah;[54] Eleazar Azikri mentions that he saved two Conversos from returning to Christianity;[55] and Hayim Vital created an amulet for a Converso for the same purpose.[56]

Vital was deeply concerned with the Conversos and their needs. In his *Ets hada'at tov* (The Tree of Knowledge Is Good), he described the groups that

---

[49] Cited in David, 'Safed as a Centre for Conversos Returning to Judaism in the Sixteenth Century' (Heb.), 188–93.

[50] David, 'The Spanish Exiles in the Holy Land'; id., 'Safed as a Centre for Conversos Returning to Judaism in the Sixteenth Century' (Heb.).

[51] Ish-Shalom, 'Information Regarding Safed in the Books of Christian Travellers' (Heb.), 202–4.   [52] See esp. Magid, *From Metaphysics to Midrash*, 79–81.

[53] David, 'Safed as a Centre for Conversos Returning to Judaism in the Sixteenth Century' (Heb.).

[54] M. Pachter, 'Homiletic and Ethical Literature of Safed in the 16th Century' (Heb.), 74–5.

[55] Azikri, *Yomano hamisti*, 149.

[56] Vital, *Sefer hape'ulot*, 66–7, 146, 153, 155, 188, 192, 200, 262, 368–9.

accompanied the Israelites on the Exodus from Egypt in terms often used to refer to Conversos.[57] Unlike the midrashic literature, and especially the Zohar, which characterized these groups in utterly negative terms, Vital considered them part of the covenant between God and the people of Israel. His mystical diary contains a fascinating vision of a man from the Spanish court who represented the Conversos and their dual loyalty to Judaism and the burgeoning Spanish royalty.[58] The narrative mentions many current events: Habsburg hegemony over Spain and much of Europe and the Dutch War of Independence, the power of the Spanish Inquisition, and the discovery of the New World. In the midst of all this stand the Conversos, nurtured by a modern political vision and inspired by the prophecies of Daniel. The dream also reflects a Converso legend that Ferdinand had Jewish origins, since a Jewish baby had been substituted for his grandparents' child; this baby went on to become the mother of the king who ordered the expulsion of the Jews from Spain.[59]

What happened in Safed was a response to profound changes in Catholicism. According to Vital's interpretation of the four kingdoms of the book of Daniel, 'there are four sects of demonic powers: Lilith, Agrat, Rahav, Na'amah. Their seats are stationed in four states: Rome, Salamanca in Spain, Egypt, and Damascus. Each one of them has its own proficiency. Lilith of Rome is in charge of idolatry, Salamanca of bloodshed, Egypt of incest, and Damascus of robbery.'[60] Salamanca is the only one of these that was not a political or military power at the time. Rome was the seat of the popes and the centre of Catholicism, and Egypt and Damascus were important centres of the Ottoman empire. All Salamanca had was a university; however, this was enough for Vital to see it as one of the embodiments of evil, because among the professors at Salamanca University was the distinguished theologian Francisco de Vitoria. De Vitoria, a descendant of Conversos, founded the philosophical school of Salamanca which made significant contributions to theology, especially the methodological innovations known as second scholasticism. The school of Salamanca did not stop at abstract theological subtleties, however, but discussed economics and international law in the

---

[57] See Magid, *From Metaphysics to Midrash*, ch. 2.

[58] See Vital, *Sefer haḥezyonot*, 4: 20–1 (ed. Faierstein, 144–6).

[59] Kriegel, 'Histoire sociale et ragots'. Kriegel notes that the story appears in Capsali's *Seder eliyahu zuta* (1523).   [60] Vital, *Ets ḥayim*, ii. 408.

light of the new geographical discoveries being made. Salamanca was the heart of the theological ferment resulting from concrete religious and political circumstances, and it was the way in which this ferment permeated and influenced Judaism that so bothered Vital.

An example of this infiltration of Catholic ideas through the Conversos that Vital feared may be found in the life of Solomon Molkho.[61] Molkho inhabited a world of fragmented identities and permeable cultural and religious borders, carrying with him the Catholic heritage he had absorbed during his Converso years. Even though he expressed loathing and indignation at his past, he could not deny its stamp on him. As a young Converso named Diego Pires, Molkho was about to start a legal career in Portugal when he had a serious religious crisis exacerbated by a chance encounter with a mysterious person named David Reuveni, who presented himself as an envoy from the ten lost tribes. This drove Pires to a new life of Judaizing under the Hebrew name Molkho. From this moment onwards his life was filled with mystical and prophetic visions and messianic expectations. After many wanderings he was burned at the stake as a heretic and a Judaizer.

Molkho contributed to his own myth by claiming that his knowledge of the Torah was not derived from books, as he was not proficient in Hebrew, nor from any master but from heavenly revelations. Though he had no link to the classical chain of tradition, usually an essential qualification for a Jewish teacher, wherever he went people gathered around him and acknowledged his spiritual authority. In Italy he encountered the Zohar, which became crucial for his later thinking, and attracted a group of disciples, whom he instructed in penitence.[62] The Portuguese ambassador to Rome described how Jews admired him 'as if he were a saint'.[63] He exchanged letters with the leading rabbis of the large Jewish community of Salonica and sent them his sermons: these would be later collected in *Sefer hamefo'ar* (The Glorious Book). Joseph Taitatsak, head of the yeshiva in Salonica, asked Molkho to instruct him in divine revelations. Though not himself a major kabbalist, Taitatsak was the halakhic master of Joseph Karo and Solomon Alkabets. Karo was impressed by Molkho's religious devotion and wished to die a martyr as Molkho did. The encounter with Molkho turned Alkabets from a philosophical biblical exegete into a mystical kabbalistic preacher and inspired him to migrate to

[61] See Benmelekh, 'Solomon Molkho' (Heb.).   [62] Ibid. 221.   [63] Ibid. 21.

Safed, where he met other disciples of Taitatsak.[64] Vital referred to Molkho as the possessor of the 'secret of remembrance', a mental technique to avoid forgetfulness.[65]

The writings of Molkho, especially *Sefer hamefo'ar*, contain several significant Catholic doctrines which were highly problematic in the Jewish context: the importance of original sin; the new Torah of the messianic era that would replace the old Mosaic one; the need to keep the secrets of the Torah from the Jews lest they use them to pursue worldly interests; the need for the Jewish people to be subordinate to others; the messiah as the saviour first of himself and later of the entire human race; the messiah as an eternal being; and the importance of repentance over righteousness and, as a corollary, the central role of former Conversos in the salvation process. The style of his sermons was very like that of wandering preachers in Italy.[66]

Even his death at the stake aroused reactions more typically Catholic than Jewish.[67] His Italian admirers spread the word that he had somehow survived, causing his death to acquire mythical dimensions. His personal belongings were collected like the relics of a Catholic saint: they are still in the Jewish museum in Prague. His special way of wearing the *tsitsit*, a fringed garment required to be worn by men, was used to support halakhic judgements on how it should be worn. Later hagiography miraculously transported him to the Land of Israel after his death, to Safed to be more precise. A contemporary Sephardi historian, Gedalyah ben Joseph ibn Yahya, wrote: 'Still there are Jews who follow him mistakenly, claiming that he is alive, and goes every Saturday to his fiancée [the Shekhinah?] at Safed.'[68]

The Catholic Influence

In the nearly eight centuries from the battle of Covadonga, which marks the beginning of the Reconquista, to the Expulsion, a period during which Jews rose to positions of prominence and power in Christian Iberian society, the Jews of Spain and Portugal had plenty of time to absorb Catholic ideas and doctrines. They were also subject to many of the same vicissitudes as the majority Catholic society, and responded in similar ways.

[64] See Benmelekh, 'Solomon Molkho' (Heb.), 21.   [65] See ibid., 226, 290–4.
[66] Ibid. 183–9, 210, 227–30, 235.   [67] Ibid. 282–305.
[68] Gedalyah ben Joseph ibn Yahya, *Shalshelet hakabalah*, cited in David, 'Safed as a Centre for Conversos Returning to Judaism in the Sixteenth Century' (Heb.), 185.

One of the central tenets of Christianity was original sin. It had appeared in the writings of Jewish polemicists 200 years before the Expulsion, but Luria made it a cornerstone of his doctrines.[69] Like St Paul and the Church Fathers, Luria focused on the sin of Adam and not, as was customary in rabbinic hermeneutics, on the collective sin of the Jewish people at Mount Sinai: the construction and adoration of the golden calf. This was intensified by the idea of reincarnation, which loaded every individual with the sins of past lives as well. Similar ideas appear in Molkho's *Sefer hamefo'ar*: originally the world was pure, but it was contaminated by Adam's sin; the messiah would return the world to its pristine status.[70] Placing sin at the centre of theological thought and presenting it as the motor of human history reveals a strong Catholic influence; however, Luria also linked it to the doctrine of reincarnation, which meant that sin did not only affect the sinner but also all of their reincarnations. The messiah would have no previous incarnations and would have a new soul: a notion very similar to the Christian doctrine of the immaculate conception, according to which Mary the mother of Jesus was born free of original sin so that she would be pure enough to give birth to the messiah.

During the sixteenth century the Catholic world witnessed the increased importance of visual imagery, manifest in the private ownership of icons, public processions, and statues of Mary. Such imagery also came to have a prominent role in Safed kabbalah. One story involves Abraham Barukhim, who was sent to the Wailing Wall by Luria as a penitential act, where he actually saw the Shekhinah.[71] Kabbalistic manuscripts often contained diagrams of the divine worlds and their interrelations, sometimes with remarkably anthropomorphic images,[72] and provided instructions on meditative techniques to guide the imagination. In the Catholic world meditative techniques to achieve personal identification with the suffering of Christ, especially the *Spiritual Exercises* of Ignatius Loyola, were becoming popular.

Vital's *Sefer hahezyonot* is full of realistic physical descriptions of journeys, by himself and others, to the divine realms. No one doubted the veracity of such accounts. Inquisition files contain similar testimonies about encounters with the souls of the departed in paradise or revelations from the dead in a

---

[69] Magid, *From Metaphysics to Midrash*, ch. 1.
[70] Benmelekh, 'Solomon Molkho' (Heb.), 183–9.
[71] *Sefer toledot ha'ari*, 229–30.   [72] Busi, *Qabbalah visiva*.

dream or heightened state of consciousness. Interaction between the worlds of the living and the dead is a regular component of folklore and was part of medieval Catholicism and Judaism. The main innovation in the sixteenth century lies in its use—in Jewish, Christian, and Converso circles—as a force for religious reform. Direct contact with the divine realms was one source of prestige for Luria and his disciples. It furnished the basis for their claim that in order to understand the Zohar—the grounds for all theological, halakhic, and ritual innovations—one needed to contact the same founts of inspiration that had inspired the composition of the book in the first place. Hence the Lurianic school's claims to the monopoly on mystical truth and the priority of the new kabbalah.[73]

Iberian Jews produced a rich and varied literature presenting Jewish tenets in theological and philosophical terminology familiar to many Conversos, which also served as a useful tool in the struggle against heretics and those who rejected rabbinic authority.[74] The mystical criticism of rabbinic and halakhic tradition was inspired by the Catholic tradition. For example, Vital's introduction to *Ets ḥayim* clearly reveals its debt to St Paul and the Church Fathers, repeating Paul's criticisms of the rabbinic tradition. It indicates a sense of deep crisis in rabbinic thought and the need for cultural and religious reform. Solomon Molkho asserted that a new spiritual, messianic Torah would replace the old Torah of rules and talmudic discussions. Knowledge of the new Torah would be achieved not by arduous study in a yeshiva but through direct contact with divine realms.[75] Samuel Aboab also attempted to marginalize theoretical discussions in favour of concrete guidance.[76] Catholic authorities stressed the importance of guiding the behaviour of the faithful, rather than the elaboration of complex theological issues. Erudite Conversos studied the works of St Paul in the search for a way to ameliorate relations between new and old Christians. Paul's ideas of grace and charity formed the basis for criticisms of rituals performed without the correct intention, worship of saints, disregard of regulations, and especially violence. Illuminist and Alumbradist groups in Spain, among which were a large number of Con-

[73] Huss, *Like the Radiance of the Sky* (Heb.), ch. 6.
[74] Kaplan, *From New Christians to New Jews* (Heb.), esp. 266, 272, 276, 291.
[75] Benmelekh, 'Solomon Molkho' (Heb.), 190–2, 227–30.
[76] Samuel Aboab, *Sefer hazikhronot*, 261.

versos, objected to the institutional attitude of the Catholic Church, in its elevation of empty ritual and dry scholasticism over the mystical aspects of faith.[77]

Catholicism developed the idea of 'sacred archaeology'. Excavations of catacombs in Spain and Italy brought to light remains of first-century martyrs—real and fictional—and increased the trade in saints' relics and led to the establishment of comprehensive collections.[78] Luria and his disciples made many journeys in the environs of Safed and often 'discovered' the tombs of figures from the Talmud and Zohar. The cult of past *kedoshim*—a source of legitimacy for current *kedoshim*—centred on their graves.

Summary

After the Expulsion, many Iberian Converso and Jewish refugees arrived in western Europe and the Ottoman empire bringing with them their particular cultural and religious heritage, which they often managed to impose on the local Jews. They were helped by the fact that they often had the backing of local authorities, their economic might and involvement in trade, their political and administrative experience in Portugal and Spain, and their international family networks. They saw themselves as distinct from and superior to the rest of the Jews: they were 'the men of the nation'.

More than any other community of the early modern period, the inhabitants of Safed were a multicultural group that included Jews from all over the world. This situation required cultural and institutional mechanisms to define the limits of the various legal traditions and to ensure basic homogeneity in communal life. The Sephardi were better equipped than any others to cope with this clash of traditions. Their wide political experience and ambition are reflected in the halakhic works of Joseph Karo and his intention to enforce his legal decisions throughout the entire Jewish diaspora.

Iberian Jewish culture had already absorbed elements of the Catholic environment prior to the Expulsion, in areas such as mystical revelations

---

[77] On the importance of the Pauline tradition in Spain and its role in Converso criticism of the church, see Pastore, *Un'eresia spagnola*, 98, 106, 117–18, 121, 141, 149, 155, 195–6, 198, 219.

[78] Prosperi, 'L'Immacolata a Siviglia e la fondazione sacra della monarchia spagnola', esp. 138, 160.

—for example, the circle of mystics who followed the teachings in *Sefer hameshiv*[79]—study in religious schools, and normative literature. Yet the exiles brought with them not only this legacy but also the heritage of the Conversos, who straddled Jewish and Christian cultures. The Iberian diaspora reveals borrowings from baroque culture, Counter-Reformation Catholicism, traditional and mystical Judaism, and the tensions of the Conversos' lifestyles, which were all mediated to the Jewish world through Safed kabbalah.

The Conversos expressed pride in their 'Jewish descent', deemed it superior to Catholic origins,[80] and even attempted to subvert claims of *limpieza de sangre* by asserting that Jewish genealogies were more ancient and nobler than those of their neighbours. The famous Converso family De Santa Maria claimed that its lineage went back as far as the Virgin Mary, a Jewess from Galilee. In their wanderings, they carried this mentality far beyond Spain, as testified in the writings of Isaac Cardoso (1603–83), the Converso physician, philosopher, and polemicist who escaped the Spanish Inquisition and settled in Verona to live openly as a Jew, and his brother, the kabbalist and follower of Shabetai Tsevi, Abraham Miguel Cardozo (1626–1706).[81] Despite recurring emphasis on the need for self-abasement and extreme modesty as basic conditions for approaching God, the personal and autobiographical writings of the Safed kabbalists are replete with expressions of pride. Honour was of great importance in Mediterranean cultures,[82] and the interaction of Catholics and Jews in contemporary Europe contained clear elements of honour rivalry: the honour of the faith, of the race, and of God. Martyrdom was held to be a matter of honour, since it enhanced the glory of God and the Jewish people.

Although Conversos were unable to practise their faith overtly, the testimonies studied by Stuczynski reveal their need to know what to believe and what not to believe—that is, to have some sort of theology—and their awareness of the differences between Judaism and Christianity.[83] In Converso society, where religion had to be practised in secret, without teachers or books, women served as the guardians of the religious heritage, passing it on to the

---

[79] See Idel, 'Magic and Kabbalah in the "Book of the Responding Entity"'; id., 'Studies in the Method of *Sefer hameshiv*' (Heb.).   [80] Pastore, *Un'eresia spagnola*, 173–4.

[81] Cardoso, *Las excelencias y calumnias de los hebreos*; Cardozo, *Selected Writings*; see Yerushalmi, *From Spanish Court to Italian Ghetto*.   [82] Nirenberg, *Communities of Violence*.

[83] Stuczynski, 'A "Marrano Religion"?' (Heb.), 114–19.

next generation.[84] In Safed, women often had religious authority through their ability to perform magic, have visions, make prophecies, cure cases of possession, or interpret dreams.[85] This is in sharp contrast to the marginal role of women in other branches of Jewish mysticism. When Hayim Vital needed confirmation of his mystical visions or interpretation of his dreams, he did not hesitate to turn to a woman. Their role even increased later with the Shabatean movement.

One of the major tensions of Converso life was the constant scrutiny from neighbours, priests, other family members, and the Inquisition. In Safed too, people kept an eye on each other's doings, words, and opinions. It was deemed necessary to reveal intimate details of sins in order to make atonement and reparation.[86] This tight control of community members was the continuation of practices of pre-Expulsion Sephardi communities. *Ḥerem* and ostracism were used, not to be lifted until the miscreant had made a public confession, expressed remorse, and begged for forgiveness in front of the entire community in the synagogue.[87]

During the sixteenth century conscience became central to religious life. For the Safed kabbalists, intention was the effective part of any ritual act. Mental states were also very important to the Conversos, as they were deprived of any means of openly expressing their religion, and they developed the belief that an internal attachment to the Jewish people was more important than external acts. Such attitudes, which were often irreconcilable with halakhah, were present in all Iberian communities.[88] Some Conversos maintained this attitude even after they migrated to northern Europe where they could practise Judaism openly. Many Spanish sages, such as Joseph Garson, were critical of this 'Jewishness of the heart', and similar attitudes could be found among Catholic theologians of Converso origin, who criticized any empty act of ritual and interpreted every act as revelatory of an inner disposition.[89]

---

[84] Levine Melammed, *Heretics or Daughters of Israel?*

[85] Chajes, 'In a Different Voice' (Heb.).

[86] *Sefer toledot ha'ari*, 107, 159–61, 173, 191, 225–9.

[87] Kaplan, *From New Christians to New Jews* (Heb.), 65–7, 69–70, 78, 85–6, 134–9, 169, 207–8, 212–13.

[88] Kaplan, 'The Intellectual Ferment in the Spanish-Portuguese Community of Seventeenth Century Amsterdam'.   [89] See e.g. Pastore, *Un'eresia spagnola*, 194–5.

The Conversos also developed their own religious practices, often with obvious Catholic antecedents. The role and importance of angels as protectors and mediators with God increased significantly in Counter-Reformation Catholicism and was declared part of the official dogma. According to Abraham ben Eliezer Halevi, addressing prayers to God through angels was a common practice.[90] However, he was highly critical of those who addressed prayers to the angels themselves, as this bordered on idolatry. He also mentioned 'newcomers' to kabbalah who prayed to a certain *sefirah* and not to God in his entirety. Conversos believed that certain magical and prophetic techniques could accelerate the advent of the messiah, who would relieve their current misery, although at the same time they formed corporations to defend their political interests.[91] The vigorous messianic activity of Solomon Molkho was inspired by Franciscan apocalyptic traditions which considered real, human history as the main arena for the messianic drama.[92]

Conversos were preoccupied with martyrdom as a true sign of the expiation of the sin of apostasy and a secure sign of eternal life.[93] Martyrdom has a long history in Judaism, as it has in Christianity. Fascination with martyrdom increased after the Expulsion, and it was part of the penitential and ascetic atmosphere of Safed.[94] The Safed kabbalists prostrated themselves fully on the ground at certain moments of the daily prayers as a physical sign of their willingness to die for God. Abraham ben Eliezer Halevi wrote a guide to martyrdom called *Megilat amrafel*,[95] and Karo's desire for martyrdom was a constant theme in his mystical diary.[96]

According to Issachar ibn Susan, a Safed kabbalist from Fez, the Conversos had little knowledge of Jewish tradition, but some of them knew the Bible very well.[97] This testimony is further supported by the Inquisition files from

[90] Kadari, 'The Polemics over Prayers Addressed to Angels' (Heb.); see also Robinson, 'Abraham ben Eliezer Halevi' (Heb.), 208–12.

[91] Stuczynski, 'New Christian Political Leadership in Times of Crisis'.

[92] Benmelekh, 'Solomon Molkho' (Heb.), esp. 25–6, 131–2, 164–75.

[93] See Bodian, *Dying in the Law of Moses*.

[94] David, 'Safed as a Centre for Conversos Returning to Judaism in the Sixteenth Century' (Heb.), 200–3.

[95] See Robinson, 'Abraham ben Eliezer Halevi' (Heb.), 212–13.

[96] Karo, *Magid meisharim*, 3–4, 10, 13, 16–17, 19, 23, 25–6, 28–9, 33–4, 49, 51–2.

[97] See David, 'Safed as a Centre for Conversos Returning to Judaism in the Sixteenth Century' (Heb.).

Spain, Portugal, and Italy. Simple people and women were versed in biblical stories and could argue forcefully with 'old Christians'. The Bible was part of the foundations of their folk religiosity.[98] Biblical exegesis—such as the translation and exposition projects of Cisneros and Arias Montano and the intensive biblical study of the monks of the Order of St Jerome, many of them former Jews—also occupied an important place in contemporary Iberian culture. The Lurianic corpus can be seen as a giant, comprehensive exegesis of the Bible, since all its important positions draw their legitimacy either from biblical verses or the Zohar, which in turn was composed as a biblical commentary.[99]

Luria's first encounter with kabbalah was mediated by a former Converso. His death, again according to Safed hagiography, was the fulfilment of the prophecy of another former Converso.[100] Alerted to his approaching end, Luria moved from Egypt to the Land of Israel and began a period of intensive activity in order to complete his life's work. This reflects the significance of the Iberian Conversos' contribution to Safed kabbalah: stories originating from the Converso milieu were taken as authoritative, even in respect of such a prominent kabbalistic figure as Isaac Luria.

[98] Frattarelli-Fisher, 'Ritratti di donne dai processi dell'Inquisizione'; ead., 'Scelta religiosa e lacerazioni familiari nelle comunità ebraiche toscane tra seicento e settecento'; ead., 'Percorsi di conversione di ebrei nella Livorno di fine seicento'.

[99] On the centrality of biblical stories to Lurianic mythology, see Magid, *From Metaphysics to Midrash*.   [100] Vital, *Ets ḥayim*, i. 21.

Safed Kabbalah and Modernity

I N THE JEWISH CONTEXT, 'modernity' refers to the results of changes in the fundamental components of life and culture in the early sixteenth century, such as community organization, exegesis of sacred scriptures, rituals, pedagogical institutions, marriage and family life, attitudes to property and poverty, demographics, migration and the establishment of new diasporas, and, last but certainly not least, the place of Jews in the majority societies in which they lived. These components are fairly readily available for analysis as they are on the whole documented. However, there were other aspects which are less so, especially thoughts and attitudes. Safed kabbalah contributed a Jewish component to the growing European interest in individualism and unconscious inclinations. The spiritual diaries of the kabbalists document their most intimate secrets and were deeply concerned with controlling the emotions—especially anger—bodily urges, and the refinement of behaviour.

I have tried to present the innovations of early modern kabbalah in various domains and not simply confine myself to its theological aspects. The 'theological' course is more convenient, since it restricts itself to the better-documented and therefore more easily analysable features, yet it marginalizes others which were considered no less significant in their life and work by the kabbalists themselves, such as the confraternities, the reparation of the self and the cosmos, ritual innovation, new interpretations of halakhah, and charging religious practices with new meaning.

This study follows in the tradition of the sociological analysis of religion and its place in the life of the community—alongside economics and the means of production, political mechanisms, geography, and folk traditions—pioneered by Max Weber, Émile Durkheim, and Ernst Tröltsch.[1] I do not

---

[1] Weber, *The Sociology of Religion*; id., *The Protestant Ethic and the Spirit of Capitalism*; Durkheim, *Les Formes élémentaires de la vie religieuse*; Tröltsch, *The Social Teaching of the Christian Churches*.

want to suggest that religion is secondary to economic activity or mainly serves social needs, but the richness of the religious experience and its profound contribution to individual and collective life can only be fully appreciated in the public context: sociological and historical. An important case in point is the role of exceptional figures (saints and mystics). In order to be considered holy people and attract disciples, they needed the endorsement of their communities. There is a mutual dependency between the community and the heroic religious figure: each side confers legitimacy, prestige, and sanctity on the other. Religion is a powerful force, and the activity of exceptional religious people can have a profound effect upon society.

The sociological approach to religion is especially revealing when applied to moments of change, asking what the contribution of religion was to these changes and how it was affected by them.[2] The sixteenth and seventeenth centuries were periods of marked change in European history: in politics, with the advent of modern centralized nation states; in religion, with the schism between the Protestant and Catholic churches; in economics, with the discovery of the New World and the start of the global economy; and in science, with new metallurgical techniques and weaponry. The political changes could not have taken place without a new balance of power and cooperation between the state and the church. In Christian Europe, the process of confessionalization led to increasingly large, coherent, and geographically defined groups accepting a single religious confession, be it Catholic or Protestant. This made it easier for secular as well as religious authorities to establish and maintain hegemony. They gained access to private domains— pastimes, sexual behaviour, the raising and educating of children—and more comprehensive control of criminals, vagabonds, and other marginal elements of society. Confessionalization involved the coercive use of religion in both Catholic and Protestant states in order to create more unified political units, as the cultural elite attempted to mould the population in its own image. Both churches wanted to establish a model of the worthy citizen of a modern state. Authority was exercised from above over larger and larger segments of the population, who were forced to accept the ideas imposed by the regime. The most obvious example is the convergence of the lines separating Catholics

---

[2] For an analysis of Jewish mysticism using sociological tools, see Wexler, *Mystical Interactions*.

and Protestants with political borders all across Europe. Similar processes were at work in the Ottoman empire and even much further east.[3]

The Jewish diaspora was not immune to the religious ferment sweeping Europe. However, in the Jewish context there is an even greater need to re-appraise the contribution of religion to the modernization process. David Sorotzkin has argued that the dominant trend in Jewish historiography considers religion as a major obstacle to Jewish modernism and sees change as imposed on Jews by the majority communities in which they lived, forcing them to adapt as best they could. However, what is needed is a global reading of political and religious changes in the early modern period.[4] Changes imposed from outside would hardly be greeted with enthusiasm by many segments of the Jewish population. As with other social changes, the process was lengthy and did not necessarily proceed in a straight line—as the progressive model of the spread of the Enlightenment assumes—and it evoked different responses from different parts of society. The kabbalistic message spread slowly to all corners of the Jewish world during the seventeenth and eighteenth centuries.

Most studies of confessionalization concentrate on the coercive aspects of the political and religious changes involved and ignore the responses to them. Church and state authorities needed the co-operation of the population for their reforms to succeed, and other local and community mechanisms were also essential: sermons, missionary campaigns, and, especially, confession in the Catholic world. This use of persuasion rather than force required the faithful to change their attitude to religion and to allocate it a more significant place in their lives. Women were assigned a more important role, as the church saw in them the principal educators of the young and the guardians of Christian family life. However, there were many instances of open or covert resistance to the church's new propaganda, and the full effects of Catholic reform were not felt until the end of the seventeenth century.[5] Similar changes took place in the Jewish world in the sixteenth

---

[3] See Subrahmanyam, 'Connected Histories'.

[4] Sorotzkin, *Orthodoxy and Modern Discipline* (Heb.). That Jewish modernity began in the eighteenth century is still considered a basic tenet of Jewish historiography (see e.g. Feiner, *The Origins of Jewish Secularization in Eighteenth-Century Europe*; *New Jewish Time* (Heb.), esp. Yovel, 'Parameters of New Jewish Time' (Heb.)).

[5] A clear example is the slow adoption of Tridentine doctrines of family life and marriage rites.

and seventeenth centuries, as beliefs and ritual practices became institutionalized, although the full consequences were not apparent until the eighteenth century.

A sociological approach to early modern kabbalah can go a long way towards explaining the modus operandi of the first generation of Safed kabbalists and those of the second who passionately committed themselves to spreading their message. None of them confined themselves to speculative writing: the explication of divine secrets was but one strand of a much broader attempt to shape collective attitudes and practices. The theoretical and the practical were two facets of the same activity, typical of the changes undergone by Jewish communities in response to the religious ferment in contemporary Europe and the Ottoman empire. Jewish mysticism moved from elitist and esoteric circles to the public domain, and the kabbalistic message was circulated with missionary zeal and much criticism of earlier attitudes.[6] Kabbalah increasingly infiltrated personal, family, and community life, even of those who did not accept its tenets. In most cases, kabbalists had little interest in systematic or detailed exposition of theological positions, and their main energy was channelled into practical actions.

A notable example of the passage from the theological to the sociological level can be found in Cordovero's *Tomer devorah*. Readers are encouraged to modify their behaviour according to a kabbalistic programme. The divine *sefirot* represent the ethical values on the basis of which God acts, and they may be made manifest in the human world as well. God and humanity act in a similar way, morality increases, and further intimacy becomes possible. This programme not only made an impressive leap in the establishment of kabbalistic ethics but provided a pioneering concretization of the ideal of the 'imitation of God'.

Change was driven by theological innovation. The Lurianic God was in constant flux: every assertion regarding his activities, nature, or image was relative, lacking any constant validity, as other assertions could be made which took their place or restricted their scope. However, these bold mythical

---

[6] A similar process took place in science in early modern Europe. Maintaining knowledge in small and elitist circles gave way to sharing it in communities and collaborating with other scientists. This was further enhanced by a change in attitude to ancient knowledge, which came to be seen as limited and inferior. See Rossi, *Philosophy, Technology and the Arts in the Early Modern Period*, 7–12.

descriptions were intended to suggest modes of interaction between Jews and God. Theurgy and the human ability to influence God were stressed repeatedly. The entire set of revelations—of lights, divine Faces, and *sefirot*—was not only about God, but mainly about the bridge between God and humanity, as it was translated into mystical techniques or patterns of meditative prayer. Even the diversified system of reparations, which affected every aspect of human life, was derived from this dynamic character. Reparations provided the possibility of repairing the individual, the world, and God. This was fuelled by the kabbalists' interest in previous incarnations and the strong bonds they believed existed between themselves and various aspects of the divinity. Their belief that good and evil human acts had consequences in the divine realms relied heavily on the earlier shift from abstract to practical theology. This also allowed large parts of the Jewish population to become involved through social institutions such as confraternities and schools.

The divine aspect most representative of these changes is Ze'er Anpin. *Ets ḥayim* provides abundant details of his birth and growth and his intercourse with his female partner. His status as the son of God, conceived by the divine Faces Abba and Imma, his human aspects, and his death and resurrection are all reminiscent of the Christological narrative, and, just as Christ's human nature and sufferings made him accessible to believers, so too did Ze'er Anpin's.[7]

The kabbalists of Safed often presented themselves as no more than interpreters of the secrets of the Zohar. It is tempting to accept this at face value and see Safed kabbalah as a continuation of medieval Jewish kabbalah; however, Luria shifted the focus from the *sefirot* to what he considered the higher mystical level of Adam Kadmon and the divine Faces. The Zohar had little to say on these aspects of the divinity, as they were deep secrets only to be revealed to the initiated. Lurianic kabbalah was a new and revolutionary theological system, and Luria was fully aware of that, but he could not declare it explicitly as he could not directly contradict the earlier traditions.

Lurianic kabbalah relied on new encyclopedic conceptions of knowledge prevalent in early modern Europe and claimed to be the key to comprehensive knowledge of the entire chain of being, from Adam Kadmon to the demonic domain. The similarity of Lurianic theology to early modern

---

[7] On Christological elements in the Jewish mystical tradition, see Idel, *Ben*.

responses to the challenge of increasing knowledge is apparent in its use of mechanical and mnemonic models and visualization techniques to classify and remember vast quantities of information. It was also highly sensitive to the developing ideas of personhood, the place of emotion in religion, the role of women, and new discoveries about the human body. It was not the secrets of divinity per se which were of importance but communicating with God. This also aroused the curiosity of non-Jews: of all Jewish literature, kabbalistic works attracted the most attention from the leading intellectuals of early modern Europe.[8]

Kabbalah also gave rise to a new cultural elite, the *kedoshim*. They had precedents in Judaism, going back to the talmudic period, but their role radically changed in the sixteenth century. They served as role models and counsellors; hagiographical literature grew up around them, especially Luria, and they joined the ranks of the traditional figures of classical Judaism: scholars, rabbis, liturgists, and community leaders. The *kedoshim* saw themselves as being of much greater significance than members of earlier generations. They materialized the Jewish heritage in their bodies, behaviour, and personalities, since each one of them could cite a long line of previous incarnations as key figures of Jewish history. Although there was a strong link between the *kedoshim* of Safed and the Sufis, the Islamic influence was secondary, providing local colour once the *kadosh* was established in the Ottoman empire: the *kadosh* arose as a consequence of the religious ferment in the sixteenth-century Catholic world. However, much work remains to be done on the *kedoshim* and their different manifestations in the Ottoman empire and Catholic Europe.

From their early days the *kedoshim* were very conscious of their public status and authority. Some of them headed religious confraternities and compiled regulations for them. The hagiographical literature described Luria as a member of a quasi-legal court, originating in pre-Expulsion Spain, which oversaw moral behaviour. One of the stories involves him in the mock-execution of a sinner, in a similar manner to that used by the Spanish Inquisition.

The battle against heresy in Safed led to censorship. Luria established lists of books that were recommended for study and books that were forbid-

---

[8] Schmidt-Biggemann, *Christliche Kabbala*; id., *Geschichte der christlichen Kabbala*.

den. Here also, the parallel with the Inquisition's distinction between permitted and forbidden books is obvious. At a later period a famous Italian follower
of Luria, Moses Zacuto, initiated the copying of Lurianic manuscripts and
removed passages of which he disapproved.[9] Kabbalistic censorship owed
much to an awareness that these works would be inherited by future generations and that it was essential that what was passed on was exact and correct.
Luria himself was too engaged in his kabbalistic activities to put his thoughts
into writing, but the following generations produced books of encyclopedic
scope. Vital and his disciples sought to create a synthesis of all Luria's utterances, in order to preserve the heritage they had received orally and provide a
theoretical basis for new practices, instructions, and religious rituals.

Safed kabbalists were deeply interested in ritual. They produced books
dedicated to the mystical sense of the commandments and the invention of
new practices. They sought to provide a new depth to ritual practices, so that
they would not be merely formal obligations but offer the possibility of intimacy with God. They saw the presence of God in every moment of human
life and therefore felt the need to provide a religious meaning for every
human act. For this reason it was the kabbalists rather than the halakhists
who were responsible for religious and cultural innovation. The kabbalists
did not intend to marginalize halakhah—which was far beyond their capabilities—but to channel it in new directions. The interpenetration of the
two domains appears in Jacob Tsemah's *Shulhan arukh ha'ari*, which lists
the halakhic commandments and charges them with kabbalistic content.
At the same time, kabbalists were critical of much contemporary halakhah,
as seen in Vital's introduction to *Ets hayim*, where he raised objections to the
rabbinic traditions similar to those raised by St Paul and the Church Fathers.
According to Jacob Katz:

The recurring claim, that the study of halakhah does not suffice without complet-
ing it with kabbalistic knowledge undermined the position of the talmudists. Many
preachers stressed the need for self-examination and encouraged purification and
repentance according to kabbalistic notions. The study of Torah was no longer
sufficient for a true relationship with God.[10]

Their awareness of the divine in every aspect of human life led the kabbalists to enlarge the classical repertoire of commandments. The sabbath was

---

[9] Avivi, 'Pure Flour' (Heb.).   [10] Katz, *Halakhah and Kabbalah* (Heb.), 100.

turned into a theatrical and emotional event when the Shekhinah was invited into people's houses and minds, and rituals of 'exile' and 'divorce' were performed in which confraternities travelled outside the city to study Torah and encounter the exiled Shekhinah and receive divine revelations. The emphasis on emotion in religious practice opened the door to new worlds of music and liturgy, under Turkish and Sufic influence. Israel Najara, for example, was gifted both in musical and liturgical composition, and his poetry is often used today in musical events outside the synagogue.

Initially, the kabbalistic message was not spread through theological texts, but through ethical literature, such as *Shulḥan arukh ha'ari*. Until the early seventeenth century most exegesis of the Zohar was only available in manuscript form and confined to the erudite elite. Although Luria committed very little to writing himself, his immense mystical creativity was synthesized into vast, comprehensive encyclopedias by later generations. These theoretically made his teachings accessible to the public. The Spanish halakhist David ben Zimra led Egyptian Jewry after the Expulsion, but for the last twenty years of his life he lived in Safed and attempted to justify kabbalistic innovations by arguing that mystical reasoning and symbolism were superior to legal formality.[11] Joseph Karo was unprecedented in using zoharic literature in his legal verdicts, either as secondary legitimation or as a decisive juridical source, and his law codes the *Beit yosef* and the *Shulḥan arukh* drew on both halakhah and kabbalah in their attempt to provide one law for all Jews, despite the enormous variety of the diaspora. David Sorotzkin describes his work as a 'search for a centre' and the establishment of a more authoritative and self-assured Jewish society.[12]

Kabbalah also responded to the problem of evil. The idea that evil is in some sense necessary was already present in the Zohar. The Safed kabbalists presented the demonic domain as a counter to the divine realms, but their main interest lay in its intimate, familiar presence in everyday life. The kabbalists' personal and autobiographical writings deal almost obsessively with evil in the individual conscience, often reading like transcripts of legal proceedings in which the internal judge rebukes the writer for personal sins and failings. According to the hagiography, people came to Luria from far beyond

---

[11] Morell, *Studies in the Judicial Methodology of Rabbi David ibn Abi Zimra*.
[12] Sorotzkin, 'The Super-Temporal Community in an Age of Change' (Heb.), 20–2.

his immediate vicinity in search of reparations for their souls. The preoccupation with sin and the urgency of repentance became a fundamental theme alongside that of the immediate presence of God, which intensified some of the kabbalists' feelings of guilt and shame, a major concern of Mediterranean society, and facilitated social control of communities, families, and individuals.

Confession was the most obvious expression of the preoccupation with sin in kabbalistic circles. It was markedly different from medieval Jewish confession and clearly inspired by Catholic practices. It was conducted in front of religious authorities, who prescribed a course of reparation that would atone for the sin. The idea that 'a person is judged every day' meant that the citizens of Safed lived in constant anxiety. From a formal procedure with set times and places, confession became a religious attitude, creating a desire for an ascetic life of constant commitment to God and control of religious consciousness. Personal confession of sins in the 'internal court of law' was to be conducted several times a day. Repentance held such a prominent place that it marginalized messianic expectations in both the Lurianic and Cordoveran schools.

The kabbalists of Safed were also deeply concerned with the body. The medical discoveries of the sixteenth and seventeenth centuries and philosophical positions such as that of Descartes on the distinction between the body and the soul had not yet reached a large public in Europe. The prevailing attitude was that every mental phenomenon had some counterpart in the body, and control of the body was held to be necessary in shaping one's personality and character. In the social sphere it provided a way for the newly emerging nation states to impose discipline on their subjects. For the Safed kabbalists there was a strong link between the divine body and the human body. The human body provided the means of acquaintance with the divine realms and their infinite complexity. Many of the depictions of Ze'er Anpin and Nukba Deze'er Anpin are very daring: all sexual fantasies were permitted. However, this attitude was not continued in later kabbalistic writings. Contemporary sexual discourse in the Catholic world also included surprisingly erotic images of encounters between monks and female saints and confessors and their clients and the sexual freedom allowed to those who were beyond sin.

Kabbalah moved into areas previously considered religiously neutral, such as using a handkerchief rather than spitting on the floor of the syna-

gogue, sleeping, deportment, and talking or remaining silent. In this, kabbalah was one of the main conduits through which ideas held to be civilized in
early modern Europe entered Judaism. However, it also retreated from many
public spheres, such as economic activity, the discoveries of the New World,
the emergent philosophical and scientific discourse, and the politics of the
new nation states.[13] Religious life was to be confined to ritual space and orthodox positions, an attitude to the secular which became more effective in later
centuries and laid the foundations for modern Judaism. It is apparent in the
halakhic literature of the Sephardi diaspora, which avoided discussion of economic activity in the new global markets and let commercial forces hold sway.
This also involved a withdrawal of Jewish thought from its previous engagement with non-Jewish intellectual activities save in exceptional cases, such as
Abraham Herrera and Joseph Solomon del Medigo, who attempted to inter-
polate the new scientific and philosophical achievements into their kabbalistic writings.[14]

Like the Catholic authorities, Safed kabbalists understood that deep
changes were happening in society and that religious reform was necessary.
Their responses to these changes were religious confraternities and education. Confraternities had their historical roots in pre-Expulsion Spain, but
also drew inspiration from the Sufic lodges scattered across the Ottoman
empire, including the two in Safed. They were led by major kabbalists, who
provided their regulatory norms and religious ethos, and spread kabbalistic
theology and practices. Few of the Safed confraternities survived the death of
their founder, but they remained popular in Italy, where they became more
open to people who did not want to live an ascetic life and united kabbalistic
doctrines with other elements of the Jewish tradition.

Jewish kabbalah, especially as it developed in Safed, had many elements
in common with contemporary Catholicism: saints and hagiographical literature; confraternities; sin, confession, and repentance; a focus on individual
conscience; control of the body; religion as a means of social control. Safed
kabbalah was an important intermediary between the Jewish and Catholic
worlds, and Catholic ideas permeated all levels of Jewish culture.

---

[13] See Garb, 'On the Kabbalists of Prague' (Heb.).
[14] Yosha, *Myth and Metaphor* (Heb.); Ruderman, *Jewish Thought and Scientific Discovery in
Early Modern Europe*, 105, 110–11, 117–56, 175, 193–8, 227–31, 350–72.

The Spanish exiles played a leading role in Safed kabbalah and its circulation throughout the Jewish world. Safed was a Sephardi town in its economic life, community arrangements, discipline, talmudic study, law courts, demography, and especially its connections with other Sephardi communities. The former Conversos, living between two religions, established a bridge between the Catholic and Jewish traditions.[15] Safed, its Conversos, and, especially, its kabbalists were part of an international network and played an important part in Jewish responses to the new challenges of a rapidly changing world.

[15] On the contribution of Conversos to the modernization of Europe, see Yovel, *The Other Within*, 287–377.

Bibliography

Primary Sources

AARON BERAKHYAH OF MODENA, *Sefer ma'avar yabok* [encyclopedic collection mainly on burial and mourning rituals] (Jerusalem, 1996).

ABOAB, ISAAC, *Menorat hamaor* [ethics] (Istanbul, 1514).

ABOAB, SAMUEL, *Sefer hazikhronot* [rabbinic and ethical guidance] (Jerusalem, 2001).

ABRAHAM BEN DAVID OF POSQUIÈRES, *Ba'alei hanefesh* [on the laws of ritual purity], ed. Joseph Kapih (Jerusalem, 1993).

ALATRINO, ISAAC BEN ABRAHAM BEN MATITYAH, *Kenaf renanim* [commentary on the Song of Songs] (Bodleian Library, Oxford, MS Reggio 22 (Neubauer 2222/5)).

ALKABETS, SOLOMON, *Derashat haperedah besaloniki lifnei aloto litsefat* [farewell sermon before leaving Salonica for Safed], ed. Mordechai Pachter, in *From Safed's Hidden Treasures: Studies and Texts Concerning the History of Safed and Its Sages in the 16th Century* [Mitsefunot tsefat: meḥkarim umekorot letoledot tsefat veḥakhmeiha bame'ah ha-16] (Jerusalem, 1994), 17–38.

AL-NAKAWA, ISRAEL BEN JOSEPH, *Sefer menorat hamaor* [ethical treatise], ed. Hillel Gershom [Hyman] Enelow (New York, 1929).

AZIKRI, ELEAZAR, *Milei dishemaya* [mystical diary], ed. Mordechai Pachter (Tel Aviv, 1991).

—— *Sefer ḥaredim* [ethical treatise], ed. Jacob J. Gruenwald (Jerusalem, 2005).

—— *Yomano hamisti* [mystical diary], ed. Mordechai Pachter, in *From Safed's Hidden Treasures: Studies and Texts Concerning the History of Safed and Its Sages in the 16th Century* [Mitsefunot tsefat: meḥkarim umekorot letoledot tsefat veḥakhmeiha bame'ah ha-16] (Jerusalem, 1994), 124–86.

AZULAI, ABRAHAM, *Or haḥamah*, 4 vols. (Jerusalem, 1981).

CAPSALI, ELIJAH, *Seder eliyahu zuta*, 3 vols. (Jerusalem, 1976–83).

CARDOSO, ISAAC, *Las excelencias y calumnias de los hebreos* (Amsterdam, 1679).

CARDOZO, ABRAHAM MIGUEL, *Selected Writings*, trans. David J. Halperin (New York, 2001).

CORDOVERO, MOSES, *Or ne'erav* [on the study of kabbalah and its prerequisites] (Venice, 1587).

—— *Or yakar* [commentary on the Zohar], 23 vols. to date (Jerusalem, 1962–95).

—— *Pardes rimonim* [encyclopedic kabbalistic synthesis] (Jerusalem, 2000).

—— *Sefer shi'ur komah* [kabbalistic treatise on the structure of the world and the *sefirot*] (Warsaw, 1885).

—— *Tomer devorah* [kabbalistic treatise on *imitatio Dei*] (Wickliffe, Ohio, 1999).

DATO, MORDECAI, *Derekh emunah* [kabbalistic miscellany] (Hebrew Union College, Cincinnati, MS 631).

DATO, MORDECAI, *Perush nevi'im* [commentary on the Prophets] (British Library, London, MS Add. 27008).

DE VIDAS, ELIJAH, *Reshit ḥokhmah* [kabbalistic ethical treatise] (Satmar, 1942).

FIGO, AZARYAH, *Sefer binah le'itim* [halakhic responsa], 2 vols. (Jerusalem, 1989).

FOA, ELIEZER NAHMAN, *Sefer ma'amarim me'inyan hateshuvah* [on penitence], ed. Avigdor Glandauer and Zvi-Ze'ev Lieberman (London, 1993).

GALLICO, ELISHA, *Kav venaki* [commentary on Proverbs] (Jewish Theological Seminary, New York, MS Ben-Na'im 42), fos. 1–228.

GARSON, JOSEPH, *Ben porat yosef* (British Library, London, MS Gaster Or. 10726).

GERONDI, JONAH, *Sefer sha'arei teshuvah im sefer hayirah viyesod hateshuvah* [on repentance] (Modi'in Illit, 2003).

HAKOHEN, ELIJAH BEN SOLOMON, OF SMYRNA, *Sefer shevet musar* [ethical treatise] (Jerusalem, 1978).

IBN YAHYA, GEDALYAH BEN JOSEPH, *Sefer hamaskil* [dialogue between good and evil inclinations] (British Library, London, MS Add. 27001 (Margoliouth 934/3)).

—— *Shalshelet hakabalah* [The Chain of Transmission] (New York, 1999).

IBN YAHYA, JOSEPH BEN DAVID, *Perush ḥamesh megilot* [commentary on the five scrolls: Esther, Song of Songs, Ruth, Lamentations, and Ecclesiastes] (Bologna, 1530).

—— *Sefer torah or* [descriptions of heaven and hell] (New York, 1993).

JOSEPH IBN SHRAGA, *Teshuvot be'inyanei kabalah* [kabbalistic responsa] (Bodleian Library, Oxford, MS Opp. Add. Qu. 40 (Neubauer 1663/6)).

KAIDANOVER, TSEVI HIRSCH, *Kav hayashar* [ethical and kabbalistic stories and customs], ed. Abraham Scheinberger, 2 vols. (Jerusalem, 1993–9).

KARO, JOSEPH, *Magid meisharim* [mystical diary], ed. Yehiel Bar-Lev (Petah Tikvah, 1990).

LAVI, SHIMON, *Ketem paz*, ed. Menahem Makover, 2 vols. (Bat Yam, 2014).

LEIB BEN OZER, *Sipur ma'asei shabetai tsevi / Beshraybung fun shabse tsvi* [life of Shabetai Tsevi], ed. and trans. Shlomo Zucker and Rivkah Plesser (Jerusalem, 1978).

Mayse bukh [Book of Stories] (Basel, 1602).

MOLKHO, SOLOMON, *Sefer hamefo'ar* [sermons] (Kraków, 1598).

MONSELICE, PINHAS BARUKH BEN PELATIYAH, *Magen ḥayim* [kabbalistic guide to preparing for sleep] (Oriental Studies Institute, St Petersburg, MS A 21; Collegio Rabbinico Italiano, Rome, MS 122).

—— *Tiferet baḥurim* [Glory of Youth] (Bodleian Library, Oxford, MS Regio 33 (Neubauer 1418)); Eng. trans. in Roni Weinstein, *Juvenile Sexuality, Kabbalah, and Catholic Religiosity among Jewish Italian Communities: 'Glory of Youth' by Pinhas Barukh ben Pelatiyah Monselice (Ferrara, XVII Century)* (Leiden, 2008), 301–427.

MOSCATO, JUDAH BEN JOSEPH, *Nefutsot yehudah* [sermons] (Venice, 1589).

OZEIDA, SAMUEL, *Derashat hesped al mot ha'ari* [obituary of Isaac Luria], ed. Mordechai Pachter, in *From Safed's Hidden Treasures: Studies and Texts Concerning the History of Safed and Its Sages in the 16th Century* [Mitsefunot tsefat:

meḥkarim umekorot letoledot tsefat veḥakhmeiha bame'ah ha-16] (Jerusalem, 1994), 39–68.

POJETTI, JACOB, *Divrei ya'akov* [homilies] (Jewish Theological Seminary, New York, MS 1588).

POPPERS, MEIR, *Or hayashar* [kabbalistic ethical treatise] (Jerusalem, 1981).

PROVENZALI, JACOB BEN DAVID, *She'ar yashuv* [commentary on the Song of Songs] (Istanbul, *c.*1577).

PROVENZALO, DAVID ABRAHAM (attrib.), *Perush leshir hashirim* [commentary on the Song of Songs] (Cambridge University Library, MS Add. 636(8)).

ROMANO, MANUELE, *Tofet ve'eden* [poetic description of hell and heaven] (Berlin, 1778).

Safed Spirituality: Rules of Mystical Piety, The Beginning of Wisdom, trans. Lawrence Fine (New York, 1984).

Sefer hadokterinah [guidance for adolescents] (Hungarian Academy of Sciences, Budapest, MS Kaufman A 266).

Sefer ha'igeron [epistles] (Biblioteca Medicea Laurenziana, Florence, MS Plut. 88.18), fos. 1–33.

Sefer ḥasidim [on the teachings of the German Pietists], ed. Reuven Margaliot (Jerusalem, 1957).

Sefer toledot ha'ari: gilgulei nusḥaotav ve'erko mibeḥinah historit; nosefu alav hanhagot ha'ari [hagiography of Isaac Luria], ed. Meir Benayahu (Jerusalem, 1967).

Sefer yetsirah [kabbalistic work] (Tel Aviv, 2011).

SHEMARYAH HA'IKRITI OF NEGROPONTE, *Perush leshir hashirim* [commentary on the Song of Songs] (Bibliothèque Nationale de France, Paris, MS heb. 897).

SOLOMON SHLOMIEL OF DRESNITZ, *Sefer ha'ari vegurav* [Luria and his disciples as reflected in the epistles of Solomon Shlomiel], ed. Ya'akov Moshe Hillel (Jerusalem, 1992).

SOMMO, JUDAH [LEONE DE SOMMO PORTALEONE], *Tsaḥut bediḥuta dekidushin* [comedy based on a midrashic aggadah], ed. J. Schirman (Tel Aviv, 1965).

TREVES [TSARFATI], ABRAHAM BEN SOLOMON, *Birkat avraham* [halakhic instructions] (Venice, 1552).

TSAHALON, ABRAHAM, *Marpe lanefesh* [practical kabbalistic handbook] (Venice, 1593).

TSAHALON, JACOB BEN ISAAC, *Otsar hashamayim* [medical treatise] (Hungarian Academy of Sciences, Budapest, MS Kaufmann 293).

TSEMAH, JACOB, *Nagid umetsaveh* [on the mystical meanings of religious practices] (Lublin, 1881).

VITAL, HAYIM, *Ets ḥayim* [encyclopedic work of Lurianic kabbalah], ed. Zvi-Michal Vidavsky (Jerusalem, 1986).

—— *Kitsur seder ha'atsilut* [on the divine emanations], ed Yosef Avivi (Jerusalem, 2009).

—— *Sefer haḥezyonot* [mystical diary], ed. Morris M. Faierstein (Jerusalem, 2005).

—— *Sefer hape'ulot* [practical, magical, and mystical guidance] (Jerusalem, 2010).

VITAL, HAYIM, *Sha'ar hagilgulim* [on reincarnation], ed. Judah Tsevi Brandwein, in *Complete Works of Isaac Luria* [Kol kitvei ha'ari] (Jerusalem, 1988).

—— *Sha'ar hakavanot* [kabbalistic meditations], ed. Judah Tsevi Brandwein, 2 vols. (Jerusalem, 1984).

—— *Sha'ar hamitsvot* [on the mystical meanings of religious practices], ed. Judah Tsevi Brandwein, in *Complete Works of Isaac Luria* [Kol kitvei ha'ari] (Jerusalem, 1988)

—— *Sha'arei kedushah* [mystical guidance] (Benei Berak, 1973).

YAGEL-GALLICO, ABRAHAM, *Moshia hosim* [short sermon describing a cure for the plague] (Venice, 1587).

—— *Perush eshet hayil* [Commentary on 'Woman of Valour' (Prov. 31)] (Venice, 1606).

—— *Sefer be'er sheva* [miscellany] (Bodleian Library, Oxford, MS Reggio 11 (Neubauer 1306/1)).

—— *A Valley of Vision: The Heavenly Journey of Abraham ben Hananiah Yagel*, trans. David B. Ruderman (Philadelphia, 1990).

YEHIEL BEN YEKUTIEL BEN BENJAMIN, *Sefer ma'alot hamidot* [ethical treatise], ed. Pesach Lebensohn (Warsaw, 1849).

ZACUTO, MOSES, *Igerot haremez* [letters], ed. Mordecai Atiyah (Jerusalem, 1999).

—— *Tofteh arukh* [long poem on hell], ed. Baruch Setzerow (Józefów, 1881).

The Zohar: Pritzker Edition, trans. Daniel C. Matt, 8 vols. to date (Stanford, Calif., 2004–14).

Secondary Literature

ABRAMS, DANIEL, 'The Cultural Reception of the Zohar: An Unknown Lecture by Gershom Scholem from 1940 (Study, Edition and English Translation)', *Kabbalah: Journal for the Study of Jewish Mystical Texts*, 19 (2009), 279–316.

—— *The Female Body of God in Kabbalistic Literature: Embodied Forms of Love and Sexuality in the Divine Feminine* [Haguf ha'elohi hanashi bakabalah] (Jerusalem, 2004).

—— *Kabbalistic Manuscripts and Textual Theory: Methodologies of Textual Scholarship and Editorial Practice in the Study of Jewish Mysticism* (Jerusalem, 2010).

ALESSIO, FRANCO, 'Conservazione e modelli di sapere nel medioevo', in Pietro Rossi (ed.), *La memoria del sapere: Forme di conservazione e strutture organizzative dall'antichità a oggi* (Rome, 1988), 99–133.

ANDREATTA, MICHELA, 'Libri di preghiera della confraternità "Le sentinelle del mattino"', *Annali di Ca' Foscari*, 44/3 (2005), 5–43.

—— *Poesia religiosa ebraica di età barocca: L'innario della confraternità Šomerim la-boqer (Mantova 1612)* (Padua, 2007).

ARRAS, DANIEL, 'La Chair, la grâce, le sublime', in Alain Corbin, Jean-Jacques Courtine, and Georges Vigarello (eds.), *Histoire du corps* (Paris, 2005), ii. 411–76.

ASAD, TALAL, *Formations of the Secular: Christianity, Islam, Modernity* (Stanford, Calif., 2003).

ASSIS, YOM TOV, 'Welfare and Mutual Aid in the Spanish Jewish Community', in Haim Beinart (ed.), *Moreshet Sepharad: The Sephardi Legacy*, trans. Yael Guiladi (Jerusalem, 1992), i. 318–45.

AVIVI, JOSEPH, *Lurianic Kabbalah* [Kabalat ha'ari], 3 vols. (Jerusalem, 2008).

—— 'Pure Flour: Rabbi Moses Zacuto's Sifter' (Heb.), *Pe'amim*, 96 (2003), 71–106.

BAER, YITZHAK, *A History of the Jews in Christian Spain*, trans. Louis Schoffman (Philadelphia, 1992).

BAR-LEVAV, AVRIEL, 'R. Aaron Berakhyah of Modena and R. Naftali Katz, the Founding Fathers of *Ars Moriendi* Books' (Heb.), *Asufot*, 9 (1995), 135–95.

BARNAI, JACOB, *Shabateanism: Social Perspectives* [Shabeta'ut: hebetim ḥevratiyim] (Jerusalem, 2000).

BATAILLON, MARCEL, *Erasme et l'Espagne* (Geneva, 1991).

BEERI, TOVA, 'Israel Najara's "Monthly Sacrifice": Themes and Content' (Heb.), *Asufot*, 4 (1990), 311–24.

BEINART, HAIM, 'The Jews in Castile', in id. (ed.), *Moreshet Sepharad*, i. 11–43.

—— (ed.), *Moreshet Sepharad: The Sephardi Legacy*, trans. Yael Guiladi, 2 vols. (Jerusalem, 1992).

BELKIN, AHUVAH (ed.), *Leone de' Sommi and the Performing Arts* (Tel Aviv, 1997).

BENARROCH, JONATAN, '"The Mystery of Unity": Poetic and Mystical Aspects of a Unique Aoharic Shema Mystery', *AJS Review*, 37/2 (2013), 231–56.

BENAYAHU, MEIR, 'The Commentaries of R. Bezalel Ashkenazi and R. Joseph Ashkenazi and Their Original Version' (Heb.), *Asufot*, 1 (1987), 47–104.

—— 'The Commentaries on *Mishneh torah* on the Original Maimonidean Copy and the Commentaries Ascribed to R. Bezalel Ashkenazi and to R. Isaac Luria' (Heb.), *Sinai*, 100 (1987), 135–42.

—— 'The Conegliano Yeshiva Based on the Manifesto Printed in Venice 1605 and the Epistles of R. Judah Aryeh of Modena' (Heb.), *Asufot*, 15 (2003), 311–25.

—— 'The Confraternity Shomerim Laboker' (Heb.), *Asufot*, 11 (1998), 101–26.

—— 'The Epistle of R. Moses ben Makhir to the Turkish Communities Regarding the *Hesger* in Ein Zeitun' (Heb.), *Asufot*, 15 (2003), 299–305.

—— 'R. Israel Najara' (Heb.), *Asufot*, 4 (1990), 103–284.

—— 'The Revival of Ordination in Safed' (Heb.), in Salo W. Baron et al. (eds.), *Yitzhak F. Baer Jubilee Volume: On the Occasion of his Seventieth Birthday* [Sefer yovel leyitsḥak ba'er bimelot lo shivim shanah] (Jerusalem, 1960), 248–69.

BENMELEKH, MOTI, 'Solomon Molkho: A Biography' [Shelomoh molkho: ḥayav verishumam behistoryah] (Ph.D. diss., Hebrew University of Jerusalem, 2007).

BEN-NAEH, YARON, *Jews in the Realm of the Sultans: Ottoman Jewish Society in the Seventeenth Century* (Tübingen, 2008).

BENNETT, PAULA, and VERNON A. ROSARIO (eds.), *Solitary Pleasures: The Historical, Literary, and Artistic Discourses of Autoeroticism* (New York, 1995).

BEN-SASSON, MENAHEM, *The Emergence of the Local Jewish Community in the Muslim World: Qayrawan, 800–1057* [Tsemiḥat hakehilah hayehudit be'artsot ha'islam] (Jerusalem, 1997).

BEN-SHALOM, RAM, 'The Jewish Community in Arles and Its Institutions: Ben Sheshet's Responsum 266 as a Historical Source' (Heb.), *Michael*, 12 (1991), 6–41.

BENVENUTI, ANNA, 'La civiltà urbana', in *Storia della santità nel cristianesimo occidentale* (Rome, 2005), 157–222.

BERGER, SHLOMO, and RESIANNE FONTAINE, '"Something on Every Subject": On Pre-Modern Hebrew and Yiddish Encyclopaedias', *Journal for Modern Jewish Studies*, 5 (2006), 269–84.

BLACKBURN, SIMON, *Oxford Dictionary of Philosophy* (Oxford, 2014).

BLAIR, ANN, 'A Europeanist's Perspective', in Gerhard Endress (ed.), *Organizing Knowledge: Encyclopaedic Activities in the Pre-Eighteenth-Century Islamic World* (Leiden, 2006), 201–15.

—— *The Theater of Nature: Jean Bodin and Renaissance Science* (Princeton, NJ, 1997).

—— *Too Much to Know: Managing Scholarly Information before the Modern Age* (New Haven, Conn., 2010).

BODIAN, MIRIAM, *Dying in the Law of Moses: Crypto-Jewish Martyrdom in the Iberian World* (Bloomington, Ind., 2007).

—— *Hebrews of the Portuguese Nation: Conversos and Community in Early Modern Amsterdam* (Bloomington, Ind., 1997).

—— 'The "Portuguese" Dowry Societies in Venice and Amsterdam: A Case Study in Communal Differentiation within the Marrano Diaspora', *Italia*, 6/1–2 (1987), 30–61.

BOESCH GAJANO, SOFIA, 'La strutturazione della cristianità occidentale', in *Storia della santità nel cristianesimo occidentale* (Rome, 2005), 91–156.

BOLOGNA, CORRADO, 'Esercizi di memoria dal "Theatro della sapientia" di Giulio Camillo agli "Esercizi spirituali" di Ignazio Loyola', in Lina Bolzoni and Pietro Corsi (eds.), *La cultura della memoria* (Bologna, 1992), 169–221.

BOLZONI, LINA, *La rete delle immagini: Predicazione in volgare dalle origini a Bernardino da Siena* (Turin, 2002).

—— *La stanza della memoria: Modelli letterari e iconografici nell'età della stampa* (Turin, 1995).

BONFIL, ROBERT [REUVEN], 'Halakha, Kabbala and Society: Some Insights into Rabbi Menahem Azaria da Fano's Inner World', in Isadore Twersky and Bernard Septimus (eds.), *Jewish Thought in the Seventeenth Century* (Cambridge, Mass., 1987), 39–61.

—— 'New Information on Rabbi Menahem Azaryah da Fano and His Age' (Heb.), in Immanuel Etkes and Joseph Salmon (eds.), *Studies in the History of Jewish Society in the Middle Ages and in the Modern Period Presented to Professor Jacob Katz on his Seventy-Fifth Birthday* [Perakim betoledot haḥevrah hayehudit biyemei habeinayim uva'et haḥadashah] (Jerusalem, 1980), 98–135.

BOSSY, JOHN, 'The Social History of Confession in the Age of the Reformation', *Transactions of the Royal Historical Society*, 5th ser., 25 (1975), 21–38.

BRAMBILA, ELENA, 'Il Concilio di Trento e i mutamenti nella legittimità', in Anna Bellavitis and Isabelle Chabot (eds.), *Famiglie e poteri in Italia tra medioevo ed età moderna*, Collection de l'École Française de Rome, 422 (Rome, 2009), 51–76.

BREDEKAMP, HORST, *The Lure of Antiquity and the Cult of the Machine*, trans. Allison Brown (Princeton, NJ, 1995).

BROWN, PETER R. L., *The Cult of the Saints: Its Rise and Function in Latin Christianity* (London, 1981).

BURKE, PETER, 'How to be a Counter-Reformation Saint', in *The Historical Anthropology of Early Modern Italy: Essays on Perception and Communication* (Cambridge, 2005), 48–62.

BUSI, GIULIO, *Qabbalah visiva* (Turin, 2005).

CAFFIERO, MARINA, 'Dall'esplosione mistica tardo-barocca all'apostolato sociale', in Lucetta Scaraffia and Gabriella Zarri (eds.), *Donne e fede: Santità e vita religiosa in Italia* (Rome, 1994), 327–73.

CAMPORESI, PIERO, *Il sugo della vita: Simbolismo e magia del sangue* (Milan, 1988).

CANOSA, ROMANO, *Sessualità e inquisizione in Italia tra cinquecento e seicento* (Rome, 1994).

CARRUTHERS MARY, *The Craft of Thought: Meditation, Rhetoric, and the Making of Images, 400–1200* (Cambridge, 1998).

CESARANI, DAVID, and GEMMA ROMAIN (eds.), *Jews and Port Cities, 1590–1990: Commerce, Community and Cosmopolitanism* (Edgware, Middx, 2004).

CHAJES, JEFFERY H., 'Accounting for the Self: Preliminary Generic-Historical Reflections on Early Modern Jewish Egodocuments', *Jewish Quarterly Review*, 95/1 (2005), 1–15.

—— *Between Worlds: Dybbuks, Exorcists and Early Modern Judaism* (Philadelphia, 2003).

—— 'In a Different Voice: The Non-Kabbalistic Women's Mysticism of Early Modern Jewish Culture' (Heb.), *Zion*, 67 (2002), 139–62.

CLAGETT, MARSHAL, *The Science of Mechanics in the Middle Ages* (Madison, Wis., 1959).

COHEN, RICHARD I., *Jewish Icons: Art and Society in Modern Europe* (Berkeley, Calif., 1998).

COMPAGNON, ANTOINE, *La Seconde Main, ou le travail de la citation* (Paris, 1979).

COURTINE, JEAN-JACQUES, 'Le Miroir de l'âme', in Alain Corbin, Jean-Jacques Courtine, and Georges Vigarello (eds.), *Histoire du corps* (Paris, 2005), i. 303–33.

CROUZET-PAVAN, ELIZABETH, 'Un fiore del male: I giovani nelle società urbane italiane (secoli xiv–xv)', in Giovanni Levi and Jean-Claude Schmitt (eds.), *Storia dei giovani* (Rome 1994), 211–77.

DAN, JOSEPH (ed.), *The Age of the Zohar: Proceedings of the Third International Conference on the History of Jewish Mysticism* (Jerusalem, 1989).

DANDELET, THOMAS J., *Spanish Rome, 1500–1700* (New Haven, Conn., 2001).

DASTON, LORRAINE, and KATHARINE PARK (eds.), *Early Modern Science*, Cambridge History of Science, 3 (Cambridge, 2006).

DAVID, ABRAHAM, 'Safed as a Centre for Conversos Returning to Judaism in the Sixteenth Century' (Heb.), in Abraham Haim (ed.), *Society and Community: Proceedings of the Second International Congress for Research on the Sephardi and Oriental Jewish Heritage* [Ḥevrah ukehilah: midivrei hakongres habeinle'umi hasheni leḥeker moreshet yahadut sefarad vehamizraḥ] (Jerusalem, 1991), 183–204.

DAVID, ABRAHAM, 'The Spanish Exiles in the Holy Land', in Haim Beinart (ed.), *Moreshet Sepharad: The Sephardi Legacy*, trans. Yael Guiladi (Jerusalem, 1992), ii. 77–108.

DAVIDSON, EYAL, 'The Sages of Safed between 1540 and 1615: Their Religious and Social Status' [Ḥakhmei tsefat bein hashanim 1540–1615: ma'amadam hadati vehaḥevrati] (Ph.D. diss., Hebrew University of Jerusalem, 2009).

DE BOER, WIETSE, *The Conquest of the Soul: Confession, Discipline and Public Order in Counter-Reformation Milan* (Leiden, 2001).

DE CERTEAU, MICHEL, *The Practice of Everyday Life*, trans. Steven Rendall (Berkeley, Calif., 1984).

DE ROSA, GABRIELE, and GREGORY TULLIO (eds.), *Storia dell'Italia religiosa*, vol. ii: *L'età moderna* (Rome, 1994).

DEAR, PETER, 'The Meaning of Experience', in Lorraine Daston and Katharine Park (eds.), *Early Modern Science*, Cambridge History of Science, 3 (Cambridge, 2006), 106–31.

DEKKER, RUDOLF (ed.), *Egodocuments and History: Autobiographical Writing in Its Social Context since the Middle Ages* (Hilversum, 2002).

DEL COL, ANDREA, *L'Inquisizione in Italia dal 12. al 21. secolo* (Milan, 2006).

DURKHEIM, ÉMILE, *Les Formes élémentaires de la vie religieuse: Le Système totemique en Australie* (Paris, 1991).

EISENBICHLER, KONRAD, *The Boys of the Archangel Raphael: A Youth Confraternity in Florence, 1411–1785* (Toronto, 1998).

ELBAUM, JACOB, *Repentance and Self-Flagellation in the Writings of the Sages of Germany and Poland, 1348–1648* [Teshuvat halev vekabalat isurim: iyunim beshitot hateshuvah shel ḥakhmei ashkenaz vepolin] (Jerusalem, 1992).

ELIAS, NORBERT, *On Civilization, Power, and Knowledge: Selected Writings*, ed. Stephen Mannell and Johan Goudsblom (Chicago, 1998).

ELIOR, RACHEL, 'The Doctrine of Metempsychosis in *Galya raza*' (Heb.), *Jerusalem Studies in Jewish Thought*, 3/1–2 (1984), 207–39.

—— 'Messianic Expectations and Spiritualization of Religious Life in the Sixteenth Century', in David B. Ruderman (ed.), *Essential Papers on Jewish Culture in Renaissance and Baroque Italy* (New York, 1992), 283–98.

—— 'The Metaphorical Relation between God and Man and the Significance of the Visionary Reality in Lurianic Kabbalah' (Heb.), in Rachel Elior and Yehuda Liebes (eds.), *Lurianic Kabbalah*, 47–57.

—— and YEHUDA LIEBES (eds.), *Lurianic Kabbalah: Proceedings of the Fourth International Conference on the History of Jewish Mysticism* [Kabalat ha'ari: divrei hakenes habeinle'umi harevi'i leḥeker toledot hamistikah hayehudit] (Jerusalem, 1992).

ELON, MENACHEM, *Jewish Law: History, Sources, Principles*, trans. Bernard Auerbach and Melvin J. Sykes (Jerusalem, 1994).

ELSTEIN, YOAV, and ARIELA KRASNEY, 'The *Mayse bukh*: Mapping and Basic Problems' (Heb.), in Avidov Lipsker and Rella Kushelevsky (eds.), *Ma'aseh sipur: Studies in Jewish Narrative Presented to Yoav Elstein* [Ma'aseh sipur: meḥkarim basiporet hayehudit] (Ramat Gan, 2006), i. 99–118.

FALK-MOORE, SALLY (ed.), *Law and Anthropology: A Reader* (Malden, Mass., 2005)
—— *Law as Process: An Anthropological Approach* (London, 1978).

FEHER, MICHEL, NADDAFF RAMONA, and NADIA TAZI (eds.), *Fragments for a History of the Human Body*, 3 vols. (New York, 1989).

FEINER, SHMUEL, *The Origins of Jewish Secularization in Eighteenth-Century Europe*, trans. Chaya Naor (Philadelphia, 2010).

FEINGOLD, MORDECHAI (ed.), *Jesuit Science and the Republic of Letters* (Cambridge, Mass., 2003).

FELDHAI, RIVKA, *Galileo and the Church: Political Inquisition or Critical Dialogue* (Cambridge, 1995).

FENTON, PAUL B., 'Abraham Maimonides: Founding a Mystical Dynasty', in Moshe Idel and Mortimer Ostow (eds.), *Jewish Mystical Leaders and Leadership in the 13th Century* (Northvale, NJ, 1998), 127–54.
—— 'Devotional Rites in a Sufi Mode', in Lawrence Fine (ed.), *Judaism in Practice: From the Middle Ages through the Early Modern Period* (Princeton, NJ, 2001), 364–74.
—— 'Influences soufies sur le développement de la Qabbale à Safed: Le Cas de la visitation des tombes', in Paul B. Fenton and Roland Goetschel (eds.), *Expérience et écriture mystiques dans les religions du livre* (Leiden, 2000), 163–90.
—— 'La Hiérarchie des saints dans la mystique juive et dans la mystique islamique', in Moshe Hallamish (ed.), *Alei Shefer: Studies in the Literature of Jewish Thought, Presented to Rabbi Dr. Alexandre Safran* (Ramat Gan, 1990), 49–73.

FINE, LAWRENCE, *Physician of the Soul, Healer of the Cosmos: Isaac Luria and His Kabbalistic Fellowship* (Stanford, Calif., 2003).

FIORAVANTI, MAURIZIO (ed.), *Lo stato moderno in Europa* (Rome, 2002).

FISHBANE, MICHAEL, *The Kiss of God: Spiritual and Mystical Death in Judaism* (Seattle, 1994)

FRAJESE, VITTORIO, *Il popolo fanciullo: Silvio Antoniano e il sistema disciplinare della controriforma* (Milan, 1987).

FRATTARELLI-FISHER, LUCIA, 'Percorsi di conversione di ebrei nella Livorno di fine seicento', *Nuovi studi livornesi*, 13 (2006), 139–71.
—— 'Ritratti di donne dai processi dell'Inquisizione: Rachele e Antonia portoghesi, Caterina schiava moresca e Sara Nunez "donna e rabbina"', in Lucia Frattarelli-Fisher and Olimpia Vaccari (eds.), *Sul filo delle scritture: Fonti e temi per la storia delle donne a Livorno* (Pisa, 2005), 343–75.
—— 'Scelta religiosa e lacerazioni familiari nelle comunità ebraiche toscane tra seicento e settecento', in Ida Fazio and Daniela Lombardi (eds.), *Generazioni: Legami di parentela tra passato e presente* (Rome, 2006), 241–58.

FRENKEL, MIRIAM, *The 'Compassionate and Benevolent': The Elite of the Jewish Community of Alexandria in the Middle Ages* [Ha'ohavim vehanedivim: ilit manhigah bekerev yehudei aleksandriyah biyemei habeinayim] (Jerusalem, 2006).

FRIGO, DANIELA, *Il padre di famiglia: Governo della casa e governo tradizionale dell' economica tra cinque e seicento* (Rome, 1985).

FRUGONI, CHIARA, *Francesco e l'invenzione delle stimmate: Una storia per parole e immagini fino a Bonaventura e Giotto* (Turin, 1993).

FUMAGALLI BEONIO BROCCHIERI, MARIATERESA, 'Le enciclopedie', in *Lo spazio letterario del medioevo*, vol. i/2: *La produzione del testo* (Rome, 1993), 653–7.

—— and MASSIMO PARODI, 'Due enciclopedie dell'occidente medievale: Alessandro Neckam e Bartolomeo Anglico', *Rivista di storia della filosofia*, 1 (1985), 51–90.

FUNKENSTEIN, AMOS, *Theology and the Scientific Imagination from the Middle Ages to the Seventeenth Century* (Princeton, NJ, 1986).

GALINSKY, YEHUDAH D., 'The *Arba'ah turim* and the Halakhic Literature of Fourteenth-Century Spain' [Arba'ah turim vehasifrut hahilkhatit shel sefarad bame'ah ha'arba-esreh: aspektim historiyim, sifrutiyim vehilkhatiyim] (Ph.D. diss., Bar-Ilan University, 1999).

—— 'Jewish Charitable Bequests and the Hekdesh Trust in Thirteenth-Century Spain', *Journal of Interdisciplinary History*, 35/3 (2004), 423–40.

GARB, JONATHAN, 'Gender and Power in Kabbalah: A Theoretical Investigation', *Kabbalah: Journal for the Study of Jewish Mystical Texts*, 13 (2005), 79–107.

—— 'Magic and Mysticism: Between North Africa and the Land of Israel' (Heb.), *Pe'amim*, 85 (2000), 112–30.

—— *Manifestations of Power in Jewish Mysticism: From Rabbinic Literature to Safedian Kabbalah* [Hofaotav shel hakoaḥ bamistikah hayehudit misifrut ḥazal ad kabalat tsefat] (Jerusalem, 2005).

—— 'On the Kabbalists of Prague' (Heb.), *Kabbalah: Journal for the Study of Jewish Mystical Texts*, 14 (2006), 347–83.

GÉLIS, JACQUES, 'Le Corps, l'Église et le sacré', in Alain Corbin, Jean-Jacques Courtine, and Georges Vigarello (eds.), *Histoire du corps* (Paris, 2005), i. 17–108.

GIL, MOSHE, *Documents of the Jewish Pious Foundations from the Cairo Geniza* (Leiden, 1976).

GILBERT, NEAL W., *Renaissance Concepts of Method* (New York, 1963).

GILLER, PINCHAS, 'Between Poland and Jerusalem: Kabbalistic Prayer in Early Modernity', *Modern Judaism*, 24/3 (2004), 226–50.

—— *Shalom Shar'abi and the Kabbalists of Beit El* (Oxford, 2008).

GINZBURG, CARLO, 'High and Low: The Theme of Forbidden Knowledge in the Sixteenth and Seventeenth Centuries', *Past and Present*, 73 (1976), 28–41.

—— 'Titian, Ovid and Sixteenth-Century Codes for Erotic Illustration', in *Clues, Myths and the Historical Method*, trans. John Tedeschi and Anne Tedeschi (Baltimore, 1989), 77–95, 197–200.

GITLITZ, MARTIN, *Secrecy and Deceit: The Religion of the Crypto-Jews* (Philadelphia, 1996).

GOITEIN, SHLOMO D., *A Mediterranean Society: The Jewish Communities of the Arab World as Portrayed in the Documents of the Cairo Geniza*, 5 vols. (Berkeley, Calif., 1967–93).

GOLDISH, MATT D., 'Halakhah, Kabbalah, and Heresy: A Controversy in Early Eighteenth-Century Amsterdam', *Jewish Quarterly Review*, 84/2–3 (1993–4), 153–76.

—— *The Sabbatean Prophets* (Cambridge, Mass., 2004).

—— and RICHARD H. POPKIN (eds.), *Millenarianism and Messianism in Early Modern European Culture*, vol. i: *Jewish Messianism in the Early Modern World* (Dordrecht, 2001).

GORMAN, MICHAEL J., 'The Scientific Counter-Revolution: Mathematics, Natural Philosophy and Experimentalism in Jesuit Culture 1580–c.1670' (Ph.D. diss., European University Institute, 1998).

GRAFTON, ANTHONY, *Bring Out Your Dead: The Past as Revelation* (Cambridge, Mass., 2001).

—— APRIL SHELFORD, and NANCY SIRAISI, *New Worlds, Ancient Texts: The Power of Tradition and the Shock of Discovery* (Cambridge, Mass., 1992).

GRAIZBOARD, DAVID L., *Souls in Dispute: Converso Identities in Iberia and the Jewish Diaspora, 1580–1700* (Philadephia, 2004).

GREEN, ARTHUR, 'The Zaddiq as Axis Mundi in Later Judaism', *Journal of the American Academy of Religion*, 45/3 (1977), 327–47.

GRENDLER, PAUL, 'The Schools of Christian Doctrine in Sixteenth-Century Italy', *Church History*, 53 (1984), 319–31.

GRIES, ZEEV, *Conduct Literature: Its History and Place in the Life of Beshtian Hasidim* [Sifrut hahanhagot: toledoteiha umekomah beḥayei ḥasidav shel habesht] (Jerusalem, 1990).

GROSSMAN, AVRAHAM, 'Characteristics of the Yeshivas in Islamic Spain' (Heb.), in Immanuel Etkes (ed.), *Yeshivas and Houses of Study* [Yeshivot uvatei midrashot] (Jerusalem, 2007), 57–73.

GUTWIRTH, ELEAZAR, 'Jewish Bodies and Renaissance Melancholy: Culture and the City in Italy and the Ottoman Empire', in Maria Diemling and Giuseppe Veltri (eds.), *The Jewish Body: Corporeality, Society, and Identity in the Renaissance and Early Modern Period* (Boston, 2008), 57–92.

HACKER, JOSEPH R., 'Communal Organization among the Jewish Communities of the Ottoman Empire (1453–1676)' (Heb.), in Avraham Grossman and Yosef Kaplan (eds.), *Kehal Yisra'el: Jewish Self-Rule through the Ages*, vol. ii: *The Middle Ages and Early Modern Period* [Kehal yisra'el: hashilton ha'atsmi hayehudi ledorotav, ii: Yemei habeinayim veha'et haḥadashah hamukdemet] (Jerusalem, 2004), 287–309.

—— 'Pride and Depression: The Polarity of the Spiritual and Social Experience of the Iberian Exiles in the Ottoman Empire' (Heb.), in Menahem Ben-Sasson, Robert Bonfil, and Joseph R. Hacker (eds.), *Culture and Society in Medieval Jewry: Studies Dedicated to the Memory of Haim Hillel Ben-Sasson* [Tarbut veḥevrah betoledot yisra'el biyemei habeinayim; kovets ma'amarim lezikhro shel ḥayim hilel ben-sason] (Jerusalem, 1989), 541–86.

—— 'The Sephardim in the Ottoman Empire in the Sixteenth Century', in Haim Beinart (ed.), *Moreshet Sepharad: The Sephardi Legacy*, trans. Yael Guiladi (Jerusalem, 1992), ii. 109–33.

HALBERTAL, MOSHE, *By the Way of Truth: Nahmanides and the Creation of Tradition* [Al derekh ha'emet: haramban viyetsiratah shel masoret] (Jerusalem, 2006).

HALLAMISH, MOSHE, *Kabbalah in Liturgy, Halakhah and Customs* [Hakabalah batefilah, bahalakhah uvaminhag] (Ramat Gan, 2000).

HALLAMISH, MOSHE, *The Kabbalah in North Africa: A Historical Survey* [Hakabalah bitsefon afrikah lemin hame'ah ha-16: sekirah historit vetarbutit] (Tel Aviv, 2001)

—— 'Kabbalistic Ethical Literature before and after the 1492 Expulsion' (Heb.), in Michel Abitbol, Yom Tov Assis, and Galit Hasan-Rokem (eds.), *Hispano-Jewish Civilization after 1492* [Hevrah vetarbut: yehudei sefarad le'ahar hagerush] (Jerusalem, 1997), 165–85.

—— 'Luria's Status as a Halakhic Authority' (Heb.), in Rachel Elior and Yehuda Liebes (eds.), *Lurianic Kabbalah: Proceedings of the Fourth International Conference on the History of Jewish Mysticism* [Kabalat ha'ari: divrei hakenes habeinle'umi harevi'i leheker toledot hamistikah hayehudit] (Jerusalem, 1992), 259–85.

—— 'The Ritual of Reading and Speaking and Its Kabbalistic Significance' (Heb.), in Howard Kreisel (ed.), *Study and Knowledge in Jewish Thought* [Limud veda'at bamahashavah yehudit] (Be'er Sheva, 2006), ii. 157–66.

HAMES, HARVEY J., 'It Takes Three to Tango: Ramon Llull, Solomon ibn Adret and Alfonso of Valladolid Debate the Trinity', *Medieval Encounters*, 15 (2009), 199–224.

HANAFI, ZAKIYA, *The Monster in the Machine: Magic, Medicine, and the Marvelous in the Time of the Scientific Revolution* (Durham, NC, 2000).

HARVEY, STEVEN (ed.), *The Medieval Hebrew Encyclopedias of Science and Philosophy* (Dordrecht, 2000).

HELNER-ESHED, MELILA, *A River Flows from Eden: The Language of Mystical Experience in the Zohar*, trans. Nathan Wolski (Stanford, Calif., 2009).

—— 'Transmigration of Souls in the Kabbalistic Writings of R. David ibn Zimra' (Heb.), *Pe'amim*, 43 (1990), 16–50.

HENNINGER-VOSS, M., 'Working Machines and Noble Mechanics: Guidobaldo del Monte and the Translation of Knowledge', *Isis*, 1/2 (2000), 233–59.

HESCHEL, ABRAHAM J., 'The Holy Spirit in the Middle Ages until Maimonides' Time' (Heb.), in Saul Lieberman (ed.), *Alexander Marx Jubilee Volume* [Sefer hayovel likhevod aleksander marks] (New York, 1950), i. 175–208.

HESPANHA, ANTÓNIO MANUEL BOTELHO, 'Cultura giuridica, libri dei giuristi e tecniche tipografiche', in Maria Antonietta Visceglia (ed.), *Le radici storiche dell'Europa: L'età moderna* (Rome, 2007), 39–68.

HOROWITZ, CARMI, '*Darshanim*, *Derashot*, and *Derashah* Literature in Medieval Spain', in Haim Beinart (ed.), *Moreshet Sepharad: The Sephardi Legacy*, trans. Yael Guiladi (Jerusalem, 1992), i. 383–98.

HOROWITZ, ELLIOT, 'Coffee, Coffeehouses, and Nocturnal Rituals in Early Modern Jewry', *AJS Review*, 14/1 (1989), 17–46.

—— 'The Eve of the Circumcision: A Chapter in the History of Jewish Nightlife', *Journal of Social History*, 23/1 (1989), 45–69.

—— 'Jewish Confraternal Piety in Sixteenth-Century Ferrara: Continuity and Change', in Nicholas Terpstra (ed.), *The Politics of Ritual Kinship: Confraternities and Social Order in Early Modern Italy* (Cambridge, 2000), 150–71.

—— 'The Jews and the Moment of Death in Medieval and Modern Times', *Judaism*, 44/3 (1995), 271–81.

—— 'Towards a Social History of Jewish Popular Religion: Obadiah of Bertinoro on the Jews of Palermo', *Journal of Religious History*, 17/2 (1992), 138–51.

—— '*Yeshiva* and *Hevra*: Educational Control and Confraternal Organization in Sixteenth-Century Italy', in *Shlomo Simonsohn Jubilee Volume: Studies of the History of the Jews in the Middle Ages and Renaissance Period* [Sefer yovel lishelomoh simonson] (Tel Aviv, 1993), 123–47.

HOSHEN, DALIA, '*Tsimtsum* and R. Akiva's School: Kabbalah and Midrash' (Heb.), *Daat: A Journal of Jewish Philosophy and Kabbalah*, 34 (1995), 34–60.

HUNDERT, GERSHON DAVID (ed.), *Jews in Early Modern Poland* (London, 1997).

HUSS, BOAZ, 'Holy Place, Holy Time, Holy Book: The Influence of the Zohar on Pilgrimage to Meron and the Lag Ba'omer Festival' (Heb.), *Kabbalah: Journal for the Study of Jewish Mystical Texts*, 7 (2002), 237–56.

—— *The Kabbalah of R. Simeon ibn Lavi* [Al adnei paz: hakabalah shel r. shimon ibn lavi] (Jerusalem, 2000).

—— *Like the Radiance of the Sky: Chapters in the Reception History of the Zohar and the Construction of Its Symbolic Value* [Kezohar harakia: perakim betoledot hitkabelut hazohar uvehavnayat erko hasimli] (Jerusalem, 2008). English edn.: *The Zohar: Reception and Impact* (Oxford, 2016).

—— 'The Zoharic Communities of Safed' (Heb.), in Zeev Gries, Haim Kreisel, and Boaz Huss (eds.), *Shefa tal: On Jewish Thought and Culture, Presented to Bracha Sack* [Shefa tal: iyunim bemaḥshevet yisra'el uvetarbut yehudit] (Be'er Sheva, 2004), 149–69.

IDEL, MOSHE, *Ben: Sonship and Jewish Mysticism* (London, 2007).

—— '*Ganz Andere*: On Rudolph Otto and Concepts of Holiness in Jewish Mysticism', *Daat: A Journal of Jewish Philosophy and Kabbalah*, 57–9 (2006), pp. v–xliv.

—— 'Italy in Safed, Safed in Italy: Toward an Interactive History of Sixteenth-Century Kabbalah', in Giuseppe Veltri and David B. Ruderman (eds.), *Cultural Intermediaries in Early Modern Italy* (Philadelphia, 2004), 239–69.

—— 'Jewish Thought in Medieval Spain', in Haim Beinart (ed.), *Moreshet Sepharad: The Sephardi Legacy*, trans. Yael Guiladi (Jerusalem, 1992), i. 261–81.

—— *Kabbalah and Eros* (New Haven, Conn., 2005).

—— 'Magic and Kabbalah in the "Book of the Responding Entity"', *The Solomon Goldman Lectures*, 6 (1993), 125–38.

—— 'Nahmanides: Kabbalah, Halakhah, and Spiritual Leadership', in Moshe Idel and Mortimer Ostow (eds.), *Jewish Mystical Leaders and Leadership in the 13th Century* (Northvale, NJ, 1998), 15–96.

—— 'On the Concept of *Tsimtsum* in Kabbalah and Its Research' (Heb.), in Rachel Elior and Yehuda Liebes (eds.), *Lurianic Kabbalah: Proceedings of the Fourth International Conference on the History of Jewish Mysticism* [Kabalat ha'ari: divrei hakenes habeinle'umi harevi'i leḥeker toledot hamistikah hayehudit] (Jerusalem, 1992), 59–112.

—— 'On Mobility, Individuals and Groups: Prolegomenon for a Sociological Approach to Sixteenth-Century Kabbalah', *Kabbalah: Journal for the Study of Jewish Mystical Texts*, 3 (1998), 145–73.

IDEL, MOSHE, 'On Rabbi Zvi Hirsch Koidanover's Sefer Qav ha-Yashar', in Karl E. Grözinger (ed.), *Jüdische Kultur in Frankfurt am Main von den Anfängen bis zur Gegenwart* (Wiesbaden, 1997), 123–33.

—— 'On the Theologization of Kabbalah in Modern Scholarship', in Yossef Schwartz and Volkhard Krech (eds.), *Religious Apologetics: Philosophical Argumentation* (Tübingen, 2004), 123–74.

—— '"One from a Town and Two from a Family": A New Look at the Problem of Dissemination of Lurianic Kabbalah and the Shabatean Movement' (Heb.), *Pe'amim*, 44 (1990), 5–30.

—— 'R. Judah Halewah and His *Tsafenat pane'aḥ*' (Heb.), *Shalem: Studies in the History of Jews in Eretz Israel*, 3 (1981), 119–48.

—— 'Reflections on Kabbalah in Spain and Christian Kabbalah', *Hispania Judaica*, 2 (1999), 315.

—— Review of Swietlicki, *Spanish Christian Cabala*, *Jewish Quarterly Review*, 78/3–4 (1988), 310–31.

—— 'Saturn and Shabetai Tsevi: A New Approach to Shabateanism' (Heb.), *Jewish Studies*, 37 (1997), 161–84.

—— 'Studies in the Method of *Sefer hameshiv*: A Chapter in Spanish Kabbalah' (Heb.), *Sefunot*, 17 (1983), 185–266.

ISH-SHALOM, MICHAEL, 'Information Regarding Safed in the Books of Christian Travellers' (Heb.), in Isaac Ben-Zvi and Meir Benayahu (eds.), *Safed* [Sefer tsefat] (Jerusalem, 1968), ii. 199–228.

ISRAEL, JONATHAN, 'The Sephardi Contribution to Economic Life and Colonization in Europe and the New World (16th–18th Centuries)', in Haim Beinart (ed.), *Moreshet Sepharad: The Sephardi Legacy*, trans. Yael Guiladi (Jerusalem, 1992), ii. 365–98.

JUHASZ, ESTHER, 'The "Shiviti Menorah": Between Abstract and Material. Studies in the Representation of the Sacred' [Ha'shiviti menorah'—bein mufshat leḥomri: iyunim beyitsug hakodesh] (Ph.D. diss., Hebrew University of Jerusalem, 2004).

JULIA, DOMINIQUE, '1650–1800: L'infanzia tra assolutismo ed epoca dei lumi', in Egle Becchi and Dominique Julia (eds.), *Storia dell'infanzia*, vol. ii: *Dal settecento a oggi* (Rome, 1996), 3–99.

JÜTTE, ROBERT, *Poverty and Deviance in Early Modern Europe* (Cambridge, 1994).

KADARI, YOAD, 'The Polemics over Prayers Addressed to Angels: R. Abraham Halevi and Jerusalem Kabbalists' [Hapulmos al odot tefilot lemalakhim: r. avraham halevi umekubelei yerushalayim] (MA thesis, Hebrew University of Jerusalem, 2008).

KADOSH, MEIR, 'Kabbalistic Laws in Responsa from the Thirteenth Century to the Early Years of the Seventeenth Century' [Hapesikah hakabalit besifrut hashe'elot uteshuvot mehame'ah hashalosh-esreh ad reshit hame'ah hasheva-esreh] (Ph.D. diss., Bar-Ilan University, 2004).

KALLUS, MENACHEM, 'The Theurgy of Prayer in the Lurianic Kabbalah' (Ph.D. diss., Hebrew University of Jerusalem, 2002).

KAPLAN, YOSEF, 'Foi et scepticisme dans la diaspora des Nouveaux-Chrétiens des débuts de l'Europe moderne', in *La Diaspora des Nouveaux-Chrétiens* (Lisbon, 2004), 21–40.

—— *From New Christians to New Jews* [Minotserim ḥadashim liyehudim ḥadashim] (Jerusalem, 2003); Eng. trans.: *From Christianity to Judaism: The Story of Isaac Orobio de Castro*, trans. Raphael Loewe (Oxford, 2004).

—— 'The Intellectual Ferment in the Spanish-Portuguese Community of Seventeenth Century Amsterdam', in Haim Beinart (ed.), *Moreshet Sepharad: The Sephardi Legacy*, trans. Yael Guiladi (Jerusalem, 1992), i. 288–314.

—— 'The Sephardim in North-Western Europe and the New World', in Haim Beinart (ed.), *Moreshet Sepharad: The Sephardi Legacy*, trans. Yael Guiladi (Jerusalem, 1992), ii. 240–87.

—— 'The Struggle Against Travellers to Spain and Portugal in the Western Sephardi Diaspora' (Heb.), *Zion*, 64 (1999), 65–100.

KARAMUSTARA, AHMET T., *Sufism: The Formative Period* (Berkeley, Calif., 2007).

KATZ, JACOB, 'Halakhah and Kabbalah as Competing Study Domains' (Heb.), in *Halakhah and Kabbalah* [Halakhah vekabalah], 70–101.

—— *Halakhah and Kabbalah: Studies in the History of Jewish Religion, Its Various Faces and Social Relevance* [Halakhah vekabalah: meḥkarim betoledot dat yisra'el al madureiha vezikatah haḥevratit] (Jerusalem, 1986).

—— 'The Interaction between Halakhah and Kabbalah after the "Revelation" of the Zohar' (Heb.), in *Halakhah and Kabbalah* [Halakhah vekabalah], 52–69.

KLEINBERG, AVIAD M., *Flesh Made Word: Saints' Stories and the Western Imagination*, trans. Jane M. Todd (Cambridge, Mass., 2008).

—— *Prophets in Their Own Country: Living Saints and the Making of Sainthood in the Later Middle Ages* (Chicago, 1997).

KOLAKOWSKI, LESZEK, *Chrétiens sans église: La Conscience religieuse et le lien confessionelle au XVII siècle* (Paris, 1969).

KÖNIG, JASON, and GREG WOOLF (eds.), *Encyclopaedism from Antiquity to the Renaissance* (Cambridge, 2013).

KRIEGEL, MAURICE, 'Histoire sociale et ragots: Sur l'"ascendance juive" de Ferdinand le Catholique', in *Movimientos migratorios y expulsiones en la diáspora occidental* (Pamplona, 2000), 95–100.

LAMDAN, RUTH, 'Deviation from the Norms of Moral Behaviour in Jewish Society in Israel and Egypt in the 16th Century' (Heb.), in Israel Bartal and Isaiah Gafni (eds.), *Sexuality and the Family in History* [Eros, erusin ve'isurim: miniyut umishpaḥah behistoryah] (Jerusalem, 1998), 119–30.

LAQUEUR, THOMAS W., *Solitary Sex: A Cultural History of Masturbation* (New York, 2004).

LAZURE, GUY, 'Possessing the Sacred: Monarchy and Identity in Philip II's Relic Collection at the Escorial', *Renaissance Quarterly*, 60 (2007), 58–93.

LE GAL, DINA, 'The Ottoman Naqshbandiyya in the Pre-Mujaddidi Phase: A Study in Islamic Religious Culture and Its Transmission' (Ph.D. diss., Princeton University, 1992).

LE GOFF, JACQUES, 'Pourquoi le XIIIe siècle a-t-il été plus particulièrment un siècle d'enciclopedisme?', in Michelangelo Picone (ed.), *L'enciclopedismo medievale* (Ravenna, 1992), 23–40.

LEVINE MELAMMED, RENÉE, *Heretics or Daughters of Israel? The Crypto-Jewish Women of Castile* (New York, 1999).

LICHTENSTEIN, YEHEZKEL SHRAGA, *Consecrating the Profane: Rituals Performed and Prayers Recited at Cemeteries and Burial Sites of the Pious* [Mitumah likedushah: tefilah veḥeftsei mitsvah bevatei kevarot va'aliyah lekivrei tsadikim] (Tel Aviv, 2007).

LIEBES, YEHUDA, 'Earth Shaker: Simeon bar Yohai's Aloneness' (Heb.), in Haviva Pedaya and Ephraim Meir (eds.), *Judaism: Topics, Fragments, Faces, Identities. Jubilee Volume in Honour of Rivka Horowitz* [Yahadut: sugyot, keta'im, panim, zehuyot. Sefer rivkah] (Be'er Sheva, 2007), 337–57.

—— Myth and Symbol in the Zohar and Lurianic Kabbalah' (Heb.), *Eshel Beer-Sheva*, 4 (1996), 192–209.

—— 'New Directions in the Study of Kabbalah' (Heb.), *Pe'amim*, 50 (2002), 150–70.

—— 'Towards a Study of the Author of *Emek hamelekh*: His Personality, Writings, and Kabbalah' (Heb.), *Jerusalem Studies in Jewish Thought*, 11 (1993), 101–37.

—— '"Two Young Roes of a Doe": The Secret Sermon of Isaac Luria before his Death' (Heb.), in Rachel Elior and Yehuda Liebes (eds.), *Lurianic Kabbalah: Proceedings of the Fourth International Conference on the History of Jewish Mysticism* [Kabalat ha'ari: divrei hakenes habeinle'umi harevi'i leḥeker toledot hamistikah hayehudit] (Jerusalem, 1992), 113–69.

—— 'Zohar and Eros' (Heb.), *Alpayim*, 9 (1994), 67–119.

LOMBARDI, DANIELA, 'Fidanzamento e matrimoni dal Concilio di Trento alle riforme settecentesche', in Michela de Giorgio and Christiane Klapisch-Zuber (eds.), *Storia del matrimonio* (Rome, 1996), 215–50.

LUALDI, KATHARINE JACKSON, and ANNE T. THAYER (eds.), *Penitence in the Age of Reformations* (Aldershot, 2000).

MAGID, SHAUL, *From Metaphysics to Midrash: Myth, History, and the Interpretation of Scripture in Lurianic Kabbala* (Bloomington, Ind., 2008).

MAHER, MICHAEL, 'Confession and Consolation: The Society of Jesus and Its Promotion of the General Confession', in Katharine Jackson Lualdi and Anne T. Thayer (eds.), *Penitence in the Age of Reformations* (Aldershot, 2000), 184–200.

MANDRESSI, RAPHAEL, 'Dissections et anatomie', in Alain Corbin, Jean-Jacques Courtine, and Georges Vigarello (eds.), *Histoire du corps* (Paris, 2005), ii. 311–33.

MARAVALL, JOSE ANTONIO, *Culture of the Baroque: Analysis of a Historical Structure*, trans. Terry Cochran (Minneapolis, 1986).

MARGOLIN, RON, 'Physiognomy and Chiromancy: From Prediction and Diagnosis to Healing and Human Correction (Zohar ii. 70*a*–78*a*: *Tikunei hazohar*, §70)' (Heb.), *Te'udah*, 21–2 (2007), 199–249.

MATT, DANIEL, '*Matnita dilan*: An Innovative Technique in the Zohar' (Heb.), in Joseph Dan (ed.), *The Age of the Zohar: Proceedings of the Third International*

Conference on the History of Jewish Mysticism [Hakenes habeinle'umi letoledot hamistikah hayehudit, 3: sefer hazohar vedoro] (Jerusalem, 1989), 123–45.

MAYR, OTTO, *Authority, Liberty, and Automatic Machinery in Early Modern Europe* (Baltimore, 1986).

MELAMED, ABRAHAM, 'The Hebrew Italian Renaissance and Early Modern Encyclopedias', *Rivista di storia della filosofia*, 1 (1985), 91–112.

MENCHI, SILVANA SEIDEL, and DIEGO QUAGLIONI (eds.), *I processi matrimoniali degli archivi ecclesiastici italiani*, 4 vols. (Bologna, 2000–6).

MENTZER, RAYMOND A., 'Notions of Sin and Penitence within the French Reformed Community', in Katharine Jackson Lualdi and Anne T. Thayer (eds.), *Penitence in the Age of Reformations* (Aldershot, 2000), 84–100.

MERCHAVIA, CHEN, *The Church versus Talmudic and Midrashic Literature: 500–1248* [Hatalmud bire'i hanatsrut: hayaḥas lesifrut yisra'el shele'aḥar hamikrah ba'olam hanotsri biyemi-habeinayim 500–1248] (Jerusalem, 1970).

MERI, JOSEF W., *The Cult of Saints among Muslims and Jews in Medieval Syria* (Oxford, 2002).

MEROZ, RONIT, 'The Circle of R. Moses ben Makhir and Its Regulations' (Heb.), *Pe'amim*, 31 (1987), 40–61.

—— 'The Middle Eastern Origins of Kabbalah', *Journal for the Study of Sephardic and Mizrahi Jewry*, 1 (2007), 39–56.

—— (ed.), *New Developments in Zohar Studies* (Eng. and Heb.) (Tel Aviv, 2007).

—— 'Redemption in Lurianic Teaching' [Ge'ulah betorat ha'ari] (Ph.D. diss., Hebrew University of Jerusalem, 1988).

—— 'Selections from Ephraim Penzieri: Luria's Sermon in Jerusalem and *Kavanah* in Taking Food' (Heb.), in Rachel Elior and Yehuda Liebes (eds.), *Lurianic Kabbalah: Proceedings of the Fourth International Conference on the History of Jewish Mysticism* [Kabalat ha'ari: divrei hakenes habeinle'umi harevi'i leḥeker toledot hamistikah hayehudit] (Jerusalem, 1992), 211–57.

MICHELI, GIANNI, *Le origini del concetto di macchina* (Florence, 1995).

MILHOU, ALAIN, *Colón y su metalidad mesiánica en el ambiente francicanista español* (Valladolid, 1983).

MODENA MAYER, MARIA, 'Il "Sefer miswot" della biblioteca di Casale Monferrato', *Italia*, 4/1 (1985), pp. i–xix, 1–108.

MORELL, SAMUEL, *Studies in the Judicial Methodology of Rabbi David ibn Abi Zimra* (Lanham, Md., 2004).

NABARRO, ASSAF, '*Tikun*: From Lurianic Kabbalah to Popular Culture' ['Tikun': mikabalat ha'ari legorem tarbuti] (Ph.D. diss., Ben-Gurion University, 2006).

New Jewish Time. Jewish Culture in a Secular Age: An Encyclopedic View [Zeman yehudi ḥadash: tarbut yehudi be'idan ḥiloni], 5 vols. (Tel Aviv, 2007).

NICCOLI, OTTAVIA, 'Éducation et discipline: Les Bonnes Manières des enfants dans l'Italie de la contre-réforme', in Daniela Romagnoli (ed.), *La Ville et la cour: Des bonnes et des mauvaises manières* (Paris, 1995), 185–218.

NIRENBERG, DAVID, *Communities of Violence: Persecution of Minorities in the Middle Ages* (Princeton, NJ, 1996).

OGREN, BRIAN, *Renaissance and Rebirth: Reincarnation in Early Modern Italian Kabbalah* (Leiden, 2009).

OLIVARI, MICHELE, 'La spiritualità spagnola nel primo trentennio del cinquecento: Osservazioni e variazioni su di un grande tema storiografico', *Rivista di storia e letteratura religiosa*, 29 (1993), 175–233.

O'MALLEY, JOHN W., *The First Jesuits* (Cambridge, Mass., 1994).

PACHTER, MORDECHAI, 'Homiletic and Ethical Literature of Safed in the 16th Century' [Sifrut haderush vehamusar shel ḥakhmei tsefat bame'ah ha-16 uma'arekhet rayonoteiha ha'ikariyim] (Ph.D. diss., Hebrew University, 1976).

—— 'The Life and Personality of R. Elazar Azkari according to His Mystical Diary' (Heb.), *Shalem: Studies in the History of Jews in Eretz Israel*, 3 (1981), 127–47.

—— 'Smallness and Greatness in Lurianic Kabbalah' (Heb.), in Rachel Elior and Yehuda Liebes (eds.), *Lurianic Kabbalah: Proceedings of the Fourth International Conference on the History of Jewish Mysticism* [Kabalat ha'ari: divrei hakenes habeinle'umi harevi'i leḥeker toledot hamistikah hayehudit] (Jerusalem, 1992), 171–210.

PACHTER, SHILO, 'Keeping the Covenant: The History of the Prohibition on Wasting Seed' [Shemirat haberit: letoledotav shel isur hotsa'at zera levatalah] (Ph.D. diss., Hebrew University of Jerusalem, 2006).

PANCERA, CARLO, 'Educazione dei costumi e insegnamento delle virtù', in Gian Paolo Brizzi (ed.), *Il catechismo e la grammatica* (Bologna, 1985), i. 287–346.

PARK, KATHARINE, and LORRAINE DASTON, 'Introduction: The Age of the New', in eaed. (eds.), *Early Modern Science*, Cambridge History of Science, 3 (Cambridge, 2006), 1–17.

PARKER, GEOFFREY, and LESLEY M. SMITH, 'Introduction', in eid. (eds.), *The General Crisis of the Seventeenth Century* (London, 1997), 1–31.

PASTORE, STEFANIA, *Un'eresia spagnola: Spiritualità conversa, alumbradismo e Inquisizione (1449–1559)* (Florence, 2004).

PEDAYA, HAVIVA, *Nahmanides: Elevation, Cyclical Time and Sacred Text* [Haramban: hitalut, zeman maḥzori vetekst kadosh] (Tel Aviv, 2003).

—— (ed.), *The Piyut as a Cultural Prism: New Approaches* [Hapiyut ketsohar tarbuti: kivunim ḥadashim lehavanat hapiyut ulehavnayato hatarbutit] (Jerusalem, 2012).

—— *Walking through Trauma: Rituals of Movement in the Jewish Myth, Mysticism and History* [Halikhah sheme'ever latra'umah: mistikah, historyah veritual] (Tel Aviv, 2011).

PELY, HAGAI, 'Kabbalah in R. Joseph Karo's Halakhic System in the Development of a Castilian Halakhic Ruling through the Sixteenth Century' (Heb.), *Kabbalah: Journal for the Study of Jewish Mystical Texts*, 26 (2012), 243–72.

—— 'Lurianic Kabbalah: Halakhic and Meta-Halakhic Aspects' [Kabalat ha'ari: hebetim hilkhatiyim umeta-hilkhatiyim] (Ph.D. diss., Ben-Gurion University, 2014).

PICONE, MICHELANGELO, 'Il significato di un convegno sull'enciclopedismo medievale', in id. (ed.), *L'enciclopedismo medievale* (Ravenna, 1992), 15–21.

POSKA, ALLYSON M., *Regulating the People: The Catholic Reformation in Seventeenth-Century Spain* (Leiden, 1998).

PRODI, PAOLO, *The Papal Prince: One Body and Two Souls. The Papal Monarchy in Early Modern Europe*, trans. Susan Haskins (Cambridge, 1987).

PROSPERI, ADRIANO, 'L'Immacolata a Siviglia e la fondazione sacra della monarchia spagnola', in Ida Fazio and Daniela Lombardi (eds.), *Generazioni: Legami di parentela tra passato e presente* (Rome, 2006), 125–62.

—— 'L'inquisitore come confessore', in Paolo Prodi (ed.), *Disciplina dell'anima, disciplina del corpo e disciplina della società tra medioevo ed età moderna* (Bologna, 1994), 187–224.

—— 'Scienza e immaginazione teologica nel seicento: Il battesimo e le origini dell'individuo', *Quaderni storici*, 100/1 (1999), 173–98.

—— *Tribunali della coscienza: Inquisitori, confessori, missionari* (Turin, 1996).

PULLAN, BRIAN S., '"Difettosi, impotenti, inabili": Caring for the Disabled in Early Modern Italian Cities', in *Poverty and Charity: Europe, Italy, Venice, 1400–1700* (Vermont, 1994), 1–21.

RASPE, LUCIA, 'Jewish Saints in Medieval Ashkenaz: A Contradiction in Terms', *Frankfurt Jewish Studies Bulletin*, 31 (2004), 75–90.

—— *Jüdische Hagiographie im mittelalterlichen Aschkenas* (Tübingen, 2006).

—— 'Payyetanim as Heroes of Medieval Folk Narrative: The Case of R. Shim'on b. Yishaq of Mainz', in Klaus Herrmann, Margarete Schluter, and Giuseppe Veltri (eds.), *Jewish Studies between the Disciplines: Papers in Honor of Peter Schäfer on the Occasion of His 60th Birthday* (Leiden, 2003), 354–69.

RAZ-KRAKOTZKIN, AMNON, *The Censor, the Editor, and the Text: The Catholic Church and the Shaping of the Jewish Canon in the Sixteenth Century*, trans. Jackie Feldman (Philadelphia, 2007).

—— 'Law and Censure: The Printing of the *Shulḥan arukh* as the Commencement of Jewish Modernity' (Heb.), in Roni Weinstein, Elisheva Baumgarten, and Amnon Raz-Krakotzkin (eds.), *Tov elem: Memory, Community and Gender in Medieval and Early Modern Jewish Societies. Essays in Honor of Robert Bonfil* [Tov elem: zikaron, kehilah umigdar baḥavarot yehudiyot biyemei habeinayim uvereshit ha'et haḥadashah] (Jerusalem, 2011), 304–33.

REGEV, SHAUL, 'Israel Najara's "Lover's Wounds"' (Heb.), *Asufot*, 4 (1990), 325–56.

REINER, ELCHANAN, 'Pilgrims and Pilgrimage to the Land of Israel, 1099–1517' [Aliyah va'aliyah leregel le'erets yisra'el, 1099–1517] (Ph.D. diss., Hebrew University of Jerusalem, 1988).

—— 'Wealth, Social Position and the Study of Torah: The Status of the Kloyz in Eastern European Jewish Society in the Early Modern Period' (Heb.), *Zion*, 58 (1993), 287–328.

REINHARD, WERNER, 'Was ist katholische Konfessionalisierung?', in Werner Reinhard and Heinz Schilling (eds.), *Die katholische Konfessionalisierung* (Münster, 1995), 419–52.

RIVLIN, BRACHA, 'Major Lines of Research into the History of the Jewish Family in Greece during the Sixteenth and Seventeenth Centuries' (Heb.), in Michel

Abitbol, Yom Tov Assis, and Galit Hasan-Rokem (eds.), *Hispano-Jewish Civilization after 1492* [Ḥevrah vetarbut: yehudei sefarad le'aḥar hagerush] (Jerusalem, 1997), 79–104.

RIVLIN, BRACHA, *Mutual Responsibility in the Italian Ghetto: Charity Confraternities, 1516–1789* [Arevim zeh lazeh bageto ha'italki: ḥevrot gemilut ḥasadim, 1516–1789] (Jerusalem, 1991).

ROBINSON, IRA, 'Abraham ben Eliezer Halevi: Kabbalist and Messianic Visionary of the Early Sixteenth Centry' (Ph.D. diss., Harvard University, 1980).

—— 'Messianic Prayer Vigils in Jerusalem in the Early Sixteenth Century', *Jewish Quarterly Review*, 72/4 (1981), 32–42.

ROMEO, GIOVANNI, *Esorcisti, confessori e sessualità nell'Italia della controriforma: A proposito di due casi modenesi del primo seicento* (Florence, 1998).

ROODENBURG, HERMAN, 'Reformierte Kirchenzucht und Ehrenhandel: Das Amsterdamer Nachbarschaftsleben im 17. Jahrhundert', in Heinz Schilling (ed.), *Kirchenzucht und Sozialdisziplinierung im frühneuzeitlichen Europa* (Berlin, 1994), 129–51.

ROPER, LYNDAL, '"Evil Imaginings and Fantasies": Child-Witches and the End of the Witch Craze', *Past and Present*, 167 (2000), 107–39.

ROSSI, PAOLO, *Logic and the Art of Memory: The Quest for a Universal Language*, trans. Stephen Clucas (Chicago, 2000).

—— 'La memoria, le immagini, l'enciclopedia', in id. (ed.), *La memoria del sapere: Forme di conservazione e strutture organizzative dall'antichità a oggi* (Rome, 1988), 211–37.

—— *Philosophy, Technology and the Arts in the Early Modern Period*, trans. Salvator Rossi (New York, 1970).

ROZEN MINNA, *A History of the Jewish Community in Istanbul: The Formative Years, 1453–1566* (Leiden, 2002).

RUBIN, MIRI, *The Eucharist in Late Medieval Culture* (Cambridge, 1991).

RUBIN, NOGA, *Conqueror of Hearts: The* Sefer lev tov *of Isaac ben Elyakum of Posen, Prague 1620* [Kovesh halevavot: sefer lev tov lerabi yitsḥak ben elyakum mipozna, perag 1620] (Benei Brak, 2013).

RUBIN, ZVIA, 'The Zoharic Commentaries of Joseph ibn Tabul' (Heb.), in Rachel Elior and Yehuda Liebes (eds.), *Lurianic Kabbalah: Proceedings of the Fourth International Conference on the History of Jewish Mysticism* [Kabalat ha'ari: divrei hakenes habeinle'umi harevi'i leḥeker toledot hamistikah hayehudit] (Jerusalem, 1992), 363–87.

RUDERMAN, DAVID B., 'The Founding of a "Gemilut Hasadim" Society in Ferrara in 1515', *AJS Review*, 1 (1976), 233–67.

—— *Jewish Thought and Scientific Discovery in Early Modern Europe* (New Haven, Conn., 1995).

RUSCONI, ROBERTO, *L'ordine dei peccati: La confessione tra medioevo ed età moderna* (Bologna, 2002).

SACK, BRACHA, *The Kabbalah of Moses Cordovero* [Besha'arei hakabalah shel rabi mosheh kordovero] (Be'er Sheva, 1995).

—— 'The Land of Israel, the Zohar, and the Kabbalah of Safed' (Heb.), in Warren (Ze'ev) Harvey et al. (eds.), *Zion and Zionism among Sephardi and Oriental Jews* [Tsiyon vetsiyonut bekerev yehudei sefarad vehamizraḥ] (Jerusalem, 2002), 51–79.

—— 'R. Moses Cordovero's Doctrine of *Tsimtsum*' (Heb.), *Tarbiz*, 58 (1989), 207–37.

SAFRAI, CHANA, and ZEEV SAFRAI, 'Rabbinic Holy Men', in Marcel Poorthuis and Joshua Schwartz (eds.), *Saints and Role Models in Judaism and Christianity* (Leiden, 2004), 59–78.

SALOMON, HERMAN PRINS, 'Mendes, Benveniste, De Luna, Micas, Nasci: The State of the Art (1532–1558)', *Jewish Quarterly Review*, 88/3–4 (1998), 135–211.

SARFATTI, GAD BEN-AMI, 'Pious Men, Men of Deeds, and the Early Prophets' (Heb.), *Tarbiz*, 26 (1957), 126–53.

SCHECHTER, SOLOMON, *Studies in Judaism: Second Series* (Philadelphia, 1908).

SCHILLING, HEINZ, 'Die Konfessionalisierung von Kirche, Staat und Gesellschaft: Profil, Leistung, Defizite und Perspektiven eines geschichtswissenschaftlichen Paradigmas', in Werner Reinhard and Heinz Schilling (eds.), *Die katholische Konfessionalisierung* (Münster, 1995), 1–49.

—— *Religion, Political Culture and the Emergence of Early Modern Society: Essays in German and Dutch History* (Leiden, 1992).

SCHINDLER, NORBERT, 'I tutori del disordine: Rituali della cultura giovanile agli inizi dell'età moderna', in Giovanni Levi and Jean-Claude Schmitt (eds.), *Storia dei giovani* (Rome, 1994), 303–74.

SCHMIDT-BIGGEMANN, WILHELM, *Christliche Kabbala*, Pforzheimer Reuchlin-schriften, 10 (Stuttgart, 2003).

—— *Geschichte der christlichen Kabbala*, 3 vols. (Stuttgart, 2012–13).

SCHOLEM, GERSHOM, 'The Bond of Fellowship of the Students of R. Isaac Luria' (Heb.), in *Lurianic Kabbalah* [Kabalat ha'ari], 262–94.

—— *Lurianic Kabbalah: Collected Studies by Gershom Scholem* [Kabalat ha'ari: osef ma'amarim me'et gershom shalom], ed. Daniel Abrams (Los Angeles, 2008).

SCHWARZ, DOV, 'Criticism of the Concept of Reincarnation during the Middle Ages' (Heb.), *Maḥanayim*, 6 (1994), 104–13.

SCORZA BARCELLONA, FRANCESCO, 'Le origini', in *Storia della santità nel cristianes-imo occidentale* (Rome, 2005), 19–89.

SECCO, LUIGI, *La pedagogia della controriforma* (Brescia, 1973).

SEIDEL MENCHI, SILVANA, *Erasmo in Italia: 1520–1580* (Turin, 1987).

SEROUSSI, EDWIN, 'From Court and *Tarikat* to Synagogue: Ottoman Art Music and Hebrew Sacred Songs', in Anders Hammarlund, Tord Olsson, and Elisabeth Özdalga (eds.), *Sufism, Music, and Society in the Middle East* (Istanbul, 2001), 81–96.

—— 'R. Israel Najara: The Shaper of Sacred Liturgy after the Spanish Expulsion' (Heb), *Asufot*, 4 (1990), 285–310.

SHALEM, SHIMON, 'Thought and Ethics in the Commentaries of R. Moses Alsheich' (Heb.), in Isaac Ben-Zvi and Meir Benayahu (eds.), *Safed: Research and Sources on the Safed Community from the Sixteenth until the Nineteenth Centuries* [Sefer tsefat:

meḥkarim umekorot al kehilat sefat min hame'ah hashesh-esreh ad hame'ah hatesha-esreh] (Jerusalem, 1962), 199–258.

SICROFF, ALBERT A., *Les Controverses des statuts de 'pureté de sang' en Espagne du XVe au XVIIe siècle* (Paris, 1960).

SLUHOVSKY, MOSHE, *Believe Not Every Spirit: Possession, Mysticism, and Discernment in Early Modern Catholicism* (Chicago, 2007).

SOROTZKIN, DAVID, *Orthodoxy and Modern Discipline: The Production of the Jewish Tradition in Europe in Modern Times* [Ortodoksyah umishtar hamoderniyut: hafakatah shel hamasoret hayehudit be'eiropah ba'et haḥadashah] (Tel Aviv, 2011).

—— 'The Super-Temporal Community in an Age of Change' [Kehilat ha'al zeman be'idan hatemurot] (Ph.D diss., Hebrew University of Jerusalem, 2007).

STENGERS, JEAN, and ANNE VAN NECK, *Masturbation: The History of a Great Terror*, trans. Kathryn A. Hoffmann (New York, 2001).

Storia della santità nel cristianesimo occidentale (Rome, 2005).

STUBER, SHIMON, 'Charity in Sephardi Communities' (Heb.), in Aryeh Morgenstern (ed.), *Avraham Spiegelman Memorial Volume* [Sefer zikaron le'avraham shpigelman] (Tel Aviv, 1979), 151–67.

STUCZYNSKI, CLAUDE B., 'A "Marrano Religion"? The Religious Behaviour of the New Christians of Bragança Convicted by the Coimbra Inquisition in the Sixteenth Century (1541–1605)' ['Dat anusim'? hahitnahagut hadatit shel ha-notserim haḥadashim bebragansah shenidonu al yedei ha'inkvizitsyah shel ko'imbrah bame'ah hashesh-esreh (1541–1605)] (Ph.D. diss., Bar-Ilan University, 2005).

—— 'New Christian Political Leadership in Times of Crisis: The Pardon Negotiations of 1605', in Moises Orfali (ed.), *Leadership in Times of Crisis* (Ramat Gan, 2007), 45–70.

SUBRAHMANYAM, SANJAY, 'Connected Histories: Notes towards a Reconfiguration of Early Modern Eurasia', *Modern Asian Studies*, 31/3 (1997), 735–62.

SVIRI, SARA, *The Sufis: An Anthology* [Hasufim: antologyah] (Tel Aviv, 2008).

SWETSCHINSKI, DANIEL M., *De familie Lopes Suasso, Financiers van Willem III* (Zwolle, 1988).

—— *Reluctant Cosmopolitans: The Portuguese Jews of Seventeenth-Century Amsterdam* (London, 2000).

SWIETLICKI, CATHERINE, *Spanish Christian Cabala: The Works of Luis de Leon, Santa Teresa de Jesus, and San Juan de la Cruz* (Columbia, Mo., 1986).

TALMON-HELLER, DANIELLA, *Islamic Piety in Medieval Syria: Mosques, Cemeteries and Sermons under the Zangids and Ayyūbids* (Leiden, 2007).

TAMAR, DAVID, 'Safed before the Arrival of Karo, Late Fifteenth–Early Sixteenth Centuries' (Heb.), in Michael Rigler (ed.), *Eshkolot tamar: The History of Safed and Its Sages and of the Great Jewish Leaders of the Last Generations* [Eshkolot tamar: meḥkarim ve'iyunim betoledot tsefat veḥakhmeiha ugedolei yisra'el badorot ha'aḥaronim] (Jerusalem, 2002), 14–26.

TA-SHMA, ISRAEL M., *Creativity and Tradition: Studies in Medieval Rabbinic Scholarship, Literature and Thought* (Cambridge, Mass., 2006).

TENTLER, THOMAS N., *Sin and Confession on the Eve of the Reformation* (Princeton, NJ, 1977).

TERPSTRA, NICHOLAS, 'Confraternities and Public Charity: Modes of Civic Welfare in Early Modern Italy', in John Patrick Donnelly and Michael W. Maher (eds.), *Confraternities and Catholic Reform in Italy, France, and Spain*, Sixteenth Century Essays and Studies, 44 (Kirksville, Mo., 1999), 97–121.

—— 'Ignatius, Confratello: Confraternities as Modes of Spiritual Community in Early Modern Society', in Kathleen M. Comerford and Hilmar M. Pabel (eds.), *Early Modern Catholicism: Essays in Honour of John W. O'Malley, S.J.* (Toronto, 2001), 163–82.

TISHBY, ISAIAH, *The Doctrine of Evil and the* Kelipah *in Lurianic Kabbalism* [Torat hara vehakelipah bekabalat ha'ari] (Jerusalem, 1942).

—— 'R. Moses David Valle and His Status within the Circle of R. Moses Hayim Luzzatto' (Heb.), *Zion*, 49 (1979), 265–302.

TOLEDANO, YA'AKOV MOSHE, '*Tikunim* and Customs of the Safed Kabbalists' (Heb.), in *Treasure House: Collected Letters from the History of the Land of Israel, Based on Old Manuscripts, with Introductions and Notes* [Otsar genazim: osef igerot letoledot erets yisra'el mitokh kitvei yad atikim, im mevo'ot vehe'arot] (Jerusalem, 1960), 48–51.

TRIVELLATO, FRANCESCA, *The Familiarity of Strangers: The Sephardic Diaspora, Livorno, and the Cross Cultural Trade in the Early Modern Period* (New Haven, Conn., 2009).

TRÖLTSCH, ERNST, *The Social Teaching of the Christian Churches*, trans. Olive Wyon (New York, 1960).

TROMBETTA, PINO LUCÀ, *La confessione della lussuria: Definizione e controllo del piacere nel cattolicesimo* (Genoa, 1991).

TURNIANSKY, CHAVA, 'Special Traits of Yiddish Literature in Italy', in Chava Turniansky and Erika Timm, *Yiddish in Italia*, 191–6.

—— and ERIKA TIMM, *Yiddish in Italia: Yiddish Manuscripts and Printed Books, from the 15th to the 17th Century* (Milan, 2003).

TURRINI, MIRIAM, and ANNAMARIA VALENTI, 'L'educazione religiosa', in Gian Paolo Brizzi (ed.), *Il catechismo e la grammatica* (Bologna, 1985), i. 347–423.

URBACH, EFRAIM E., 'Halakhah and Prophecy' (Heb.), *Tarbiz*, 18 (1947), 1–27.

VISMARA, PAOLA, *Settecento religioso in Lombardia* (Milan, 1994).

VOORBIJ, JOHANNES B., 'Purpose and Audience: Perspectives on the Thirteenth-Century Encyclopedias of Alexander Neckam, Bartholomaeus Anglicus, Thomas of Cantimpré and Vincent of Beauvais', in Steven Harvey (ed.), *The Medieval Hebrew Encyclopedias of Science and Philosophy* (Dordrecht, 2000), 31–45.

WACHTEL, NATHAN, *La Foi du souvenir: Labyrinthes marranes* (Paris, 2001).

WALLACE, WILLIAM A., 'Mechanics from Bradwardine to Galileo', *Journal of the History of Ideas*, 32/1 (1971) 15–28.

WEBER, MAX, *The Protestant Ethic and the Spirit of Capitalism, with Other Writings on the Rise of the West*, trans. Stephen Kalberg (New York, 2009).

—— *The Sociology of Religion*, trans. Ephraim Fischoff (London, 1965).

WEINSTEIN, RONI, 'Abraham Yagel Galico's Commentary on "Woman of Valour":
   Commenting on Women, Family and Civility', in Roni Weinstein, Elisheva
   Baumgarten, and Amnon Raz-Krakotzkin (eds.), *Tov elem: Memory, Community
   and Gender in Medieval and Early Modern Jewish Societies. Essays in Honor of Robert
   Bonfil* [Tov elem: zikaron, kehilah umigdar baḥavarot yehudiyot biyemei
   habeinayim uvereshit ha'et haḥadashah] (Jerusalem, 2011), 118–35.

—— 'Childhood, Adolescence, and Growing Up in the Jewish Community in Italy
   during the Late Middle Ages' (Heb.), *Italia*, 11 (1995), 77–98.

—— 'Halakhic Research. Between the Yeshiva and the Academy: The Case of
   R. Joseph Karo' (Heb.) (forthcoming).

—— '"An Honourable Death is Better than a Shameful Life": Honour Ethos, Family
   Life, and Community Control in Jewish Italian Society during the Late Middle
   Ages and Early Modern Period' (Heb.), *Proceedings of the Twelfth World Congress
   of Jewish Studies, Division B: History of the Jewish People* (Jerusalem, 2000),
   111–25.

—— 'Joseph K. (Karo) in Front of the Law: A Suggestion for Global Reading of
   Early Modern Jewish Codification', in Rivka Feldhay (ed.), *Baroque Culture*
   (forthcoming).

—— *Juvenile Sexuality, Kabbalah, and Catholic Religiosity among Jewish Italian Communities: 'Glory of Youth' by Pinḥas Barukh ben Pelatiyah Monselice (Ferrara, XVII
   Century)* (Boston, 2008).

—— 'Kabbalah and Jewish Exorcism in Seventeenth-Century Italian Jewish Communities: The Case of Rabbi Moses Zacuto', in Matt Goldish (ed.), *Spirit Possession in Judaism: Cases and Contexts from the Middle Ages to the Present* (Detroit,
   2003), 237–56.

—— *Marriage Rituals Italian Style: A Historical Anthropological Perspective on Early
   Modern Italian Jews* (Leiden, 2003).

—— 'Mock and Clandestine Marriages, Deceits, and Games in Jewish Italian Communities during the Early Modern Period', in Mark Crane, Richard Raiswell,
   and Margaret Reeves (eds.), *Shell Games: Scams, Frauds, Deceit (1300–1650)*
   (Toronto, 2004), 145–60.

—— 'The Rise of the Body in Early Modern Jewish Society: The Italian Case Study',
   in Maria Diemling and Giuseppe Veltri (eds.), *The Jewish Body: Corporeality,
   Society, and Identity in the Renaissance and Early Modern Period* (Boston, 2008),
   15–51.

—— 'Rituel du mariage et culture des jeunes dans la société judéo-italienne 16e–17e
   siècles', *Annales: Histoire Sciences Sociales*, 53/3 (1998), 455–79.

—— '"Thus will *giovani* do": Jewish Youth Sub-Culture in Early Modern Italy', in
   Konrad Eisenbichler (ed.), *The Premodern Teenager: Youth in Society 1150–1650*
   (Toronto, 2002), 51–74.

—— 'What Did Little Samuel Read in His Notebook? Jewish Education in Italy
   during the Catholic Reformation Period' (Heb.), *Italia*, 13–15 (2001), 131–68.

WEISMANN, RONALD F. E., 'Cults and Contexts: In Search of the Renaissance Confraternity', in Konrad Eisenbichler (ed.), *Crossing the Boundaries: Christian Piety
   and the Arts in Italian Medieval and Renaissance Confraternities* (Kalamazoo,
   1991), 201–20.

—— 'From Brotherhood to Congregation: Confraternal Ritual Between Renaissance and Catholic Reformation', in Jacques Chiffoleau, Lauro Martines, and Agostino Paravicini Bagliani (eds.), *Riti e rituali nelle società medievali* (Spoleto, 1994), 77–94.

—— *Ritual Brotherhood in Renaissance Florence* (New York, 1982).

WERBLOWSKY, R. J. ZWI, *Joseph Karo: Lawyer and Mystic* (Philadelphia, 1977).

WESTREICH, ELIMELECH, '"Be Fruitful and Multiply" in Jewish Law in the Ottoman Empire during the Sixteenth Century' (Heb.), *Te'udah*, 13 (1997), 195–240.

WEXLER, PHILIP, *Mystical Interactions: Sociology, Jewish Mysticism and Education* (Los Angeles, 2007).

WOLFSON, ELLIOT R., 'Assaulting the Border: Kabbalistic Traces in the Margins of Derrida', *Journal of the American Academy of Religion*, 70/3 (2002), 475–514.

—— *Language, Eros, Being: Kabbalistic Hermeneutics and Poetic Imagination* (New York, 2005).

—— *Luminal Darkness: Imaginal Gleanings from Zoharic Literature* (Oxford, 2007).

—— 'Weeping, Death, and Spiritual Ascent in Sixteenth Century Jewish Mysticism', in John J. Collings and Michael Fishbane (eds.), *Death, Ecstasy, and Other Worldly Journeys* (New York, 1995), 207–47.

YAHALOM, JOSEPH, 'R. Israel Najara and the Revival of Hebrew Poetry in the East after the Expulsion from Spain' (Heb.), *Pe'amim*, 13 (1982), 96–124.

YATES, FRANCES A., *The Art of Memory* (London, 1966).

YAYAMA, KUMIKO, 'The Singing of Bakashot of the Aleppo Jewish Tradition in Jerusalem' [Shirat habakashot shel yehudei ḥalab biyerushalayim], 2 vols. (Ph.D. diss., Hebrew University of Jerusalem, 2003).

YERUSHALMI, YOSEF HAYIM, *From Spanish Court to Italian Ghetto. Isaac Cardoso: A Study in Seventeenth-Century Marranism and Jewish Apologetics* (Seattle, 1981).

YOSHA, NISSIM, *Myth and Metaphor: The Philosophical Exegesis of R. Abraham Kohen Herrera on Lurianic Kabbalah* [Mitos umetaforah: haparshanut hafilosofit shel rav avraham kohen hererah lekabalat ha'ari] (Jerusalem, 1994).

YOVEL, YIRMIYAHU, *The Other Within: The Marranos' Split Identity and Emerging Modernity* (Princeton, NJ, 2009).

—— 'Parameters of New Jewish Time' (Heb.), in *New Jewish Time. Jewish Culture in a Secular Age: An Encyclopedic View* [Zeman yehudi ḥadash: tarbut yehudi be'idan ḥiloni] (Tel Aviv, 2007), i. 233–40.

ZARDIN, DANILO, 'Relaunching Confraternities in the Tridentine Era: Shaping Consciences and Christianizing Society in Milan and Lombardy', in Nicholas Terpstra (ed.), *The Politics of Ritual Kinship: Confraternities and Social Order in Early Modern Italy* (Cambridge, 2000), 190–209.

—— 'Riforma e confraternite nella Milano di Carlo Borromeo', in *Il buon fedele: Le confraternite tra medioevo e prima età moderna*, Quaderni di storia religiosa (Verona, 1998), 235–63.

—— 'Il rilancio delle confraternite nell'Europa cattolica cinque-seicentesca', in Cesare Mozzarelli and Danilo Zardin (eds.), *I tempi del concilio: Religione, cultura e società nell'Europa tridentina* (Rome, 1997), 107–44.

ZARRI, GABRIELLA, 'Christian Good Manners: Spiritual and Monastic Rules in the Quattro- and Cinquecento', in Letizia Panizza (ed.), *Women in Italian Renaissance Culture and Society* (Oxford, 2000), 76–91.

—— 'Dalla profezia alla disciplina (1450–1650)', in Lucetta Scaraffia and Gabriella Zarri (eds.), *Donne e fede: Santità e vita religiosa in Italia* (Rome, 1994), 177–225.

—— 'Il matrimonio tridentino', in Paolo Prodi and Werner Reinhard (eds.), *Il concilio di Trento e il moderno* (Bologna, 1996), 437–83.

ZELDES, NADIA, '*The Former Jews of This Kingdom': Sicilian Converts after the Expulsion, 1492–1516* (Leiden, 2003).

ZFATMAN, SARA, '*Mayse bukh*: Some Parameters of an Old Yiddish Genre' (Heb.), *Hasifrut*, 28 (1979), 126–52.

ZOHAR, RAVIV, *Decoding the Dogma within the Enigma: The Life, Works, Mystical Piety and Systematic Thought of Rabbi Moses Cordoeiro (aka Cordovero; Safed, Israel, 1522–1570)* (Saarbrücken, 2008).

Index

Printed and bound by CPI Group (UK) Ltd, Croydon, CR0 4YY

09/06/2025

14685812-0002